Touchstones: Reflections on the Best in Children's Literature

Volume Two:

Fairy Tales, Fables, Myths, Legends, and Poetry

Children's Literature Association

210 Education • Purdue University
West Lafayette, IN 47907

Table of Contents

Foreword

Like the living nightingale in Hans Christian Andersen's "The Nightingale," a touchstone helps us to distinguish the real from the artificial, the true from the false.

All literature is not created equal. Some is better, and the essays in this book seek to show why and how some myths, legends, folk tales and poetry are better, why and how some works of literature are deemed touchstones.

As these essays show why and how the works they discuss are touchstones, they will also give us pleasure and insight.

They will give pleasure because we enjoy reading about literature that we already know. We will take pleasure in the careful and controlled structures of these essays, the neat turn of a phrase or a sentence. We will find pleasure in the fact that some other person admires and finds stimulating a literary work that we admire and find stimulating. We will find pleasure in the creative act of reading.

These essays will give us insight into pieces of literature that we are already familiar with. And because we are familiar with the subjects, these touchstones, we may think there is little for us in them. We may have read the works under discussion a dozen times or more; we may be so familiar with them that we no longer see them clearly. Just as Fra Lippo Lippi wanted through his paintings to show the people of Florence a scene they may have passed a hundred times and not looked at or appreciated, the writers of these essays have looked at their subjects and will show us ways of seeing, reading, understanding, and appreciating that we have not before.

The essays themselves are touchstones. As we read them, we can better judge the quality of our own and other essays. The writer-critics represented in these essays have spent hours and days reading the works they discuss; they have read what others have had to say about them; they have thought about them; and as they created these essays, that magic occurred, which kindles and rekindles as we put words on paper, and which comes into play and gives us new insights, new dimensions, and new perspectives. These essays, then, are thoughtful, provocative, and well-wrought works of critical art, touchstones.

We owe, therefore, thanks to these writers, who have given us many hours of their lives to produce the essays that make up this second volume of *Touchstones.*

We owe thanks to Perry Nodelman for editing these essays. He, too, has spent many hours carefully and objectively reading them, giving them a consistent and finished quality yet maintaining their diversity and individuality as only good editing can do.

We owe thanks to the Publications Committee and the Board of Directors of the Children's Literature Association for their support and encouragement, for without them, this book would not have come to fruition.

We owe thanks to Jill May and her staff for the hours they have spent in taking care of all the details that go with publishing a book, the infinite details that most of us have only the faintest knowledge about.

Above all, we owe thanks to those people who created the poetry, to those who preserved in spoken and written word the myths, legends, and folk tales, and to Time, the true touchstone.

Malcolm Usrey, President
Children's Literature Association, 1985 and 1986
Clemson University

September, 1986

Introduction: A Recycling of Glorious Garbage

by Perry Nodelman

Like the expensive and often beautiful stock of any half-decent antique store, most of the subjects of this volume were once, quite literally, garbage. As a result, it is a messy volume. The first volume of this series was more unified, more orderly, altogether neater than this second one, simply because all the articles in it were about the same thing: children's novels. While those novels are as various as they are similar, they are nowhere near so varied as the astonishing grab bag represented in *this* volume, which contains essays about subjects as different as the ancient epics of Homer and experimental lyric poems of recent decades; as different as the exploits of King Arthur and the exploits of Brer Rabbit. In fact, the only thing that the twenty essays in this volume have in common with each other is that each of them is about one of the various collections of poems, myths, fables, legends and fairy tales named by the Children's Literature Association as touchstones for children's literature.

Poems and myths and legends and fable and fairy tales; that assortment of different genres is a rich mixture all by itself, and it reveals the variety of experiences available to children in the literature we recommend to them. The works discussed here offer a wide repertory of story forms and story patterns, and an even wider repertory of styles and kinds of language, from epic solemnity to the nursery whimsies of A. A. Milne.

What makes this assortment especially interesting is that it illustrates an important fact about children's literature—that so much of it was not originally intended for children at all. In an important sense, much of this work *is* garbage—literature discarded by grownups for whom it has become useless or old-fashioned, and left behind to be scavenged by wise children with more interest in real value than in mere faddishness. Some of the materials discussed in these essays—the Homeric epics and the Greek and Norse myths—were not originally even intended to be literature: their first audiences would probably be horrified by the sacrilegious attitude implied toward the articles of their religious faith by our recommending these materials merely because they are entertaining stories—as horrified as pioneers might be by the comparatively frivolous decorative uses to which antique collectors put their discarded cow-bells and butterchurns. And the original audiences for the folk tales that were later collected

1

by Perrault, the Grimm Brothers, and Joseph Jacobs would surely be astonished by our contemporary conviction that these stories should be the exclusive property of mere youngsters. Even the poems discussed here that were actually written newly for children are often in verse forms and rhythmical patterns that adults had already declared tasteless, and had ceased to use in the important verse meant to be read by other adults. Nowadays, these verse forms, and these stories, and even these once unquestionably true explanations of the nature and meaning of existence, are indeed more or less the exclusive property of children; and that tells us much about how children's literature preserves and recycles a rich stew of varying forms and traditions that would otherwise be lost, discarded as useless garbage.

That so many diverse materials from so many diverse and now discarded cultures should still today remain the literary property of children, children whose culture and whose experience of living are quite different from any of those original ones, says much about how once persuasively true descriptions of reality can live on in the fantasy worlds of the imagination. No longer the potent actual force he once was, Jason can come to mean something rich and strange in an imaginary world of literature, and can thus broaden the sometimes confining horizons of the lives of many children.

That history of retrieval and recycling also says much about how some works of literature come to be considered classics, or touchstones, and enter the canon of important literature. For though it was anonymous adults who once decided that the children in their care might like to hear the tales of previous generations of German peasants or the stories of ancient Greek heroes, it was obviously the children themselves who enjoyed those stories enough to want to hear them again and again, and who thus kept them current as children's literature. In a discussion of how some works of music are singled out to be played over and over again while others are lost to history, Joseph Kerman says, "repertories are determined by performers, canons, by critics" (184). The stories and poems discussed in this volume are far more significantly a repertory than a canon; they were chosen by performers—parents and nannies and other adults who liked to read them or tell them to children—and they were obviously then chosen again and again as favorites by the audiences for those performances: children themselves. Critics like the ones represented in this book can identify those works as touchstones and discuss their virtues only because the audience and the performers had already made them part of the repertory.

The eclecticism of that audience of children is made clear by the variegated nature of this repertory; a canon carefully selected

2

according to the carefully thought out principles of any one adult critic would certainly have contained works far more like each other—more like a tastefully matched set than a glorious assortment of reusable discards. As I edited these essays and thought about the works they discuss, my main problem was organizing the volume. I finally decided that there was no sensible way to impose order on this disorderly grab bag—that in fact, to do so would be to misrepresent it. To list the works chronologically, or to divide the book into separate sections that kept poetry and fairy tales apart from each other, would be to distort the way all this wonderful variety intrudes itself into the imaginations of children. Consequently, I've chosen the most arbitrary and meaningless of sequences: the essays appear in the order of the last name of the author (or compiler) of the works they discuss. Readers who decide to read the contents of this book from beginning to end will be as delightfully tossed and torn between quite different sorts of literary experiences and cultural assumptions as are the lucky children who are given access to all these works in the most random of ways—one night hearing about how Christopher Robin patriotically goes down with Alice to watch them changing the guard at Buckingham Palace, the next hearing of the starkly grand exploits of the Norse gods, the next hearing about how a beautiful young lady loses her slipper and finds love at an elegant French ball.

The novels discussed in volume one of this series are fine fiction, and many of them can be identified as touchstones simply because they are daringly innovative; nevertheless, they are all based firmly in the traditional forms and patterns, and even in the specific stories and settings, of the materials discussed in this volume; and it's not surprising that so many of the illustrators whose work will be discussed in the third volume of the series have chosen to illustrate some of these same traditional materials. The reason is clear: the works discussed in this second volume are the foundations of the tradition of children's literature. Because it was in fact these materials that children could claim as their own once adults had decided to discard them, they were the first children's literature. When adults later decided to actually write literature specifically for the enjoyment of children, they modelled their work on the literature children already had, these myths and fairy tales and rhymes. Consequently, the essays in this volume do as much to explain the touchstones discussed in the other two volumes of this series as do the essays specifically devoted to the other works in those other volumes.

That they do so in such a variety of ways, that in the process they discuss matters as random as the geography of Norway and the patriarchal assumptions of traditional religious ideas, merely

3

confirms once more the complexity of the apparent simplicities of children's literature. As the essays in this volume reveal, exploring these apparent simplicities can only persuade us of the immense richness this literature can bring to the lives of children.

REFERENCES

Kerman, Joseph. "A Few Canonic Variations." *Canons.* Ed. Robert von Hallberg. Chicago and London: Univ. of Chicago Press, 1984. 177-196.

Aesop's *Fables:* Beyond Morals

by Joanne Lynn

All of us, whether we've ever owned an Aesop or not, have at least a handful of fables rattling around in our heads: the fox mutters "sour grapes," the tortoise forever beats the hare, the dog keeps cows from getting at the hay in the manger, the boy learns too late not to cry "wolf!" Aesop and his fables are probably better known than Homer and his epics. The fables entered western European literature in written form shortly after Homer's epics, and in the popular mind, Aesop shares a reputation for wisdom and venerability with Homer, Socrates and the wisdom books of the Bible. Though the original collections of fables were meant for adults, these days we mostly think of Aesop as tales for children. Partly because of their verbal brevity and their visual appeal (since the invention of the printing press, Aesop's fables have often been accompanied by illustrations), we take for granted that the fables are part of the canon of children's literature.

The book chosen to represent Aesop as a touchstone of children's literature, *Aesop's Fables* as selected and retold by Louis Untermeyer and illustrated by Alice and Martin Provenson (Golden Press, 1965), is a handsome enough edition; it meets the criteria of clarity of text and illustration that are appropriate to a children's version of adult oral literature. Unfortunately, it is also out of print. Not to worry. The charms of Aesop and the reasons for including fables in a canon of children's literature go far beyond the limits of a particular edition.

Almost any of a number of editions, new or old, will do for adults concerned with passing along Aesop to children, for, in whatever form they are first encountered, Aesop's fables belong in the human voice and in the head. What interests me here more than which edition a child owns is why these brief and sometimes astringent little narratives should continue to be part of a child's literary heritage. Aesop's fables remain viable as children's literature not solely because of their longevity in the culture, not because of their "morals," not even, as some have claimed, because they are "about animals." Aesop's fables belong to children because the concerns of Aesop's fables make common cause with the condition of childhood. Aesop speaks for the underdog, the common man, the politically and socially disenfranchised. The dry wit and self-respecting sanity of the fables counter intrinsic powerlessness—with humorous acceptance, not docility, with wry common sense, not fear. These qualities, rather than those more frequently cited, make Aesop's place in the canon secure, regardless of the form in which children first encounter him.

Caxton was surely aware of their broad base of popularity as well as their traditional cachet when he chose to print these fables with the fifteenth-century Ulm woodcuts as an early venture in a new medium. Every age from Hesiod's time to our own has held them a vital part of the culture, and has circulated them in a variety of versions, mostly for adult audiences. When, as Daley tells us, Hesiod illustrated his pessimistic view of absolute power in *Works and Days* with the fable of the hawk and the nightingale, he assumed his eighth-century audience knew the tale well (17). The anonymous "biography" of Aesop often attached to collections of fables emphasizes Aesop's lowly origins. With delicious irony, the legend shows the master storyteller born dumb, this eventual advisor to despots and kings born a slave, this deformed, phallic body, the "property" of an absent-minded philosopher whose mind needs Aesop's aid. Certainly by the time Caxton began to print his translation of Aesop from the French in 1483, "Aesop's Fables" had become the common property of all ages, and the term had become generic for collections of brief prose narratives illustrating a keen observation of human nature. Derived probably from a number of sources, their origins now seem to defy discovery. Reasons for their persistence in the culture invite speculation.

Some assume that the chief reason for inclusion of Aesop's fables in the canon is simply that for ages they were part of the school curriculum. True, they have been schoolboy fodder for a long time. From at least Roman times through the nineteenth century they were considered an appropriate part of the education of young males. Both Phaedrus' first century text and La Fontaine's *Fables* were memorized, recited, and paraphrased as part of the school curriculum. Quintilian recommends them for just this purpose in his first-century A. D. textbook:

> The pupils of the elementary teacher should learn to paraphrase Aesop's fables, the natural successors of the fairy stories of the nursery, in simple language, and subsequently to set down this paraphrase in writing with the same simplicity of style: They should begin by analyzing each verse, then give its meaning in different language, and finally to proceed to a free paraphrase in which they will be permitted now to abridge and now to embellish the original so far as this may be done without losing the poet's meaning   (Daly 15-16).

These are still excellent linguistic and interpretive exercises. But the purpose of passing on the fables has changed considerably. Quintilian's text was designed to train young men as orators in the forum, and La Fontaine's served to educate future courtiers and statesmen. Yet the fables have not served merely to educate a male elite. Their audience has always been wider and deeper.

Received opinion assumes that this wider and deeper audience includes children because Aesop teaches good behavior, socializes the child, smooths the path to adulthood by means of "morals." Never mind that the early collections of Aesop were written down without explicit morals. (In fact, orators on both sides of the political fence can use the same anecdote to different ends.) Caxton introduced each fable with a generalization about what the story was intended to illustrate, and reiterated the point in the form of a moral at the end. But Caxton's conclusion that "he is wyse/ whiche fayneth not to desyre that thynge the whiche he may not haue/" (Lenaghan 122) differs a good deal from Untermeyer's mild injunction about rationalization: "There is comfort in pretending that what we can't get isn't worth having" (Provenson 23). Fortunately, though some children's literature texts still retain the unqualified view that Aesop is useful for teaching morals, recent studies of Aesop for children, such as those by Barbara Mirel, Kristin Lehman, and Anita Wilson in a recent special section of the *ChLA Quarterly* devoted to the fables, challenge the assumption. By showing how those who retell the fables always manage to find "morals" that mirror their own values, these studies reveal how unimportant a part of the effect of these fables are the specific messages we attach to them.

If we consult our own childhood acquaintance with Aesop honestly, in fact, we're likely to have to decide that "morals" do not fully account for the influence and charm of Aesop. I'm sure I was told "The Boy Who Cried Wolf" as a hopeful corrective to my tendency to tell "stretchers," but, city kid that I was, I was far more interested in the boy's good fortune at having sheep to look after.

My childhood acquaintance with fables—whether I heard them aloud (Sunday school teachers forever wanted to tell us "The Wind and the Sun") or pored over them in a battered set of *The Book of Knowledge*—left me with that same wonderful sense of puzzlement that I associated with fairy tales: How could a young man climb up Rapunzel's hair without it pulling and hurting awfully? Why would a fox want to eat grapes anyway? For me, and for the children I have known best, the fables stuck with us because they suggested a sometimes inexplicable adult world that had nevertheless to be coped with. Like the folktales, fables fascinated because they were faintly puzzling, numinous, compelling because of, not in spite of, their creation of a faintly familiar world in which justice did not necessarily prevail, a world which raised more questions than it answered.

Many commentators on Aesop for children assume that Aesop's fables mean beast tales, and that their popularity with children results from a child's natural affinity with animals. A substantial proportion of fables does employ animals as chief characters, but another sizeable proportion features human beings instead. Of the "animal" group, a number of the "animals" are actually insects, reptiles or amphibians, even an occasional fish. In addition, some fables allot the speaking parts to inanimate objects or natural phenomena: plants, trees, rivers, axes, pots, sun, moon, and wind. If one examines actual texts, then, the "affinity with animals" argument will not bear scrutiny. Human characters offer even less possibility of identification. Most are peasants, ordinary folk of other eras: in Greek prose versions, fishermen, potters, shepherds; in Caxton, hunters, farmers, woodcutters, or the generic "man," or "old woman," an occasional teenage boy. Significantly absent from the cast are the aristocrats of epic and märchen: kings, knights, courtiers. Or the professional types of old comedy: lawyers, doctors, teachers, priests.

In Phaedrus, of 332 tales, 179 feature animals protagonists alone, while in 135 at least one human character stars. The remaining eighteen feature inanimate objects. In Caxton a similar proportion prevails: of 133 tales, seventy-one feature animals, fifty-four employ human characters, and inanimate objects perform in the remaining eight. By comparison, in the Provenson edition for children the proportion shifts radically in favor of animals: of thirty-four tales, only five feature human beings, and three, inanimate objects. The largest group by far, twenty-six tales, employs animals. Still, one cannot then argue that children's collections feature more animals because children like them. Adults, after all, have made the selections. Decisions have just as likely been made on unexamined adult assumptions about children's preferences as on the preferences themselves.

Another false notion about the fable is that the animals take on stereotypic, and thus predictable, roles: the Fox is always cunning, the Lion always noble, the Wolf always the predatory villain. While this may be true of certain medieval fabliaux (a different generic form), it is not particularly true of Aesop's fables. Though the fox is often a cunning predator, he is just as often the victim of flattery or pride, or even stupidity. The ass is not always an ass; he sometimes outsmarts the man. Though the lion usually represents power, he can be foiled or fooled. The characters of fables are chosen for their emotional distance from, rather than their closeness to, their audience. The key factor is displacement. Because the fable's chief reason for being is to make a sharp and potentially unpalatable observation about human nature, characters must keep their impersonal distance from auditor/reader (child or adult) in order for the point to penetrate without emotional resistance. In an introduction to the fables, G. K. Chesterton once declared that their characters must be like abstractions in algebra, or like pieces in chess. Thus the cat who flatters the beasts with an invitation to a feast is not a domestic house pet, a resourceful Puss-in-Boots, nor even a real villain. (In Provenson the "beasts" become mice, rabbits and birds; the occasion is the cat's ninth birthday party.) The tale is cautionary, of course: a warning against credulity. The child is not invited to identify with cats, birds, or mice as such, but to absorb the action. The characters of fables are neither people nor animals we know in any realistic sense; they are metaphors for aspects of human nature. Thus the fabulist has the liberty of continually shifting the terms of his tenor and vehicle in the service of his view of human nature.

Just what version of human nature does Aesop offer? A hardheaded, pragmatic, predominantly cynical one, if we consider the entire body of fables as they were collected from classical times to Caxton. Such a view runs counter, one might think, to sentimental notions of childhood and childhood's needs. But despite the Wordsworthian perception of childhood as a time of spiritual insight, or the twentieth century's insistence on a "child centered" universe, the real situation of childhood inevitably shares with serfs, slaves and yeomen of past ages the condition of powerlessness and vulnerability. The child necessarily lives in a world of baffling power, apparent injustice, almost certain irrationality. Like the disenfranchised adult he needs means of psychic survival: an ability to cope with inexplicable tyrannies and a route to escape into fantasies of the cunning and victorious underdog. The fables serve these needs.

As we have seen, the early collections of Aesop's fables served adults, or adults-in-training as orators. Consequently, the majority of fables in the old collections are inapplicable to, or downright inappropriate for, children. Little by little, subsequent collections have culled the vulgar or the salacious. Thus Caxton leaves out the fable of the boy who vomits after overindulging on entrails, but retains "The Wulf whiche made a fart" (149). Later editions eliminate both. Nor does Caxton include the amusing tale of human self-deception, "the Youth and the Woman" (Daly 226) in which a strong youth lusts after the older woman he has carried on his shoulders out of pity. He satisfies both their consciences by telling her he intends "to chisel off some of [her] flesh." Instead of registering conventional horror as he continues to bear her along the way, she responds with feigned compassion: "If I am still heavy and burdensome for you, put me down again, and chisel off some more." The quasi dirty joke may disturb modern feminists, who will note perpetuation of a myth of the lustful older woman, but the honest will admit its comic truth. While these omissions need not be lamented in children's collections, their shrewd earthiness underscores the cynical realism that nonetheless remains in modern collections for children like the Untermeyer-Provenson edition.

This edition, like the Caxton (1484) and James (1848) fables chosen for the Everyman edition (1915), features plenty of tales warning against pretension and greed, tales advocating loyalty, truthfulness and industry. These tales represent what most people now think of as the wisdom of Aesop, a wisdom not exclusively the property of the disenfranchised. It's not surprising that such "lessons" comprise a healthy proportion of fables in modern collections for children. Yet, an astonishing number of tales deal shrewdly and realistically with power—and how to cope with it— from the underdog's point of view: acceptance, resignation, cunning, persistence, escape into fantasies of revenge. The "morals" inculcated by the fables collected for children turn out to be not so much guides to adult conduct as internal recognitions of a state much like children's own.

The Provenson illustrations to Untermeyer's spare text instinctively reinforce the notion that the fables deal with power relations. In a sense, two texts illuminate the point: Untermeyer's text proper, a modern economic, formal idiom consonant with the best tradition of Aesop redactions, and the Provenson illustrations, a visual retelling, often taking more space than the verbal text. The verbal text is illustrated on facing pages or on double-page spreads following the retelling. The paintings and drawings are usually accompanied by conversational balloons in which an animal "chorus" comments on the action in a breezier, less formal idiom. Animals are stylized, anthropomorphic; perspective and proportion are arbitrary, impressionistic. The period is vaguely

Edwardian; settings mix U.S. rural with eastern European urban (Russia? the Balkans?) and an exotic near east (Greece? Turkey? North Africa?). These choices allow appropriate distancing, yet suggest times when and places where power was or is more arbitrary than we like to believe of our own place and time. In the illustrations, as in the verbal text comedy diffuses but does not disguise the pragmatic, sometimes cynical, point.

Predictably, the collection contains familiar fables ridiculing pretension and greed. In one of the best-known, "The Jackdaw's Fine Feathers" (47), the ridiculous, clumsy jackdaw makes a public fool of himself while an audience of birds mouths platitudes. The Provenson illustrations of "The Lioness and the Vixen" particularize pointedly. The imposing lioness in flowered print hosts Mrs. Fox, gloved and hatted, perched on a Victorian side chair. She surveys her spoiled brood as they clamor: "I want a balloon," "Look at me ride," "I have party shoes on." Mama Fox coos, "I love a big family, don't you?" Her social superior, Mrs. Lion, merely smiles smugly, offering her one "quality" cub without comment. In "The Ass in the Lion's Skin" (32-33), the fox exposes pretensions, as he does also in "The Fox and the Crow" (60-61). Sporting jaunty Tyrolean garb, he flatters the more formally dressed crow to his defeat.

Fables on greed, honesty and industry are also illustrated with mild visual social satire. The Provensons' visual interpretations emphasize the social reality of being a little guy. In "The Goose That Laid the Golden Eggs" (34-35), a derbied mustachioed gent in pink coat attacks the straw-bonneted goose who warns: "STOP! THINK!" In "The Dog in the Manger" (44-45), the selfish dog barks at smocked and overalled farmhands, headed by the stolid bull. The bridge in "The Dog and His Shadow" (37) crosses a river flowing through an eastern European city. Several bourgeois bystanders (hen, sow, cat, vixen) comment on the foolish behavior of the greedy dog, a dandified "gentleman." "The Boy and the Wolf" (17) takes place in a vague version of Turkey; thus the villagers who provide the negative injunction to honesty are not parental authority figures, but the voice of reasonable common sense.

That fable dearest to the heart of puritan values and Victorian capitalism, "The Grasshopper and the Ant" (12) is illustrated only by two small ink drawings: the grasshopper's portrait in a large, ornate frame, the ant's, small and plain. Its not too surprising that this fable celebrating the virtues of amassing of worldly goods has been visually underplayed, given the devastating effect of Ciardi's reversal of meaning in *John Q. Plenty and Fiddler Dan* and Joyce's ant and "gracehoper" of *Finnegan's Wake*, not to mention Thurber's subversion in "The Moth and the Star." The very familiarity of such fables has laid them open to parody and satire which questions the values they have come to support.

A much larger group of fables than these which feature everyday "sins" dramatizes coping with power, in ways noted above: acceptance, resignation, cunning, persistence, escape into fantasies of revenge. In "The Lion's Share" (Provenson 20-21), the lion ends a cooperative hunt by appropriating the whole kill: "For the mighty man is never faithful to the poor," concludes Caxton (6) in his version, "The Lion, and the Cow, the Goat and the Sheep." Untermeyer interprets more tentatively: "Some people believe that Might makes Right" (21). Both versions illustrate matter-of-fact acceptance that the little guy doesn't stand much of a chance. "The Hungry Wolf and the Lamb" demonstrates the same naked tyranny. What in Caxton reads as a clearly political fable, "the frogges and Iupyter" (90-91), ie. be content with a do-nothing stupid leader (log), or risk a rapacious one (stork who eats frogs) Untermeyer reduces to "Be content with what you have" (42-43). The familiar fable of "Belling the Cat" may be extended to generalize about human cowardice, but it is the practical cowardice in the face of genuine power, that wisdom which is the better part of valor. The narrative in all cases presents a realistic, even cynical, view of what happens when the weak confront the strong.

"The Lions and the Hares" (71) is blatantly about power. Untermeyer's moral has tried to give the generalization an ethical flavor: "Actions speak louder than words." But the hares' impassioned plea for rights, justice, equality—which would have seemed an unrealistic absurdity to Aesop's audience—is likely to make more sense to twentieth-century children than the lions' very realistic observation that they, after all, have the power whether the hares like it or not. The Provenson illustration has turned it into a political comment that works against the printed moral. The lions are Tammany boss and henchman. Boss Lion flaunts a cigar. Both tower over the mob of demonstrating hares who bear placards: "Lettuce unite!" "We want justice and dessert." "The bill of fare must be changed." The bad puns in the cartoon may diffuse the original point with humor, but the Provensons seem to recognize that Aesop clearly meant the fable as a sardonic description of the underdog's world. Though political ideals may have changed since Aesop's day, the vulnerability of childhood has not.

A number of fables comfort the weak with images of strength achieved through cooperation, adaptation, cunning, persuasion or persistence. "The Strong Bundle of Sticks" (52-53) urges strength through unity. "The Wind and the Sun" (63) advocates gentle persuasion. "The Oak and the Reed" (62) recommends

11

pliant adaptation, "The Crow and the Pitcher" (67) rewards cunning inventiveness, and the cherished "Hare and the Tortoise" (84-85), a dogged persistence. These fables represent successes, but success built on manipulation and acceptance rather than on dominance: a survival kit for the ruled, not the rulers.

According to some fables, the weak can also protect themselves by healthy scepticism: In "The Nurse and the Wolf" (66) the wolf, not the child, is taken in by the nurse's empty threat to her charge. The "Cunning Cat's" guests (Provenson 74-75) see through his ploy to make them the main course. The mice in "The Mice and the Cat on the Wall" (22) outsmart and outwait a tyrannous cat. In "The Fox and the Mask" (82-83), the fox sees through the appearance of a noble being (the mask) to the empty reality. In "The Hungry Lion and the Fox," the aging lion displays cunning, but is balked by the logic of a young fox. Though "The Wolf in Sheep's Clothing" is usually offered as a warning against duplicity, it can, like "The Boy Who Cried Wolf" be read as a caution against credulity, a warning against deceivers.

Still other fables in this volume counsel the weak to accept their place realistically. The fable that La Fontaine turned into a rueful satire on class, "The Iron Pot and the Clay Pot" is omitted from Provenson, but "The Eagle and the Tortoise (40-41) makes the same point: stick to your last; don't try to play with the big guys. "The Town Mouse and the Country Mouse" (which can be interpreted as a pitch for the simple life) clearly advocates keeping 'em down on the farm even if they've seen Paree. Only one fable in the Provenson edition, "The Tricky Fox and the Stork" (86), offers the sweet comfort of revenge when the stork reciprocates the fox's invitation to dine on soup served in a flat plate with an invitation to dinner served in a narrow necked jar. The revenge is mild and doesn't counteract the general point that Aesop's fables are for and about the little guy.

All this discussion of Aesop's fables as power politics should not obscure Aesop's most endearing and enduring quality: humor. The Aesop legend, as well as early "portraits" such as the German woodcut Caxton featured in his edition, shows us a funny, vulgar, misshapen little guy who wins against odds with his wits, who prevails over the rich and the powerful. His grotesquerie suggests Priapus, Punch, and other comic subversives. When the Provenson edition was published in 1965, many were outraged by the modern visual interpretations, and particularly by the comic book technique of the double-page spreads. Nonetheless, the grotesquerie and pure corn of these illustrations are very much in keeping with the internal, eternal Aesopian humor. Humor has always been and always will be the underdog's best weapon and defense. Whatever is offered by sobersided analyses (including this one), whatever taint of didacticism that clings to the idea of Aesop's fables, a plunge into re-reading fables with children or on one's own will quickly restore the joyous element of safe rebellion with its dose of comic common sense.

REFERENCES

Aesopus. *Aesop's Fables: An Anthology of the Fabulists of All Countries.* Ed. Ernest Rhys. London: Dent; New York: Dutton, 1913.

_____. *Aesop's Fables.* Ed. Louis Untermeyer. Illus. Alice and Martin Provenson. New York: Golden Press, 1965.

_____. *Aesop's Fables.* Trans. V. S. Vernon-Jones. Illus. Arthur Rackham. Introd. G. K. Chesterton. 1912. New York: Crown, n.d.

Bottom, Olivia. "'Strange and Mervayllous Historyes': William Caxton, First English Printer." *ChLA Quarterly* 9 (Summer 1984): 62-63, 72.

Bush, Joan. "Fables and Illustrations." *ChLA Quarterly* 9 (Summer, 1984): 70-72.

Ciardi, John. *John J. Plenty and Fiddler Dan: A New Fable of the Grasshopper and the Ant.* Philadelphia: Lippincott, 1963.

Daly, Lloyd W. *Aesop Without Morals.* New York: T. Yoseloff, 1961.

Lehman, Kristin. "Tolstoy's Fables: Tools for a Vision." *ChLA Quarterly* 9 (Summer, 1984): 68-70.

Lenaghan, R. T., ed. *Caxton's 'Aesop'.* Cambridge, Mass.: Harvard U Press, 1967.

Maharg, Ruth A. "The Modern Fable: James Thurber's Social Criticisms," *ChLA Quarterly* 9 (Summer, 1984): 72-73.

Miner, Robert B., Jr. "Aesop as Litmus: The Acid Test of Children's Literature." *Children's Literature* 1 (1972): 9-15.

Mirel, Barbara. "Tradition and the Individual Retelling," *ChLA Quarterly* 9 (Summer, 1984): 63-66.

Perkins, Agnes. "The Five Hundreth Anniversary of Aesop in English: Introduction." *ChLA Quarterly* 9 (Summer, 1984): 60-62.

Pflieger, Pat. "Fables into Picture Books." *ChLA Quarterly* 9 (Summer, 1984): 73-75, 80.

Wilson, Anita C. "To Instruct and to Amuse: Some Victorian Views of *Aesop's Fables.*" *ChLA Quarterly* 9 (Summer, 1984): 66-68.

Hans Christian Andersen's Fairy Tales and Stories: Secrets, Swans and Shadows

by Jon Cech

Among the 156 "tales and stories" that Hans Christian Andersen wrote between 1835 and 1872, a dozen or so are among the best-known, most frequently anthologized and reprinted retellings of fairy tales or literary fairy tales of any canon. Indeed, such stories as "The Ugly Duckling," "The Princess and the Pea," and "The Emperor's New Clothes" have been retold so often, and in so many different forms, that they have become part of the public domain of our oral folk tradition. Bo Grønbech claims that Anderson's tales have been translated into over a hundred languages; only the Bible and Shakespeare have been translated into more. Not long after the appearance of the first of Andersen's tales, one of his friends had quipped that Andersen's novels and plays might make him famous in Denmark, but his fairy tales would make him immortal. The friend's intuitive pronouncement has not been far off the mark.

This enormous success could not have been more unlikely, more unexpected than it was for Andersen, the son of a poor washerwoman and a melancholy cobbler from the Danish coastal town of Odense. When the fourteen-year-old Andersen left for Copenhagen in 1819, with thirteen thalers in his pocket and without an education, a trade or prospects, only two people in the world believed he would ever amount to anything: the local fortune-teller and Andersen himself. In *The Fairy Tale of My Life,* Andersen tells how, in her anxiety, his mother had consulted this "wise old woman," who had, after reading her cards and Andersen's coffee grounds, reassured her with the now famous prediction: "Your son will become a great man, and in honor of him Odense will one day be illuminated" (22). Andersen begged his mother to let him go to Copenhagen to seek his fortune there; he had dreamed that something wonderful would happen to him. "First one has to endure terrible adversity," he told his mother. "Then one becomes famous" (Stirling 53).

And suffer he had and did. The facts are well-documented in the numerous biographies of Andersen and in his diaries and *The Fairy Tale of My Life,* the autobiography which he revised frequently during his life. The grinding poverty of his childhood and youth, the desperate, depressing struggle for this lad from the wrong social class to climb the ladder of literary success, the unhappiness in his romantic life, the restless travelling, the hysteric phobias (of rabies, hotel fires, or being accidentally thought dead while asleep and buried alive), the "black" moods that swept over him—all are revealed by his biographers and more often than not by Andersen himself. He was, he informs us, the ugly duckling, the lowest in the town's pecking order—awkward, painfully sensitive, vulnerable—the brunt of crude jokes and coarse criticism. Famous as he later became, he never quite got over those early traumas, or the later scars. But they became the fuel of his fantasies and the substance of his stories. Reginald Spink quotes Andersen's own words to support that idea: "Most of what I have written is a reflection of myself. Every character is from life. I know and have known them all" (70). Spink observes:

> Andersen never stopped telling his own story; that was the way he abreacted. Sometimes he tells it in an idealized form, sometimes with self-revelatory candour. In tale after tale—"The Tinder Box," "Little Claus and Big Claus," "The Steadfast Tin Soldier," "The Swineherd," "The Ugly Duckling"—he is the hero who triumphs over poverty, persecution, and plain stupidity, and who sometimes, in reversal of the facts, marries the princess ("Clodpoll") or scorns her ("The Swineherd"). (100)

For Andersen, the creative process was an act of remembering, of stating and then transforming biographical facts in order to somehow exorcise the demons that haunted him, those shadows that never quite stopped threatening to take over the poet and his identity.

But there are lives and there are lives. Not every *roman à clef* becomes a best-seller, let alone a classic; and not every reified life experience succeeds as a work of literature. In many of his fairy tales and stories, Andersen offered his readers a theme and its variations which was not only personal to him, but also had and continues to have a universal appeal: the rags-to-riches, duckling-to-swan theme. Every swineherd or common soldier is a potential prince, and every ugly duckling a swan, if they are true to their own good, decent nature. This idea, which appears with such frequency in Andersen's works, creates an immediate bond of identification and sympathy between Andersen and his readers, especially his younger readers who, like numerous heroes and heroines in Andersen, are struggling and are desperately in need of stories that frame the chaotic and conflicting emotions of this experience. In his tales Andersen is the champion of the underdogs, the downtrodden, the spurned, the impoverished—in short, those with every reason to hope for whatever transformations will lead to a better life.

Of course, this sense of hope, of a brighter and ultimately happy future (if one perseveres and remains good and kind in the process of enduring) is at the very core of the traditional fairy tale, as Bruno Bettelheim has pointed out in *The Uses of Enchantment*. Andersen had drawn his inspiration and the vehicle for expressing this theme from the traditional fairy tales that, he tells us in the notes he wrote to accompany his stories, he "had heard as a child, either in the spinning room or during the harvesting of the hops"

(1071). Unlike other Romantic artists who also used the form and subject matter of the folk fairy tale, Andersen did not have to learn about his material second hand through study or from collecting trips in the countryside. He was steeped in its traditions; the world of the fairy tale "was his own world and had been so since birth" (Grønbech 95). This oral/aural sense of story, he felt, was important to capture, and he tried to do this, beginning with his first volume of stories which appeared in 1835. Of the four stories in this volume ("The Tinder Box," "Little Claus and Big Claus," "The Princess and the Pea," and "Little Ida's Flowers"), only the last was an original creation. The others were based on tales from the oral tradition, but elaborated upon in Andersen's inimitable style. His life-long friend, Edvard Collin, remembers how Andersen, during visits to his house, would tell the Collin children

> stories which he partly made up on the spur of the moment, partly borrowed from well-known fairy tales; but whether the tale was his own or a retelling, the manner of telling it was entirely his own, and so full of life that the children were delighted. He, too, took delight in letting his humor run free. He spoke continually with plenty of phrases that children used, and gestures to match. Even the driest of sentences was given life. He didn't say, "The children got into the carriage and then drove away," but, "So they got into the carriage, good-bye Daddy, good-bye Mummy, the whip cracked, snick, snack, and away they went, giddy up!" People who later heard him reading aloud his tales would only be able to form a faint impression of the extraordinary vitality with which he told them to children.
> (Grønbech 89)

We hear this surging verbal energy in the swaggering first paragraph of Andersen's first published fairy tale—"The Tinderbox.":

> A soldier came marching down the road: Left. . . right! Left. . . right! He had a pack on his back and a sword at his side. He had been in the war and he was on his way home. Along the road he met a witch. She was a disgusting sight, with a lower lip that hung all the way down her chest.

Andersen wrote to a friend as he was finishing this first collection, which he called *Fairy Tales for Children*, to explain what he was doing: "I want to win the next generations, you see!"(Grønbech 89) But by 1843, he had changed the title of those little volumes, containing three or four stories each, to *Fairy Tales*; and, within another ten years, they became, simply, *Stories*. But it had not taken Andersen twenty years before he "found out how to write fairy tales." Within a few years of beginning the stories, he wrote to a friend to say: "Now I tell stories of my own accord, seize an idea for the adults—and then tell it for the children while still keeping in mind the fact that mother and father are often listening too, and they must have a little something for thought" (Grønbech 91-2).

We see Andersen's concern with reaching the adult listening to (or reading the tale) throughout the fairy tales and stories. Andersen can't resist such an "adult" touch in "The Ugly Duckling," for example, when an old duck comes to call on the mother duck who has just hatched out her brood (except for the ugly duckling's egg). She brags to her guest that each of the new ducklings "looks exactly like their father." But then she quickly adds: "That scoundrel hasn't come to visit me once" (217). In "The Nightingale," after the bird has been summoned to the emperor's palace and has made the monarch weep with his music, Andersen, with his tongue in his cheek, describes the trickle-down effects of the concert:

> "That was the most charming and elegant song we have ever heard," said all the ladies of the court. And from that time onward they filled their mouths with water, so they could make a clucking noise, whenever anyone spoke to them, because they thought that then they sounded like the nightingale. Even the chambermaids and the lackeys were satisfied; and that really meant something, for servants are the most difficult to please. Yes, the nightingale was a success.   (207)

But there is more than just "a little something for thought" for the adults in many of the stories that Andersen began to include in these collections. Take, for instance, "The Sweethearts," a tale about a wooden top and the leather ball with which he is in love. She rejects his attentions, telling him that "mother and father were a pair of morocco slippers, and . . . I have a cork inside me." The ball gets lost on her ninth bounce, but the top, still very much in love with her, stays on as a favored plaything in the house, eventually getting rewarded with a coat of gold paint. Years later when he, too, is lost one day, he winds up in the same trash can as the ball. Her years of exposure have left her unrecognizable, but she proudly announces herself as before. At that moment the maid finds the top and retrieves him from the trash, never noticing the ball. And Andersen leaves the reader with the biting (and male chauvinist) commentary about life and love: "You get over it when your beloved has lain in a gutter and oozed for five years. You never recognize her when you meet her in the garbage bin" (215).

Similarly, stories like "The Shadow," have pushed beyond the boundaries of the literary fairy tale to become psychological fantasies directed toward an older reader. This story, one of Andersen's darkest and most enigmatic, examines what happens when a young scholar, an intellectual, sends his shadow across the street to the house of a beautiful woman, who turns out to be Poetry, while he himself remains aloof and detached, engrossed in his philosophical treatises and reveries on the other side of the street. Years pass, the scholar travels and writes, and the shadow, meanwhile, takes on a human form and a life of its own, becoming richly successful because it can peep into mankind's deepest secrets and because "he knew how to tell about some of what he had seen and how to hint at the rest, which was even more impressive" (342). Through an ironic reversal of events befitting a writer like Kafka, the philosopher becomes the shadow's shadow; the shadow goes on to marry the princess, and the philosopher, in the closing lines of the story, is executed. As the shadow has told the philosopher when he objects to the absurdity of becoming the shadow's servant, "that's the way of the world, and it isn't going to change" (341).

Andersen was criticized for writing such pessimistic and unfamiliar tales—such "philosophical" stories. He responded to his critics in the notes to his collected stories by arguing that "through the years. . .(he) tried to walk every radius, so to speak, in the circle of the fairy tale." The problem lay, Andersen felt, with some of those who had grown up with his earlier stories and thus expected a particular kind of tale from him. Somehow they had "lost the fresh spirit with which they once approached and absorbed literature (1087). To an extent, that is still true today. The popular notion of Andersen is that he is a writer or adapter of fairly traditional fairy tales; he has yet to receive the recognition he deserves as one of the pioneers and important innovators not only in the form of the literary fairy tale, but also in the forms of fantasy (what Andersen collectively referred to as the "wonder tale"). Tales like "The Millennium" (which begins: "They will home on wings of steam, the young citizens of America will fly through the air, across the great ocean, to visit old Europe.") are at the threshold of science fiction. "Auntie Toothache," the last story that Andersen wrote, is a grotesquely absurd visit to a nineteenth century Twilight Zone, where a young poet is visited in his dream by the archetypal spirit of tooth problems. Andersen serves up the malaise to us in the form of an aunt who, in the waking world, has over-indulged the poet with sweets and with encouragement to keep writing his sentimental verse. In the young man's nightmare, though, "Auntie Toothache" treats him to an "Ode to Pain" on his wisdom teeth and forces him to admit that her power is "greater than poetry, mathematics, philosophy, and all the rest of the music. . .stronger and more penetrating than all other feeling that has been painted on canvas or carved in marble. . .older than all the others. . .born right outside the gates of paradise, where the wet winds blow and the toadstools grow" (1066). She leaves only when the poet, in a dental delirium, agrees to stop writing verse forever. Andersen wrote this sardonically witty story when he returned to Odense in December of 1867 to be made an honorary citizen of the town— the highest accolade that his neighbors could bestow on him—and to be feted at an evening banquet when, as the gypsy had predicted, the city would be illuminated to celebrate his accomplishments. On the day of the festivities, Andersen was suffering from an excruciating toothache, the victim of one of life's supreme poetic injustices. But as so often happened with Andersen, he transformed that bitter experience immediately into art.

Almost as often as Andersen allows his characters to triumph, it seems, he offers stories in which fortunes are frustrated (as above), love is unrequited, or at the farthest extreme, lives are lost. There are too many dead or dying children in Andersen to suit many modern tastes (see "The Mother," "The Little Match Girl," and "The Angel"), and too many lovers who don't attain their heart's desire and are left in a kind of emotional limbo. Perhaps the most famous of these impossible loves is that of "The Little Mermaid," whose sacrifices for the prince go unnoticed and unrewarded, and who is left, despite the objections of generations of readers and all the logical and emotional directions of the story, without the "love of a human being," "an immortal soul," and thus without a way to "God's kingdom"—at least not until she serves a three hundred year penance with the other "children of the air." But after condemning her, Andersen offers a kind of reprieve:

> "You may be able to go there before that," whispered one of the others to her. "Invisibly, we fly through the homes of human beings. They can't see us, so they don't know when we are there; but if we find a good child, who makes his parents happy and deserves their love, we smile and God takes a year away from the time of our trial. But if there is a naughty and mean child in the house we come to, we cry; and for every tear we shed, God adds a day to the three hundred years we already must serve.
>
> (76)

This was not one of Andersen's better endings, and readers have often objected to its heavy-handed manipulation.

A similarly dispiriting story is "The Little Fir Tree," often considered to be one of Andersen's most autobiographical fables. In this story Andersen creates a character (the little tree) who wants, in a sense, what every person—certainly every child wants—"to grow, to grow . . . to become tall and old; there's nothing in the world so marvelous" (226). And when it hears from the sparrows in the forest about Christmas and the special place of the tree in the festivities, it can't wait to be carted away to be decorated, even though the wind and the sunshine advise it to set aside these desires and "be happy with us . . . be glad you are young; enjoy your youth and your freedom, here in nature (227). Of course the tree is chosen the next year, plays its rather terrifying role in the celebration, and then is quickly removed to the attic, where it is stored for the winter. There it whiles away the days telling a story it heard on Christmas Eve to the mice who come to stay the winter in the house. But unlike the main character in the tree's story (ironically titled "How Humpty-dumpty Fell Down the Stairs but Won the Princess Anyway"), there is no ultimate triumph or happy ending for the little tree. As it is being consumed on a spring-cleaning bonfire, it thinks "of a summer day in the forest, or a winter night when stars are brightest, and it remembered Christmas Eve and Humpty-dumpty: the only fairy tale it had ever heard and knew how to tell. Then it became ashes" (233).

Andersen is commenting here on the vain, fleeting nature of fame, in contrast to the stability of an existence that is more accepting, modest, and rooted—a lesson he was having to deal with in his own rather itinerant, unsettled life, and in terms of the ups and downs of his literary fortunes, which often sent him into tantrums or depressions. He is clearly trying to tell another kind of "fairy tale"—one that expressed the other, dark side of his artistic vision. This pessimistic bleakness in Andersen, which sometimes seems so cruelly moralistic (as it does, say, in "The Red Shoes") seems out of keeping with the sympathy that Andersen is so intent on creating for many of the other protagonists in his tales.

There are other contradictions, problems, and ambiguities in Andersen's work. One doesn't always know, for instance, why Andersen ridicules the pomposity and pretentions of the aristocracy on one page and then forgives them on the next. In "The Nightingale," Andersen satirizes the ways of the Emperor of China's court and the Emperor's own shallow willingness to settle for the artifical nightingale's song. The nightingale, who is really the figure of the poet and the perceptive proletarian center of the story, tells the Emperor at the end: "I love your heart more than your crown." But then it adds: ". . . and yet I feel that the crown has a fragrance of something holy about it" (211). One explanation for this waffling is that Andersen himself was a son of the working class who aspired to be and ultimately became the darling of the salons and courts of Europe. In a sense, he was living the contradiction that he wrote about. These and other problematic contradictions arise throughout Andersen's stories to baffle or puzzle the reader because Andersen seems frequently less interested in maintaining a consistent point of view or tone than in letting loose mercurial impressions and almost free associations.

What, then, makes Andersen's tales "classics"? Why should they be considered "touchstones"? A very obvious reason is that many of Andersen's tales continue to be *read,* and to affect those who read them deeply. Regardless of how we might react to them individually, many of his stories are passed from generation to generation, through edition after edition, becoming household names and a part of our universal, literary vocabulary. Ursula Le Guin speaks for many when she writes that she "hated all the Andersen stories with unhappy endings. That didn't stop me from reading them, and rereading them. Or from remembering them" (104).

The secret to this success lies, perhaps, in the fact that Andersen was connecting with exactly that in his readers—secrets. On one level, Andersen was tapping the secret, emotional realms of his own troubled experience, often writing from his own despair out of what Keats might have called "negative capability." But Andersen succeeded in projecting these incidents onto a larger, more public screen, through forms and symbols ostensibly reserved for children but which Andersen was keenly aware would usually be introduced to children by adults. Ultimately, Andersen meant his stories to be for everyone, and to deal with the secrets that all of us keep in common but are unable or unwilling to tell. Etymologically speaking, the words for "secret" and "sacred" share the same Germanic roots: what is secret is also personally sacred to us, from those deepest yearnings to the most petty jealousies and vanities.

On the one hand, there is Andersen's composite hero, the duckling/swan, swineherd/prince, nightingale/poet, soldier/king. He frequently must undergo great suffering and trials but nevertheless remains steadfast and true to his principles and, thus, to his own inner nature and its humanity. This is the duckling's way, and the tin soldier's, and little Gerda's in "The Snow Queen." Andersen is able to touch those chords of sympathy within his readers because, on some fundamental level, they, too, have shared these feelings and have hoped for the same optimistic resolution. Often this character is flawed, wounded, incomplete, but through his perserverance, kindness, and love he compensates for these inadequacies and becomes whole, metaphorically if not literally. At times this character is a poet, like the nightingale, whose songs "sing not only of those who are happy but also of those who suffer. . . of the good and of the evil that happen around you, and yet are hidden from you" (211). Sometimes she is disguised as a little child, whose stalwart love can melt the icy heart of her friend, a captive in the Snow Queen's palace. But whoever he or she is, this persona with dozens of faces expresses those profoundly human desires to love and be loved, and to seek a way to fulfill those feelings.

On the other hand, Andersen also explores those other, darker reaches of the psyche that we do not like to admit exist within ourselves. These shadowy realms appear in many of the tales, and they are Andersen's way of dealing with the dark side of his own soul. At its grimmest, in such tales as "The Shadow," Andersen is wrestling with the need for the artist to be aware of the nether reaches of the psyche, even if these shadows may contain evil. To repress, to deny, to not confront these forces, as Ursula Le Guin argues, is to be ultimately ruled by them, to become their victim as an artist and as a human being.

> "For the shadow," Le Guin insists, is not simply evil. It is inferior, primitive, awkward, animallike, childlike; powerful, vital, spontaneous. It's not weak and decent, like the learned young man from the north (in "The Shadow"); it's dark and hairy and unseemly; but, without it, the person is nothing. What is a body that casts no shadow? Nothing, a formlessness, two-dimensional, a comic-strip character. The person who denies his own profound relationship with evil denies his own reality. He cannot do, or make; he can only undo, unmake. (107)

Yet there is another dimension to Andersen's exploration of the shadow: humor. A finely tuned sense of humor gives many of Andersen's stories a vitality that holds them from the abyss of bitter gloom, despair or unrelieved seriousness. Andersen's humor can be very dark indeed, as in "A Drop of Water," where he has his main characters, who are looking through a magnifying glass at a miniature but surprisingly vicious city they have discovered there, try to decide whether or not they are observing a microcosm of "Copenhagen or some other big city" or just plain "ditch water." In "Big Claus and Little Claus the humor is deliciously macabre, when Big Claus ironically ties himself up in what will become his own shroud and violently demands that Little Claus push him into the river. In "The Tinder Box" Andersen's humor is suggestively risqué: when the soldier has the magic dog fetch the sleeping princess for him, he cannot resist kissing her, for "he was a soldier all over."

Finally, in "The Emperor's New Clothes," Andersen provides us with the kind of humor that manages to touch everyone's pet vanities. No one knew better than Andersen about the serious side of this kind of public embarrassment; he had felt it keenly since he was an awkward child walking down the center aisle of the church in the squeaky new boots of which he was so proud. This particular story—one of Andersen's most famous—was also rooted in the facts of the writer's life. Haugaard retells the incident from Andersen's diaries:

> A foreign artist arrived in Copenhagen and announced in the newspapers that he had come to paint portraits of the most famous Danes, and he hoped that these great personages would come to the studio he had just rented. The very next morning who should appear at his door but Andersen and one of the actors from the Royal Theatre, a man known for his self-love and conceit. Andersen looked at the actor and could not help laughing, both at him and at himself.   (74)

"To write the Emperor's New Clothes," Haugaard goes on, "one must be able to be as foolish as the emperor—although I admit that it is more important to be as wise as the child who saw that he was naked. But only the genius can be both at the same time and, therefore, be able to write the story."

P. M. Pickard writes that Andersen used "so much courage in displaying so much vulnerability" (78). This struggle of opposing elements within Andersen is at the paradoxical heart of his works—as it evidently was in his life. Throughout his works, Andersen tried to preserve a precarious balance between competing sides of his nature: the courtly and the colloquial, the exalted and the mundane, the realistic and the Romantic, the conservative and the iconoclast, the hopeful and the pessimistic. These and other dramatic oppositions give Andersen's stories their rich complexity and expressive range. Andersen took real emotional and artistic chances in his tales "for everyone." Because he did, Andersen was instrumental in creating a children's literature that could become a vehicle for carrying both traditional messages and values as well as an author's personal visions. Andersen wrote, as Keats puts it, "on the pulses," casting light on the shadows, telling his own, and our own, secrets, giving them a song and wings.

REFERENCES

Andersen, Hans Christian. *The Complete Fairy Tales and Stories.* Trans. Erik Christian Haugaard. New York: Doubleday, 1974.

_____. *The Fairy Tale of My Life.* 1868; rpr. New York: Paddington Press, 1975.

Grønech, Bo. *Hans Christian Andersen.* Boston: Twayne, 1982.

Haugaard, Erik Christian. "Portrait of a Poet: Hans Christian Andersen." *The Open-Hearted Audience: Ten Writers Talk about Writing for Children.* Ed. Virginia Haviland. Washington: Library of Congress, 1980.

Le Guin, Ursula. "The Child and the Shadow." *The Open-Hearted Audience.*

Pickard, P. M. *I Could a Tale Unfold: Violence, Horror and Sensationalism in Stories for Children.* New York: The Humanities Press, 1961.

Spink, Reginald. *Hans Christian Andersen and His World.* New York: G. P. Putnam's, 1972.

Stirling, Monica. *The Wild Swan: The Life and Times of Hans Christian Andersen.* New York: Harcourt, Brace and World, 1965.

Asbjornsen and Moe's Norwegian Folktales: Voice and Vision

by Kay Unruh DesRoches

My interest in the folktales collected by Asbjornsen and Moe began in Norway, where I was studying the language in order to pursue my research in the work of the great playwright Henrik Ibsen. My studies took me to the Gudbrandsdal district—Peer Gynt country. I was completely unprepared for what I saw and felt there. In a week of hiking over the boulder-scattered moors and spongy marshes of the Gudrands valley, through dense pine forests, up and down steep mountain slopes, and sleeping in rain-sodden make-shift shelters or in abandoned mountain huts, I began to understand that I was experiencing "culture shock." I discovered later that my very intense response was not unusual, even for Norwegians. On a folk-tale collecting expedition of his own in 1862, Ibsen noted in his diary the horror he felt at the remoteness, isolation and harsh conditions of life in this area. He records a detail which we recognize from his play *Brand:* far below him, in the shadow of a precipice so sheer that he could not conceive the possibility of a way down, he saw a church and parsonage which, because the rock face it hugged, angled out slightly, was protected from the inevitable avalanches. One could add that the parsonage was probably occupied, and the church attended, although the dwellings of the parishoners were nowhere visible. On his first visit to this same valley, Werenskiold, the illustrator whose pictures still appear in editions of the Norwegian folktales, reports that he sensed behind the primitive life on the great feudal farms a living image of the Middle Ages; "and behind the large forest, the troll world of the Jutenheim mountains." Although the towering landscape of this part of Norway is truly formidable, it was this sense of a living presence I found so unsettling.

But I experienced this feeling in other parts of Norway, too. From the Arctic Circle north I was alert to sights and sounds which sent shocks into my system: the sudden rumbling of the glacier underfoot; the wildness of the Lofoten mountains and the hidden, secret harbours and settlements with their tiny graveyards commemorating storms and avalanches, where the names of children and women far outnumber those of the men and boys; the pregnant silence as we chugged down the narrow passage of the Trollfjord; the bleak shale slopes lining long miles of Lyngenfjord; the sparse and isolated houses hidden in mists and

24

rain and the sudden appearance of reindeer shapes crossing the road and surrounding us as we moved deeper into the north; the unearthly displays of northern lights as they danced and sang across the sky. No doubt all this exists in the North of my own country, Canada; but there it remains the cultural property of a largely unassimilated minority who live within a more-or-less oral tradition. Thus it has not been made a living presence for the literate majority—as it has been made in Norway.

As I discovered when I read them, that landscape is very much alive in the Norwegian folktales or *eventyr:* the trolls, the *huldre,* the *blaulyse,* the *draug* all express something of the Norwegian's relationship to that landscape. Caught and isolated within rock, mountain, forest, and endless miles of inhospitable coastline, the folk imagination seems to have interiorized that landscape and given it a voice, a voice which reverberates through the stories. I hear it in the tone: the broad humour; the blunt, almost sardonic laugh at the end of the story which so readily becomes vulgar. I hear it in the storyteller back of the writing. Particularly, I hear it in the sly sense of being in cahoots with something unspoken, as though the very act of storytelling was part of a pact to check the trolls and their magic—a pact I participate in when I listen.

In one of Henrik Ibsen's early unfinished plays, a *skjald* (minstrel) who lives in the mountains with the *huldre* folk comes down into the village to sing. When the tavern owner senses he will sing of things he does not want to hear, the *skjald* reminds him that listening to the songs will bring good luck, whereas refusing to listen will bring bad luck. Asked to say briefly what he has to say and then leave, the *skjald* counters that he cannot: "by song alone and story do I work, that's all." Nor is there any cause for wonder; Walter J. Ong suggests that this is a mark of an oral tradition:

> In a primary oral culture, to solve effectively the problem of retaining and retrieving carefully articulated thought, you have to do your thinking in mnemonic patterns, shaped for ready oral recurrence. Your thought must come into being in heavily rhythmic, balanced patterns, in repetitions or antitheses, in alliterations and assonances, in epithetic and formulary expressions, in standard thematic settings (the assembly, the meal, the duel, the hero's "helper", and so on), in proverbs which are constantly heard by everyone so that they come to mind readily and which themselves are patterned for retention and ready recall or in other mnemonic form. Serious thought is intertwined with memory systems.
>
> (34)

Folklorists have been alert to the differences between genuine oral patterning and literate structuring long enough to develop a considerable body of literature on the subject; but for the untrained ear of the reader who comes to folktales by way of books, there is no easy way of distinguishing an authentic record of an oral delivery from that of a literate or even a residually oral delivery. In any case I am not, here, concerned about authenticity; I am interested in tone, which means I will have to make some assumptions about what the storyteller's voice sounded like. Yet when they recorded the tales, Asbjornsen and Moe obviously made an effort to retain some aspects of the oral performances they heard; even though the original voice of the storyteller may be only residual, it is there, and it must be considered if the tales are to be seriously considered as literature.

We know Asbjornsen must have been afraid of losing this voice because of the way in which he tried initially to frame the tales so that an actual person was telling them. For all its fabrication, this kind of a reconstruction allows us to glimpse what the collector's relationship to the storyteller might have been, and, more importantly, how the collector saw the storyteller's relationship to the tales. One such story is "An Evening in the Squire's Kitchen," actually a group of tales told within a story frame. The narrator/collector is reading in a corner of the Squire's parlour on a miserable winter's evening, acutely aware of the stuffiness and affectation of the squire's attempts at intellectual discourse. In contrast, peals of genuine laughter filter in from the kitchen. When he can endure it no longer he joins them, "leaving [the squire] behind in the room in company with the dimly burning candle and his own disturbed thoughts." In the kitchen, all is "Light, life and merriment":

> A great fire blazed on the large open hearth and lighted up the room even in its farthest corners. By the side of the hearth presided the squire's wife with her spinning wheel.... Along the edge of the hearth sat the children and cracked nuts. Round about them was a circle of girls and wives of the neighbouring tenants [spinning and carding]. In the passage outside the door, the threshers who had done their day's work, were stamping the snow off their feet before they came in,—their hair full of chaff. They sat down by the big old-fashioned table, where the cook soon brought them their supper, consisting of a large bowl of thick porridge and a bowl of milk.

> The smith was leaning against the wall by the hearth; he was smoking on a long cutty-pipe, and on his countenance, which bore traces of smithy-soot, lay a dry, serious expression, which told he had been telling some story, and that to his own satisfaction.   (74-75)

This is no doubt an idealization, but it hits on a principle worth noting: storytelling requires listeners of a particular kind. As the story develops, everyone in the kitchen becomes a participant in the event. All feel free to interject, question, add, even offer alternate versions; and all assume that the stories they hear and tell have their roots in real life. Whether the stories are formless accounts of encounters with ghosts, demons, trolls, or patterned animal fables and romantic fictions, they all fasten on landscape familiar to them—a mound, a forest, a *seter*, a churchyard, a boulder. At the end of the story, we are left with the impression that these folktales are not told for entertainment alone, but as evidence and confirmation of the nature of the world. We are made aware by the storyteller's personal experience that this world of faery is not simply a fictive invention called "fairyland"; the world we enter when we join the listeners is the world in which the storytellers and their listeners are born, live and die, and where they sometimes, and often to their harm, come into contact with inhabitants from the other world.

In his "Introduction" to *Folktales of Norway*, Reidar Thorwald Christiansen considers the use of the term "fairytale" for "folktale" to be misleading and strongly prejudiced in favor of modern unbelievers:

> Even today firm believers exist, although they are growing rarer every year. They are not inclined to talk about such things, partly from their fear of ridicule, but also from the semi-religious aura which surrounds references to the other race...[Stories] were not told as entertainment but as constantly renewed proof of the necessity not to deviate from the traditional code of behaviour. This code had to be observed in order to avoid running any risks from contacts with their invisible neighbors.   (xxxv)

The "dry, serious" satisfaction of the storyteller in Asbjornsen's reconstruction is tied to the fact-like fiction that the teller is privy to special knowledge. And so he is—at least he is in an oral tradition where the tale-teller is the communal reservoir of knowledge and wisdom.

But the stories we read have neither those tellers nor those listeners; nor did Asbjornsen and Moe "hear" what those peasants in the kitchen "heard". The stories we read in our folktale collections are written versions of oral recitations. This imposition of a literate form on an at least residually oral voice and an active belief creates a tension which accounts for much of the appeal of these tales. One place where we can see this tension is in the endings of many of the stories.

The tension develops because of a difference between what I will call the "narrative ending" and the "verbal ending". The end of a narrative is that point to which the events have logically (or magically) been driving, and which completes them by means of an appropriate resolution. Walter J. Ong points out that one effect of literacy is the capability to structure stories chronologically, according to a narrative idea. The result is, of course, a plot with an Aristotelean structure of beginning, middle and end, which, Ong points out, is the plot model we most admire and have come to expect of a narrative. In *The Genesis of Secrecy*, Frank Kermode calls this kind of plot "followable" or "guided"; he adds that "to make arrangements for such guidance is to have an ulterior motive, whether it is aesthetic, epistemological or ethical" (118). A "narrative ending" is one which is integrated into the plan of the whole and which convinces us by satisfying our expectation of unity.

This plotting of events to imitate a narrative idea is absent from many of these stories, especially those which appear to be more directly connected with the oral tradition. Because the end of the story in no way coincides with the completion of a narrative plot, a "narrative ending" would be inconceiveable. Yet there must always be a point at which the teller wishes to bring the tale to a close—to silence. *The Iliad* ends in such a way: its ending, "Such were the funeral rites of Hector, tamer of horses" is without plot value when judged by Aristotelean criteria. It is easy to see that the words sum up what has gone before; but they do not sum up the epic, only the previous episode. Nor can we ever be certain that such a work is completed; that "continuations" to *The Iliad* have appeared periodically suggests that not all readers have found the ending to be satisfactory. An ending, then, can simply be a means of entering into silence. This is what I mean by a "verbal ending".

The usual form of the verbal ending in the Norwegian folk tales is a rhymed couplet or nonsense verse which makes it clear that the storyteller will proceed no further. "The Pancake" is a case in point. The story follows the adventures of a pancake which has been given volition by the housewife's slip of tongue ("'wait till it turns itself', she said"). When the pancake becomes conscious of the intentions of the seven hungry children, it flips itself out of the frying pan, and rolls off; but it finds the voracity of the children duplicated in all it encounters, so that it must keep rolling. When the time has come to end the tale, the teller has only to bring in the pig (or whatever) to trick and eat the pancake before he recites: "Since the pancake can go no further, this tale can be no longer".

Here we have an accumulative series of encounters which can be brought to an end or continued by the whim of the storyteller or the willingness of the audience to continue the joke. There is no need to justify the story's end, and little point in following the sequence of events in order to interpret them, since no "ulterior motive"—or idea—is evident in the telling. We can see this same principle again in the "Snip, snap, snout,/Now the tale's told out" of "The Three Billygoats Gruff".

So, too, with "The Charcoal Burner," although we notice here that the verbal ending also becomes the punch-line to a joke. This rags to riches story differs from others of its type in that the charcoal burner wins his rewards by means of a confidence trick. Poor, illiterate, and lazy, he decides to become a parson for reasons of status; and being black already, he has only to buy cassock and ruff and do as other parsons do. When he sees them all heading for the king's manor, he joins them, identifying himself as "the wise parson and true prophet" who surely can find the thieves who stole the king's most costly ring. By a combination of luck, stealth, sloth and stupidity (or mother-wit, depending on perspective) he manages to win the reward: a parsonage. The story includes a second and a third episode which bring him the deanship, and, finally, the second highest rank in the kingdom. Like "The Pancake," this story, too, is aggregative: it could end after any one of the episodes. The joke is actually told when the charcoal burner "catches" the thieves; subsequent episodes merely add to the fun which is had at the expense of the clergy, the king and book-learning. All our expectations of an unmasking are frustrated: "Trip, trap trill,/he got more than his fill," sings the storyteller at the end, mocking us as the parishioners, who knew their parson to be a con-artist, were also mocked. This would be more than our middle-class consciences could bear if we were to read it as an end to the tale instead of as an end of the tale. A tension is thus created between the verbal ending and our literary expectations, which shocks us into the recognition that we have been reading with both a literary and a moral bias.

We find another form of the verbal ending in "The Golden Castle Which Hung in the Air," a typical Ash Lad quest-story. Here a verbal ending has been tacked on to a narrative plot:

Then a house they did build,
And shoes they did patch,
And wee princes they had,
From cellar to thatch.

Events, causally interlocked and sequentially told, have been brought to narrative completion when the Ash Lad rights the wrong he has done to the donkey who helped him find the princess of his dreams. The Ash Lad weds the princess, and the donkey, who turns out to be a prince, weds her sister. This narrative ending leaves the verbal ending without any apparent function. But it is there, nonetheless, and its presence has the effect of focusing our attention on the storyteller. It reminds us that this tale was not told in the way we have just read it. But more importantly, it gives the stories a second voice—an oral voice which, however residual, pulls away from the authorial, or "written" voice.

This double voice is significant, especially in light of the storytellers' frequent claim to be giving an eyewitness account of the events. We notice, for instance, that the teller, by means of the verbal ending, ties the events of the tale to events in his or her social world:

> And since then, no one has ever heard that the trolls have been about in the Hedal Woods sniffing after Christian blood.
> ("The Boys Who Met The Trolls In The Hedal Woods" 12)

> So the wedding was held, and it was so grand and fine, and they celebrated so that people are still talking about it.
> ("The Golden Bird" 55)

The verbal ending can also tie the teller directly to the events: he is able to tell the story because he was there:

> Oh yes, it could just be that squire Per wanted her as his queen. So there was a wedding and a feast which lasted eight days, and then I wasn't with squire Per and his queen any longer, that's the truth.
> ("Squire Per" 126)

In *The Genesis of Secrecy* (101-123), Frank Kermode talks about the "fact-likeness" of a narrative—that the claim to reporting merely makes a narrative history-like, not historical: "there is a difference between making a text sound as if what it reports had occurred, and making it report what had occurred." Even the latter, he says, implies a fiction, in that history itself is a narrative invented to explain facts. Kermode is here discussing the question of historicity in the Gospel narratives, but much of what he says is equally applicable to folk narrative. Folktales assure their readers that the fiction is fact, but since our primary target, as literary critics, is meaning ("what is written"), not truth ("what is written about"), we perceive the assurances as "illusion, the effect of a rhetorical device." The claim of the storyteller to be giving an eyewitness account of the events thus becomes part of the tale's meaning, not its truth. As readers we have no difficulty penetrating the barely disguised fiction implicit in the verbal ending of "Squire Per."

But the double voice is significant in another way. As previously indicated, the tale Asbjornsen and Moe have written is not the story that was told them, nor the story they recorded. Undoubtedly they wrote the story with the intention of accurately reporting the performance (what had occurred—the truth). Undoubtedly, also, their primary aim was to write the story, and story-writing is an act of fiction—to use Kermode's phrase, a "sense-making" act: "Fictions are for finding things out, and they change as the needs of sense-making change" (*The Sense of an Ending* 39). The tale collector and story writer are thus involved in contradictory purposes: the former must be inclusive (reporting what occurred) and the latter must be selective (shaping what occurred). The solution, of course, is mimesis—"make it sound as if what they report had occurred." Thus, at the root of the folktale as we know it there is always an irony.

The *skjald*, on the other hand, belonging to a different (oral) cultural and belief system must have been unaware of the distinction between fact and fact-likeness. He would have had no comprehension of fact as a concept separate from event, a point about oral consciousness confirmed by Ong, who notes that, "For an oral culture...knowing means achieving close, empathetic, communal identification with the known" (45). Citing as an example the "controlled" transcription of *The Mwindo Epic* where the singer Candi Rureke recited for twelve days all the episodes he knew about the hero Mwindo, Ong points to the strong identification of the performer and listeners with the hero,

> an identification which actually affects the grammar of the narration, so that on occasion the narrator slips into the first person when describing the actions of the hero. So bound together are narrator, audience and character that Rureke has the epic character Mwindo himself address the scribes taking down Rureke's performance.... In the sensibility of the narrator and his audience the hero of the oral performance assimilates into the oral world even the transcribers who are de-oralizing it into text. (46)

We have seen the close identification between knower and known in the verbal endings and in the storyteller's claim to have been an eyewitness. But there is an element of irony in the storyteller's claim, which is puzzling. The objectivity necessary for analysis (and thus for consciously created discrepancies) being unavailable to him in an oral culture, there is no possibility that the irony we note in the storyteller's voice was intended by the *skjald*.

It is "writing," Ong notes, "which separates the knower from the known and sets up conditions for objectivity" (46). The point to be noted here is again ironic: the *skjald's* "truth" (evident in the close identification of knower and known) turns by the act of writing it into the fiction of a storyteller whose very presence in the tale is ironic. As a creation of the story, he is both a spokesman for the *skjald's* truth and an ironic comment upon it. We, the readers, perceiving that the purposes of both *skjald* and tale collector have been frustrated, delight in the irony created by the storywriter and the storyteller.

If we can accept this, then we can begin to see how the tension between the two voices creates also a tension between the content (what is written about), where the writer is in control, and the story (what is written), where the storyteller is in control. In "The Ash Lad and the Good Helpers" we can see several ways in which tension is created. The story is built on a set of the most improbable events imaginable: a king challenges the young men of his kingdom to build him a ship which runs as well on land as on water; a bent wizened old man puts a spell on all three brothers who will attempt to meet the challenge; the third brother who has "built" the ship is instructed to take with him anyone who asks—a skinny knave who satisfies his hunger for meat by eating rubble, one with hearing so keen that he can hear the grass grow; one with sight so sharp that he could hit a troll's eye at the world's end, and so on—companions qualified to accomplish the impossible. Which is what they proceed to do, in order to force the king to live up to his promise of his daughter and half the kingdom. The story has become a magnificently told tall tale, with an ending that matches it exactly: "And, as they were rushing about groping for a bullet wadding, they mistook me for one, and gave me porridge in a flask and milk in a basket, and shot me straight here so I could tell you how it all came about." The slyness of that ending could easily escape one: yes, the teller has entered his tale and claims to have been an eyewitness. In Ong's terms this would be a case of identification. But an identification with what? A world so topsy-turvy that he could identify with it only if he were prepared to capitulate wholeheartedly to its anarchy, which of course he hasn't done, as the act of storytelling suggests. Again we are aware of an ironic perspective. But whose perspective is it? We had assumed it was ours, but we now see that the storyteller is also aware of an irony. By responding with laughter, we recognize our complicity; we too have capitulated, but to irony, not to anarchy, and thereby participate in the joke. Once again we have penetrated the disguise of "fact-likeness".

But if we persist, we find the fiction unveiled to be made of the same stuff as the disguise itself. The content of the story is magical, but the story is told with so much realistic detail that it in turn becomes "fact-like," making us forget the improbability of the situation:

> When they had sailed a little farther they met a fellow who was lying on a sunny hillside sucking a barrel tap.
> "What sort of a fellow are you?" asked Espen Ashlad. "And what's the good of lying there sucking that barrel tap?"
> "Oh, when one hasn't got the barrel, one must make do with the tap," said the man. "I'm always so thirsty that I can never drink my fill of beer or wine," he said and then asked if he could come along.

As the ordeals become more impossible, they are wedded to more homely details. The water which must be fetched from the world's end in *ten minutes* is to be used for the princess' *tea* and carried in a *pail;* the man who can hear grass grow now hears the water-fetcher *snoring* at the world's end; the winter the man blows out of his mouth produces a *chilblain* on the king's face. This attention to realistic detail becomes part of the voice of the storyteller, and gives us the same ironic perspective we get from the verbal endings.

In most cases our response to the irony is laughter. This is not to say that the tales are genuinely structured comedies; but it does suggest that comic conventions are at work. As I was reading Ong's *Orality and Literacy* I was struck by the number of correspondences there appear to be between what he identifies as the characteristics of oral narrative and what literary theorists understand to be the characteristics of comedy: both are highly conventionalized; both deal in flat character types; both assume the primacy of the group rather than the individual; both exteriorize rather than interiorize their action—to the extent that gross physical action is central to both; both are performance-oriented rather than information-oriented, which keeps concepts "situational and operational within a living human lifeworld"; both organize action episodically (Ong 36-55). I can offer no explanation for these correspondences; but if there is a natural affinity between them, we could accept the tendency of these tales to move always toward comedy as the natural expression of the storyteller's style rather than a conscious comedic shaping of the stories by the author/writers. In fact, it is my impression that the storyteller is so much in contol in the Norwegian stories that Asbjornsen and Moe—short of excising him altogether—could do little else than give him his head. The result is the use of conventions which we normally consider more appropriate to comedy than to romance.

A comparison between the German and Norwegian versions of the familiar golden goose story might help to clarify my point. Although both stories give us a poor man with three sons, a golden goose, a string of people fastened to the goose, a king and his too serious daughter, and a final wedding, the tone of the stories and the way in which they are developed are remarkably different.

The Grimm version is structured in such a way that the "point" or moral remains always in sight. The hero of the story is Dummling, the typical simpleton, youngest of three brothers; he succeeds where others fail, not because he is more clever than they, but because he is unselfconscious and therefore true to his own nature. Because he has no sense of tomorrow, he is able to concentrate on the needs of the moment; because he is unable to see danger ahead, he stands firm where others tend to run. Being the youngest and least valued member of the realm, he also tends to have developed a natural sympathy with all that is undervalued. All of this serves him admirably on his quest.

True to type, Dummling is willing to share his few crumbs with the hungry little man who asks for food, and his reward is the magical golden goose. This one choice leads him, by the logic of reward and the power of chance, to the ultimate prize: the King's daughter and half the kingdom. Completely in the control of the writer/narrator who selects and arranges all its parts according to a plan, the story underplays anything which might distract from the idea of reward, so that even the comedy striving at times to assert itself is merely reported, not developed.

In contrast, the Norwegian "Taper Tom Who Made the Princess Laugh" seems intent on evoking laughter, not only from the princess but also from us—an effect of the telling, not what is told. In this story the hero is also a simpleton, but instead of focusing on the reward for an action, this story focuses on the action itself—a contest—which makes the hero active, not passive. Taper Tom nags and whines until his father gives him permission to try his luck; then he talks the king into hiring him to carry wood and water; finally, he swaps the fine fish he caught for the golden goose: "if it's the way you say, I can use it for a fishhook", he says. At each stage he makes a choice which leads him by degrees to his goal. Even the reward is conceived of in terms of action, since what he aims for is not so much the princess as the princess' laughter.

These structural differences affect the tone in that they allow for much more involvement on the part of the storyteller in the Norwegian story. He is not just "giving information" as is the writer/narrator of the Grimm tale; he is dramatically involving us in each moment. Consider the part about the second son in the two stories:

> Next went out the second son to work; and his mother gave him too a pasty and a bottle of wine. And the same little old man met him also, and asked him for something to eat and drink. But he too thought himself vastly clever, and said, "Whatever you get I shall lose; so go your way!" The little man took care that he should have his reward; and the second stroke he aimed against the tree hit him on the leg; so that he too was forced to go home.

Here in the Grimm's version, the second son is part of the familiar threesome pattern; the repetition prepares us for the third son who will complete the pattern by breaking it. It is a convention which we enjoy primarily for its familiarity. But in Asbjornsen and Moe's version, although all the conventions are observed, there is an addition of detail which directs the focus onto the story itself:

> When [the first son] had come safely home, the second son wanted to set out. He was a schoolmaster, and a strange figure of a man he was, too. He had legs of unequal length, and that with a vengeance. One minute he was as short as a boy, and then he stood up on his long leg and became as tall as a troll. And he was really a champion at running.
>
> Yes, he too set out for the king's manor and said he wanted to make the king's daughter laugh. That wasn't at all unlikely, thought the king, "but heaven help you if you don't!" he said. "We cut the strips broader for each one who tries!"
>
> The schoolmaster strode out on the field. There he placed himself outside the princess' window, and he preached and said mass like seven parsons, and read and sang like seven sextons who had been in the parish there. The king laughed so he had to hold onto the porch post, and the king's daughter almost cracked a smile, but she caught herself and was just as gloomy and serious again, and so it went no better with Paul the schoolmaster than it had with Per the soldier—for they were called Per and Paul, you might know. They took him and cut three strips out of his back, and rubbed in salt, and then they sent him home again.

All three sons are developed by contest criteria: the first is a clumsy soldier; the second is a deformed schoolteacher; the third and youngest is a dreamer. Though they are individually characterized, they remain true to type, with no attempt made to interiorize them: the differences are strictly physical and external in that they refer to appearance, occupation and method. From first to last the storyteller is involved in the physicality of the situation:

> So the smith said, "it would be fun to hold back the whole flock of geese, as many as they are." For he was a strong man. And so with his tongs he grabbed the old man by the seat of his breeches, and the old fellow began to shout and wriggle.
> But Taper Tom said, "Hang on if you want to come along!"
> So the smith also had to go along. And for all he bent his back, and dug his heels in the ground and wanted to get loose, it helped not one bit. He was stuck as fast as though he had been screwed into the big anvil in the smithy, and whether he wanted to or not, he had to dance along.

This attention to physical detail takes the emphasis from the tale's allegorical content and places it instead on its action—the contest.

Contest, as Susanne Langer has pointed out, is the form conflict takes in comedy. A character in conflict, whether with himself or with an external force, invites an emotional response by involving other characters, and therefore the reader, in a system of values. But value is hard to apply to an action that falls outside the scope of our emotional responses; the glee with which we watch the simpleton hero brutally vanquish his opponents is possible only when we are distanced enough to remain emotionally uninvolved. A contest offers that distance because it is a game and therefore is played by rules, not laws. In a contest the comic hero is removed from moral imperatives, and likewise, our own emotional attachment to right and wrong is replaced with an intellectual appreciation of good and bad. Furthermore, the goodness or badness of a character's actions becomes a strictly "internal" matter not to be judged by an "outside" referential except insofar as the story violates our sense of propriety (which, one may add, is an aspect of aesthetics and rhetoric, not morality.) By this I do not mean that we do not judge; all art requires that we judge. I mean that the conventions of a work determine the criteria for judgment; therefore we judge differently when we watch a contest than when we become involved in a conflict.

In general, Norwegian folktales are built upon contest and employ comic conventions that allow the distance necessary for laughter. We are not incensed when the charcoal burner is rewarded for deceit, or when a boy who has "used" a troll to help him with his task proceeds to chop him to pieces, as in "The Ash Lad Who Had An Eating Match With The Troll"; nor are we horrified in "The Old Woman Against The Stream" when an exasperated husband drowns his nagging wife in order to shut her up. We understand that the conventions are those of comedy; and however grotesque it may be, we recognize that the old woman has won when she fools the old man by floating upstream after her death.

The comic conventions and the ironic tone set these stories apart from the quest/romance fantasies which we tend to use as our models for fairy tales. Because they are not "plotted", the events tend to be more noticeably episodic and accumulative (this happens and then that happens) instead of causal and sequential (this happens because of that). Further, the contest serves as a natural way of arranging separate episodes and holding them together as an event as well as serving as a comic device. Finally, because the storyteller's ironic voice is felt so immediately in the Norwegian stories, a comic manner is developed which allows the stories to gather comic overtones. Within these terms the structure of "Taper Tom" tends towards the comedic whereas that of "The Golden Goose" tends toward a more typical quest/romance.

Comedy and romance are not mutually exclusive genres; they must, however, part company when the story moves too far toward irony. Irony calls our attention to discrepancies: between the way the world appears to be and the way it is, and between the ideal and the real—what ought to be and what is. In *Anatomy of Criticism*, Northrop Frye places irony as the polar opposite of romance. Both represent the ultimate discrepancy between the realities of life and the desires of dream, but in romance the dream is realized, and in irony the dream is exposed as a sham. Thus, irony can coexist with romance only so long as it does not destroy our belief in the ideal. When the irony becomes too strong for the web of belief, the ideal (fantastical) element must be assimilated into the real. Then we glimpse the demonic forces of this world where we had previously seen only the personalities and powers of the "other world".

As we have seen, the Norwegian *eventyr* balance the real with the ideal by holding them in a tension which allows neither to assert itself. But sometimes the irony becomes too strong, as in "The Old Woman Against The Stream," or "The Devil and The Bailiff", or "Butterball", and the stories become demonic, and not a little frightening, for all that we are encouraged to laugh.

No one understood better than the two illustrators, Werenskiold and Kittelsen, how the ironies in these stories work. They create in their illustrations the tension that exists always between the real world in which these events occur and the magical events themselves; between tone and content.

The illustrations for "Three Princesses in the Mountain-in-the-Blue" are typical of Werenskiold's work. In a picture showing the princesses in this typical quest/romance, their dresses, their shoes, and their long pigtails put them into provincial, middleclass Norway; and their attitudes proclaim them to be high-spirited girls in their teens. The illustrations of humble cottage and splendid manor depict rural Norway; both are isolated, weathered establishments, differing mainly in size. Furthermore, although the diminutive size and great head of hair of a "little lame man on crutches" in another picture mark him as traditionally elvish, he is shown in realistic action: he has a crutch in each hand with which he is flailing a man who is lying on his back on the floor and kicking out as best he can, desperately warding off the blows to his face with his hands and arms. This focus on familiar action neutralizes the strangeness of the "visitor" without making him a recognizeable denizen of this world. In other words, Werenskiold implies an ironic presence in the fantastic content; we see it in the realistic detail, the focus on action, and the realistic settings into which he places magical beings.

Kittelsen's drawings are different from Werenskiold's mainly in his willingness to allow the "strangeness" to assert itself. But if his illustrations have more the quality of dream, and frequently nightmare, he never loses the tension between the romance and the lusty telling of the tales. In "White-Bear-King-Valemon" the illustrations are dream-scapes, but the final cartoon-like drawing of a whole troll colony catapulting off a bridge into a river below allows us the perspective which exists in the telling, if not in the story. Like his partner, he frequently throws the emphasis on comic detail.

But where Kittelsen excels is in creating a vision of the demonic. The trolls as he sees them are ultimate representatives of an ironic vision. The menace they represent is always overlaid with their monstrous stupidity, or what Bergson calls "absence of mind," which makes them comic as often as not. In the "Golden Bird", when the fox-turned-parson easily tricks the three irate trolls into believing that the young prince had passed by in the time of his grandmother's grandmother, they break into a fit of laughter:

> "Ha, ha, ha, ha!" they said holding on to each other. "If we've been asleep that long, we might as well turn right back and go to sleep again," they said, and then they went back the same way.

Kittelsen shows us the mindless laughter of faces and bodies that resemble but are not quite human. In the fox's sly and self-satisfied expression we see another aspect of the human face which is quite as unsettling.

In troll drawings like this one, Kittelsen's ironic perception does not encroach so far on romance that the latter is quite destroyed. We are shown the underside of this vision in "The Tabby Who Was Such A Glutton". In the second of Kittelsen's three illustrations for this story, the giant, menacing cat, intent on eating up the world, stalks right out of the picture towards us with its evil eyes and razor-sharp teeth fixed on us—its next meal. In this picture, the illustrator has caught something which strikes me as the essence of these tales—a voice, a tone, a laugh. In response to that voice, we laugh, too. But if the stories make us laugh, they also make us conscious that we are laughing. Kittelsen's illustrations of the tabby are not at all funny; they are genuinely frightening. Yet our laughter in response to the fantastic energy with which the storyteller tells of the cat's gluttony, and recites his list of victims each time one has been added, is also genuine. The comic irony amuses us, but serves at the same time to underline the grotesque; a very thin line separates the story from the *skjald's* unconditional belief. The writers and readers of these tales cope with this tension by means of the irony in the storyteller's voice.

I sensed this the first time I read these stories. A friend and I had travelled to a small farmhouse on the southern coast of Norway, very isolated, and very old. It was nested in the hills, not far from the open sea. During the afternoon we had walked down to the sea to buy some crabs from the fishermen's traps, and had listened for several hours to stories being passed back and forth among them, until the storm that had been brewing all day made it impossible to hear them any longer. My Norwegian did not always serve me well enough to catch what they were saying, but I came away with an overwhelming sense of voice and tone—and storm. I had been hearing something I had never heard before, and what I wanted was a collection of *Norske Folkeventyr,* so I could read at leisure what had passed me by. We found a copy of Asbjornsen's *Huldre-Eventyr og Folksagn* (Folktales and Legends) and with that my companion left me for two days, alone in this isolated farmstead in the midst of a howling storm.

In those two days the *eventyr* came alive as fairy tales had never done before. The rocks I had clambered over in the morning had become giant shapes that moved unnervingly; the tall pines that had creaked and groaned comfortingly in the afternoon began to shriek their questions and answers from hilltop to hilltop; the pounding of the sea against the rocks had lost its late afternoon romance and become menacing. Through that terrifying night and the next day, I kept my tenuous hold on reality by reading the *eventyr.* The storyteller's voice, mocking, often sardonic, frequently obscene, spoke louder and more comfortingly to me than any voice I had ever heard in literature.

Needless to say, a respect for these tales was born that night, a respect which has only grown with reading and thinking.

REFERENCES

Asbjornsen, Peter Christen and **Jorgen Moe.** *Norwegian Folk Tales.* Trans. Pat Shaw Iversen and Carl Norman. Oslo: Dreyers Forlag, 1960.

Booss, Clair, ed. *Scandinavian Folk and Fairy Tales.* New York: Avenel Books, 1984.

Christiansen, Reidar Thorwald, ed. *Folktales of Norway.* Trans. Pat Shaw Iversen. Chicago: University of Chicago Press, 1964.

Frye, Northrop. *Anatomy of Criticism.* Princeton, New Jersey: Princeton University Press, 1957.

Grimm, Jacob and **Wilhelm.** *Complete Grimm's Fairy Tales.* Trans. Margaret Hunt and James Stern. New York: Pantheon Books, 1944.

Ibsen, Henrik. "The Grouse of Justedal." *Ibsen,* Volume I. Ed. James Walter McFarlane and Graham Orton. London: Oxford University Press, 1970.

Kermode, Frank, *The Genesis of Secrecy.* Cambridge, Mass: Harvard University Press, 1979.

_____. *The Sense of an Ending.* New York: Oxford University Press, 1967.

Langer, Susanne K. *Feeling and Form.* New York: Scribners, 1953.

Ong, Walter J. *Orality and Literacy.* London: Methuen, 1982.

Richard Chase's *Jack Tales:* A Trickster in the New World

by Nina Mikkelsen

In 1935, years before Richard Chase became a well known critic of American literature, he was a twenty-one year old schoolteacher in Virginia, with a developing interest in Anglo-American folk traditions, especially folk songs. At this point, he met Marshall Ward, a man from the mountains of western North Carolina who told him about a certain type of story, handed down in his family by his great-grandfather, Council Harmon, but not told, as he stressed, the same way it was read "in books."

The Jack Tales, says Chase in the Preface to the book he published eight years later, is the result of this chance encounter with Ward and many evenings afterward spent with Ward's relatives, listening to and recording the tales of a boy who killed giants and scared away robbers in England, and as it turned out, did many of the same things in America (but not always in the same way).

It is to Chase's credit as a folklorist that he was able to uncover the tales in this North Carolina family, a discovery that produced something of a missing link in English holdings. Such a trickster hero had been observed in the German Grimm tales, and also in Irish, Spanish, French, and even Jamaican stories. But there were only a few such tales in Joseph Jacobs' English collection, compared to the many Chase was to discover in the American South. Apparently, those bound for the New World years before had packed up Jack with other keepsakes and carried him along to America, to take on the traits and personality of his new relatives in the years ahead.

Chase describes Ward and his family of Southern mountain people as "honest, industrious, and intelligent," with "rare qualities of kindliness and poise" (viii). And if it is true that storytellers leave their own imprint on the stories they tell, it may be said that Appalachian Jack, as we come to know him in these stories, was a true kinsman of the Wards. Humor and rich imagination mark the stories, the teller, and Jack, as particularly American, and as one of the few American folk characters that can compare to his animal cousin, Brer Rabbit, in popularity. If Jack's English cousin, in Chase's words, was "the cocksure, dashing young hero of the 'fairy' tale," then the Jack that Chase uncovered was conversely the "easy-going, unpretentious rural American" (ix), a trickster, as in Europe, and always the youngest-born underdog, but self-propelled rather than dependent on supernatural magic, and lucky primarily because he was shrewd and resourceful.

In collecting and publishing the tales, Chase had certain choices to make, choices that directly affect what we have today as we open the book. He could have produced the actual transcriptions of what he heard listening to the Wards tell stories. But since, as Chase says, no two individuals ever tell a tale quite the same way twice, such a choice might have meant publishing hundreds of tales in order to obtain the best of each. Chase thus chose to produce "composites" (correlating the best of many tellings as one version), similar to the procedure of the Brothers Grimm and Jacobs. He was also careful to describe the changes he made and

41

to include in his Notes one story that is an actual transcription. Folklorists thus have a record of the storytelling style of this particular era, while children have something substantial for their library shelves.

"We have all not had grandfathers like Council Harmon," Chase explains concerning his choice, "and yet we can, as we rediscover these things, learn them from books" (xi). And although he recommended to adults of 1943 that they tell the stories without the book, what is important for us some forty years later is that, because Chase so scrupulously recorded the natural rhythms of language for this time and place, they come to life as they are read aloud, and children ask to hear them again and again.

The plain style that Chase heard from his Appalachian informants was no doubt similar in kind to what Jacobs heard from English tellers half a century earlier. Yet Chase's egalitarian attitude toward maintaining the flavor of this speech was much more typically American than Jacobs, who speaks of the "unsuspected capacity for fun and humour among the unlettered classes" (vi) who told the tales. Chase seems almost to apologize for changing dialect that was confusing "to the ready eye" as he insists strongly that "the idiom has been kept throughout" (xi). Jacobs, on the other hand, speaks easily of having rewritten the tales, especially those in dialect, and seems to apologize for having "left a few vulgarisms in the mouths of vulgar people," insisting that "children appreciate the dramatic propriety of this as much as their elders" (viii).

The result is in Chase a printed story much closer to the sounds of the oral folk tradition, as this passage from "Jack and the Bean Tree" reveals, when placed next to the same sentence as Jacobs records it:

He kept on goin'—up and up and up.
He cloomb all day, till it was way late
in the evenin' 'fore he got to the top.
Then, just about dark Jack came to a
big pike-road up there.   (Chase 32).

So Jack climbed, and he
climbed, and he climbed, and
he climbed, and he climbed,
and he climbed, and he climbed
till at last he reached the sky.
And when he got there he found
a long broad road going as
straight as a dart.   (Jacobs 62).

Traditional storytelling patterns are also preserved by Chase when he relies on the principle of addition (the natural mode of oral expression, according to Walter Ong) rather than allowing subordination (the natural mode of literary presentation) to become the dominant structure. Notice this passage from Grimm's "The Bremen Town-Musicians" in which embedded clauses introduced by as and so carry the meaning, compared to Chase's parallel story, "Jack an the Robbers," where independent clauses piled one upon the other roll the action along:

> "What are you gasping so far, you big
> fellow?" asked the donkey.
> "Ah," replied the hound, "as I am old,
> and daily grow weaker, and no longer can
> hunt, my master wanted to kill me, so I
> took to flight."   (Grimm 144).

> "Hello," says Jack. "What
> you a-howlin' so for?"
> "Oh, law me," says the old
> dog. "The boys took me coon-
> huntin last night, cut a tree
> where the coon had got up in it.
> I got hold on the coon all right
> but my teeth are all gone and
> hit got loose from me. They
> said they were goin' to kill me
> today, get shet of me."   (Chase 42).

That Chase was able to capture the natural storytelling style of the Wards and the Harmons may account for the popularity of the stories with children today. But the wealth of detail Chase chose to include, in contrast to Jacobs, is also important. If, as Jacobs implies, children enjoy the vulgarity of vulgar people, then perhaps the more they have of it, the better for liking a book. In Jacobs' version for example, the scene above involves only a few spare lines that trip along like a nursery rhyme and give no motivation for the animals' journey:

> They went a little further and they met a dog.
> "Where are you going, Jack?" said the dog.
> "I am going to seek my fortune."
> "May I go with you?"
> "Yes," said Jack, "the more the merrier."
> So on they went, jiggelty-jolt, jiggelty-jolt.
> (Jacobs, "How Jack Went to Seek His Fortune" 24)

43

Chase and the Grimms, on the other hand, give us a great many more details about why these animals went on their journey. In the Grimms' tale each except the rooster is old and each has always worked hard only to be unappreciated at the last. So they leave to escape being killed. In the Chase stories, however, the details fall into something of a contrastive binary pattern. Each animal is old, hard working, and in a weakened state now, in contrast to Jack who is young and strong, but lazy. An emergent adolescent, he stands between the playful child and the working adult, and is not eager to assume responsibility. And he leaves home after his father whips him for not helping with domestic chores. Thus Jack wants easier work at the same time they *require* it. The ox is not strong enough to plow. The donkey is too weak to haul wood. The cat and dog have bad teeth (or no teeth) and cannot catch rats and raccoons. Finally, and worst of all, the rooster is about to be cooked.

All the animals and Jack enter a robbers' enclave and await their return to stake their own claim. Each takes a post of his own choosing, but the reader expects no action from these "pathetic" creatures. We laugh as the cat sinks into the comfort of the hearth and the donkey takes his "stand" (last stand) on the porch. (We laugh at what we think is their cowardice.) The dog says he will get behind the door and fight—from there. The rooster carols gently, "If you boys need any help now, just call on me, call on me-e-e!" (44)

Then, in a firecracker burst of action, they surprise us. When the robbers come, each does his part. The cat scratches. The dog bites. The donkey kicks. The ox gores. The rooster gives a big crow. The men think *men* are in the house and run away, leaving Jack and his trickster friends there having "a big time." But the details here are not given as they are in Grimm solely to show that the old can still outwit the young—although that implication is strongly present, since Jack takes no actual part in the fighting. They are given instead to trick and surprise us, to make us laugh; and perhaps Jack, standing for the moment off-stage, stands laughing with us.

So it is not only a natural storytelling style, but also, the wealth of understated mountain humor and imaginative detail Chase was able to capture that sets these tales off from those of both Jacobs and Grimm, and that may account for their popularity with children today. Yet there seems to be something more fundamental at stake here, especially if we consider that the Chase story does not end as the Grimm, with the animals remaining permanently in their new home.

The American version concludes with "the last time I was down that way, Jack had gone on back home to his folks. He was out in the yard a cuttin' his mother a big pile of stovewood." (The animals seem to have taught Jack a lesson about hard work and responsibility. He has joined ranks with them.) What seems to be running through the tale, therefore, is a trickster hero and the impetus, an emotional readiness, that sends him out into the world with the quest to succeed and bring him back successful in the end (having completed the "passage" from one stage of maturity to the next).

Consider the story from a different angle. In the German version, a donkey whose master forced him to carry corn-sacks to the mill "for many a long year" (144), becomes in the American one a boy who, even at twelve, refuses, as does Grimm's donkey, to be placed in the donkey's position. When whipped, he becomes, as a real donkey, stubborn. But, similar to Grimm's literary donkey, he does not refuse to budge. He hits the road to seek his fortune and as it turns out, wins it from the robbers. The Jacobs version, on the other hand, gives no motive for Jack's leaving home, except that he is seeking his fortune. English Jack is not learning responsibility; he is ready for it. German "Jack" (the donkey) has long known responsibility. Only American Jack seems to be in this position of initiate, as he is in almost every one of the stories.

Thus, unlike the English and German versions of this tale, three cultural symbols rise to importance here: the emergent adolescent crossing to adulthood, the trickster using initiative to gain his ends, and the road as passage to opportunity. Even when tellers record this same tale today, some forty years later, the same three symbols are evident. Notice, for example, how Jackie Torrence, well-known Southern storyteller, records this tale; Torrence even extends the introduction of Chase's one hundred words to seven hundred, in order to emphasize these same three elements of the original story: the adolescent standing at the crossroads of childhood play and adult responsibility, his finding a solution to his problem in trickster tactics, and his escape by the road.

Well, Jack was about ten, eleven years old. He's one of the laziest little ol boys you've ever seen in your life. Well sir, one morning, Jack's dad went over to his bedroom, said "Jack, git up."

Jack said, "I don't think I want to git up this morning."

"Git up now Jack. I got something I want you to do."

"No," Jack said. "I don't want to get up."

"Come on now, Jack. Git up."

So Jack's dad walked over to the bed and gave him a whack right on the back.

"Oh," Jack said. "I'm gonna get up. Wait a minute. Wait a minute." So ol Jack got up, pulled on his bib overalls, put on his hat, never did care nothin about shoes. So he walked into the kitchen and he said, "Pa, what is it?"

He said, "Now listen here, Jack. I got to go to town on business. And I'll be back about twelve noon. And I want you to cut that wood at the woodshed."

Jack said, "But I don't want to cut that wood."

"Jack!"

"Yes sir."

When Jack's Dad got out of sight Jack laid that ax down and laid down beside it and went right back to sleep. Well Jack was figuring he'd get up mid-ways of the morning and git that wood cut up. It wasn't much. But Jack slep up until twelve noon. And his Dad was coming down the road...

"Oh, I don't want to get a whippin," Jack said. "What am I gonna do? What in the world am I gonna do? I'm goin out the back door and I'm gonna run away. That's what I'm gonna do."

But there wasn't no back door on the woodshed. Wasn't even a window back there. Jack had to dig him a hole up beneath the wall, crawl out. When he crawled out of there, Jack took off down the road, he's goin so fast why you could see nothin' but dust. Jack was makin dust. He's picken em up, puttin them down, as fast as he was gettin away...

Although Torrence's ending is a little different from Chase's, it still speaks of—actually emphasizes—the adolescent passage to adult responsibility:

Jack went back home. His Mama and Daddy gave him a little whippin for runnin off there, not cuttin the wood. But they also bought Jack a little ol farm, put all those ol useless animals on there. They tell me that Jack is takin care of those animals to this day. And that's the end of that.

Of these three elements or symbols—the road, the adolescent crossing to sexual maturity, and trickster tactics—it is the road that appears early in the stories, to provide escape from home, unlimited opportunity, boundless, continuous movement, and to act as the supporting structure or impetus for the other two. Jack takes to the road to try his luck, make his fortune, find work, or win a wife. But because these are children's stories, "Hit the road, Jack," means Jack comes back grown into a responsible son, a wealthy man, or a new husband. As an adolescent or emergent adolescent, Jack thus escapes responsibility for a time in order to grow into it, because the road leads to freedom and at the same time, destination.

So the road is something of a microcosm for the American dream—not that the road as symbol is absent from the European tales of Hans or English Jack. There, as here, the road as setting is the male counterpart to the female's traditional place by the hearth. European Jack walks it too. It is his path to adventure, prosperity, and locating a wife. But because America with so much land and opportunity has always been the land of roads, the road takes on greater importance in these tales. It is both springboard for daring action and passage to manhood. If Jonathan Culler is correct that "we must read a novel on the assumption that we have been told all that we need to know: that significance inheres at precisely those levels where the novelist concentrates" (232) (and if we can substitute the words "story" and "storyteller" here), then significance would appear to reside in economics, for Jack's road nearly always leads to wealth or the dream of it.

Money is an important factor in almost each of the stories: proving your worth with money before marriage, making your fortune, making the most of your money or increasing your wealth. The dream of wealth without hard work is also important in these stories, which were collected in the depression years of hard-to-come-by work. The phrase "independent rich" is a common one. Six stories end with the phrase "and he was doing real well."

The teaching responsibility of stories told for children is also obvious here. At the end of one story, Jack decides to go home and save his money instead of spending it. At the end of another, Little Jack (the wily trickster) pays the doctor bill of Big (brawn without brains) Jack, inculcating the value that in a society with as yet non-existent social programs such as welfare or the dole, the more intelligent take care of the less able.

Yet as strongly as it is implied that money leads to happiness here, what the stories really say is that money is only the outer manifestation of something much more rudimentary—what money cannot buy, but what, if possessed, nearly always brings money: initiative, risk taking, facing a challenge, sometimes facing anything with nothing for collateral but the bare facts. In "Jack and the Doctor's Girl," for example, comedy arises from the blunt dead-pan "logic" in the Ma Barker-type gang Jack encounters when he takes off over the mountain to make his fortune and marry the doctor's daughter.

> The old lady says, "No, not kill him while he's asleep. Wake him up first. I never did like to see nobody killed in their sleep."

One of 'em shook Jack right good, says, "Wake up, stranger! What's your name?"

Jack sort-a roused up, says, "My name's Jack."

"Well, Jack, get up from there. We got to kill ye. That's our rules here. We don't want nobody messin' in our business." (117)

Jack replies, "Well, you all can kill me if ye want. But I ain't got a thing except what clothes I got on. I got no money." This is the frontier ideal of raw courage in the face of danger. This is a *man* (a crazy man in his nonchalance, it seems, but still a man who wins laughter and applause for his constant willingness to attempt whatever task is given him). Here, with typical folk tale impossibility, he is to steal three fat oxen for a good price, then twelve horses from under twelve men, a rabbit from the pot while everyone watches, and finally, sheets from under the sleepers, for the price of the girl. These are the terms. They are also the rites of passage to maturity and marriage, if he can meet them.

First, to be a provider in marriage, he must have money (be enterprising). He must earn one thousand dollars to win the girl. He meets this task by seizing opportunities as they present themselves. He uses what turns up in the road as a resource that tricks the farmer and helps him steal the oxen for the robbers.

He has money then, but the doctor wants something else. He sets up three more hurdles or tasks that Jack must jump before winning the girl (representing the unforeseen conflicts and challenges of adult life). Again Jack shows persistence, a willingness to try. Again he sees a way, perception rather than magic providing success for the American trickster. He drugs the twelve men, diverts the attention of those watching the rabbit so that he can retrieve it from the pot, and steals the sheets from the doctor's bed by impersonating the doctor. (Children often enjoy speculating about how Jack will deliver himself in these seemingly impossible situations.)

"The Doctor's Girl" is significant for illustrating how trickster talents and tactics aid the protagonist in his passage to maturity. (In the end Jack marries the girl and goes to work.) In this story, both of these cultural symbols, the trickster and the sexual passage, are equally powerful themes. Most of the stories of the book, however, fall into one of two categories, the pure trickster tale or the tale of sexual initiation in which trickster tactics may or may not be of primary importance.

Two stories in the trickster category are the well known "Jack and the Giant's Newground" and the less well known "Big Jack and Little Jack." In the first, Jack is typically poor, "awful lazy sometimes," and off on a "fine smooth road" to try his luck in another part of the country. The giants, large, gullible, and stupid, are really simple for Jack to knock down one by one (and a sound business venture for a thousand dollars a head), but children might well enjoy hearing of the clever set of tactics Jack uses to do it, just as they enjoy the vicarious thrill of seeing the weak overcome the strong (and powerful). They also may recognize similar incidents from different stories, such as Squeezing the Stone (in Scandinavian tales, it is a cheese; here it is milk Jack pours into his leather vest pocket), turning the giants against one another so that they destroy themselves (used also by Tolkien in *The Hobbit*) and the witch or giant's wife burned in her own oven ("Hansel and Gretel").

The less familiar "Big Jack and Little Jack" is similarly based on a contrasting binary pattern of large/empty headed—small/crafty, familiar to children from many folk tales, including the Brer Rabbit ones. Here as in the rabbit stories, the underlying meaning has more serious sociological implications. In this story, the King bargains with all who come to work for him that anyone who becomes angry with him can cut three strops from his back ("long enough to make shoestrings") and that he can exact the same "justice." The King keeps control this way, maintains total power, for those who cannot voice disapproval cannot make trouble in this otherwise smooth operation.

The first one on the scene is Big Jack (big and stupid like the giants). He collects praise from the King for his honesty, but no wages and no food (in today's terms, benefits), and finally he is knifed in the back for feeling indignation. Enter Little Jack (small but wary) who sees what has happened to his less fortunate "brother" and goes as trickster to bring down the King.

Once on the job, this Jack steals a sheep to feed himself, and it is significant that he steals on three occasions, not just one, and that the first and second time, the King tolerates it. (It is economically more desirable for the powerful to live with occasional thievery, it is implied, than to promote fair wages and benefits at all times.) It is also significant that even after the third time he is caught stealing, Jack is not fired, but merely transferred to a different line of work under this King. Firing would indicate that the King had some standards. But his morals are remarkably fluid on this point. As long as everyone pretends to be happy (displaying good manners, positive attitude, no anger) breaking the law can be overlooked. The King is in good shape economically too.

After Jack plays his second trick, however, and trades the King's horse for a mule (that is, he depletes the King's property to get even with him), the King's economics suffer a little. So he places Jack in a job of less responsibility, one which offers less possibility for Jack bringing him an economic loss. As apple picker, Jack moves in for the kill—plays dumb, so that when the King climbs up the ladder to teach him how to pick, Jack takes the ladder away and strikes a bargain for food. But once in the King's kitchen, it turns out, Jack has an even better plan in mind. He tricks the King's wife into kissing him. The King can "afford" to be less flexible where his wife is concerned. (Money is not the object.) He *is* angry now. Thus Jack gets his own turn with the knife.

With stories such as this one, it is not difficult to see why Blacks, long submerged in a society that supported the code of subterfuge for maintaining power, frequently chose to adapt the Jack tales for their own telling. But such tales also show us how any people, locked into such systems of *noblesse oblige*, found the trickster tactic of lawbreaking an acceptable way, often the encouraged way, of survival.

The second category of tales in the book, those of sexual initiation, form something of a cycle within the entire sequence of eighteen stories, beginning with "Jack and the Bean Tree", which reveals the child's sexual awakening and continuing through "Old Fire Dragaman," which celebrates a successful male-female relationship.

"Jack and the Bean Tree" needs little introduction, following as closely as it does Jacobs' version. Thus, the Freudian implication Bruno Bettelheim assigns to the English version cannot be ignored in the American one. Here we see the mother who suppresses her son's aspirations to male sexuality—ridicules what he says in relation to this newly discovered magic tree, his emergent physical power, and angrily strikes him for what she considers is lying. If we are to accept Bettleheim's interpretation, fantasy takes over at this point when reality proves disappointing (his mother fails to recognize his aspirations). So he ascends to the giant's house in his dreams, thus giving himself hope for the great things he will one day accomplish.

Once above in the giant's house, Jack (American Jack) obtains stronger belief or confidence in bodily strength and budding sexuality, represented by objects of obvious masculine power, the rifle and knife, as well as belief in mental powers for mastering life, as expressed by a coverlid. Serving the same function as the magic harp in Jacobs' story, but translated to mountain culture here, this quilt suggests the same meaning of beauty, art, and creativity that Bettleheim applies to the harp of the English story.

"Jack and the North West Wind" can also best be viewed in the light of the Freudian theories that Bettelheim presents as he speaks of the English "Jack and His Bargains" as a dramatization of the wish and the fear of sexual passage in emergent adolescence. Here Jack receives three magic objects from an old man, a Woden-like character who appears in several stories and seems to represent the adult mental power waiting within the child to give reasoning and emotional power (trust of oneself, confidence). From the old man, Jack receives first a tablecloth that will always provide food, then a rooster providing golden eggs (wealth) and finally a club or stick, representing physical survival, as well as, in Freudian terms, masculine power.

Lazy Jack is most impressed by this club which will cut his wood magically for him. But before he receives it, he loses both the tablecloth and the rooster and is just about to lose the club. (Forgetful and unwary, the trickster here is tricked by others more watchful than he.) Thus it is implied, he is not yet ready for his sexual initiation. Significantly, the club at last awakens Jack, so that he asserts himself, regains the stolen objects, and keeps the club. And because his own physical power has enabled him to do so, he attains the autonomy needed for successful passage to adult-hood—stands ready, in fact, for the courtship that will take place in such a story as "Jack and the King's Girl."

Here Jack is older and not so lazy anymore. He cuts the wood *before* starting off to his uncle's, in contrast to the way he left in "Jack and the Robbers." And here he has taken on the task of winning the King's daughter, who had never laughed (in Freudian terms, repression)—not an easy task, but a common one in folktales. He makes four visits to his uncle (four forays into the world of courtship). Each time on the way there and back·he passes the King's house (and the girl), and each time he leaves for home, his uncle gives him a present. Here as before, a series of objects—a needle, a sword, a colt, and a heifer—provide symbolic associations for sexual initiation.

First he is given a darning needle, indicating his chronological readiness for marriage (he must either learn to sew for himself or find a wife). He does not seem to know how to carry the needle, so he puts it over his shoulder. As he passes the King's house, the girl is intrigued: "Law me! I never did see a man tote a needle that-away" (84). A child has a similar reaction. And the difference in adult and child responses to the story at this point reveal something of the communal function that storytelling had in an earlier day. For children are likely to see Jack as the same noodlehead Jacobs presents in "Lazy Jack." But adults can enjoy a subtle humor rising out of the structural pattern, and Jack's deceptive double identity as noodlehead/trickster.

The King's daughter advises Jack to put the needle through his shirt. Then on a second visit to his uncle, Jack is given a sword which he sticks through his shirt, like a needle. ("That dummy does everything backward!" a child cries out at this point.) For her part, the girl is similarly astonished, tells him he should have carried the sword on his shoulder. "Next time I will" (85), he replies.

On the third visit Jack is given a colt. ("Watch that dummy put it on his shoulder," the child says.) And when he "got down close to the King's place," he "got right down under the colt and got it up on his shoulder" (86). She is appalled, calls him a fool now, tells him he should ride a colt.

Finally he is given a heifer. ("Watch him ride it!" says the child.) And he does. Close to her house, he "remembered." (Remembered her advice/remembered his plan.) He jumps over the bawling calf. Watching him ride, she is dumbfounded, laughs at last, and he wins her. For he is the trickster, we see, weaving his own comic script as innocent clown.

Chase's stories recount the ups and downs of the male-female relationship, as old as the Appalachian hills on which they rise, and still new for the next child reader. They tell of growing into adulthood in many ways; in "Old Fire Dragaman", that growth is symbolized as descent into consciousness. Although the story has received attention because of its supposed link with "Beowulf," a connection Chase admits which may be far-fetched, what is equally or more important is its link to Grimm's "The Gnome." In comparing the two tales, we can see what makes Chase's stories especially American, and it would seem, also timeless.

In the Grimm tale, there is both a dwarf and a dragon. The dwarf, serving as mental capacity or knowledge, consciously leads the youngest son down to a dragon who lives under the ground and keeps three princesses as prisoners there. In the Chase tale, on the other hand, the dwarf and dragon have been combined as a giant called Old Fire Dragaman, who comes and goes above ground and inadvertently leads Jack down to a similar place below ground where he also keeps three girls as prisoners.

In this rural mountain atmosphere where physical prowess was tantamount to survival, the dwarf may have been "dwarfed" by the giant (and dragon) as what the young boy in his fantasies needed to deal with and conquer. According to Freudian theory, however, the oedipal boy projects his frustrations and anxieties onto a giant, monster, or dragon. And in fairy tales where everything takes place in a fantasy land, as Bettleheim states, "the child need not feel guilty or anxious about casting Father in the role of a dragon or evil giant..." (114):

> The boy can love his real father even better after having gotten out all his anger at him through a fantasy of destroying the dragon or the bad giant.

Such fairy-tale fantasies—which most children would have a hard time inventing so completely and satisfactorily on their own—can help a child a great deal to overcome his oedipal anguish. (115)

The Chase story, combining as it does the character of dwarf and dragon in one character, the Fire Dragaman, allows us to see Bettleheim's theory more clearly. Jack confronts the oedipal "father" both above ground and below ground, and finally resolves his own oedipal "conflict" by destroying this anxiety when he destroys the father, distanced as a dragon.

Above ground, the Grimms' Hans and Jack work in similar ways to show their readiness for this oedipal task. In the Grimm tale, two older brothers of Hans are cowardly, each giving the dwarf just what he wants to avoid confrontation. Hans stands up to him, refuses to serve him, finally even beats him. Then he attains the knowledge needed to find the dragon and slay him. In the Chase story, each of the older brothers similarly crouches in fear before the giant, who then takes their dinner. When Jack offers him dinner, however, he refuses it. (Generosity conquers brute force; cowardice plays into its hands, it is implied.)

In both stories, the older brothers plot against the younger one, suggesting that cowardice (insecurity) breeds selfish behavior, but the younger still succeeds in finding his way down to the imprisoned maidens under the ground. In Grimm, the dwarf (psychic or intellectual power) leads Hans down into the well. In the Chase story, Jack follows the giant (the father figure or model) and discovers the underground place for himself.

In both stories the older brothers leave the younger one trapped under the ground, and in each case the youngest-best is able to rise to the surface (find his way back to consciousness and win his mate) through psychic power, symbolized in Grimm by the elves that seize him by the hair and fly him to the earth again. In Chase, the girl herself gives Jack a wishing ring before she is taken above ground by the older brothers, and he later uses this to transport himself magically home (wishes to be home), thus symbolizing the will power needed to bring about sexual maturity.

The Chase tale, seen side by side with the Grimm, gives us a clear picture of the American Jack character; there are so many parallels that the differences are definitive. The values of courage to find the female, slay the dragon (oedipal father) and will himself home (accept the power of manhood) are clearcut in each. But in Chase, mutual dependence is seen as the foundation of marriage, when the youngest girl shows Jack the chest with the sword to kill the giant and the magic ointment to protect him from the giant's blows. (In the Grimm story, Hans kills the dragon with his own hunting knife.)

Chase's female character thus is seen playing a larger, a more decisive role in her own destiny and in Jack's. She, not the elves, gives Jack the wishing ring, thus underlining her consent and her desire. Also, in presenting him with the sword, she transfers her allegiance from the oedipal father to the prospective mate and helps Jack do the same, as he takes the blows (protected by the magic ointment, they are light) and deals them out for her.

In the Chase story, furthermore, sibling rivalry is treated with more humor and tolerance than in the Grimm, in which the King has the two older brothers hanged for their mischief. Here when Jack returns, the brothers "were still a-fightin' over that youngest girl," and says the teller, "last time I was down there they'd done built 'em three pole cabins and they were all doin' pretty well" (133).

At first glance, for the adult the Jack tales may seem strange, today almost alien with their rural dialect, the language patterns of an oral tradition, their at times almost blatant sexual suggestiveness, in contrast to the more subtle and intriguing sexual allusions we have become conditioned to expect from Grimm. On the other hand, the more obvious sexual symbolism of the American tales is what in fact gives much greater credulity to Bettleheim's Freudian theories and helps us to see more clearly how folk tales of entirely different times and places can exercise similar power to inculcate strategies for a child's sexual initiation.

In other words, the differences that at first startle the adult here may in fact be what draws in the child, the male child, at any rate, his attention centered as it is in symbols of masculine prowess. (Boys listening to these stories like to categorize and list all the weapons and magic objects Jack accumulates in these tales—his rooster, his ax, his tablecloth that makes food, his sword, his silver dagger, his three strops from the King's back.) And if Jack goes about his trickster business with shrewdness and bold risk taking more often than with magic power, the child reader at least finds these wish fulfilling adventures quite "magical". As one boy said of "Old Fire Dragaman", "I liked the way it had a mystical creature, the giant. I liked how they fought. He could spit fireballs. That is my cup of tea!"

And female readers are not left behind, because so many clever girls appear alongside Jack in the stories. We do not easily forget the youngest daughter of "Old Fire Dragaman". There is a simple grace in this girl who with timeless knowledge shows Jack how to save them from the dragon, and with quiet charm gives him the ribbon to weave through her hair. Forthright and unaffected, she compares well to her female counterpart in Grimm and is the perfect partner for Jack, who in this particular tale, above all the others, shows us the Southern Mountain traditions of his people and his own "rare qualities of kindliness and poise."

"Old Fire Dragaman" may in fact stand as best representative of all the stories, introducing as it does the sexual passage in the larger context of growing up generally, matching the child's existent center of interest in magical physical powers to the symbolic center of approaching emotional maturity. This is the special value of the Jack tales today for children, I feel, and the reason they continue to please.

REFERENCES

Bettelheim, Bruno. *The Uses of Enchantment.* New York: Alfred A. Knopf, 1976.

Chase, Richard. *The Jack Tales.* Boston: Houghton Mifflin, 1943.

Culler, Jonathan. *Structuralist Poetics.* Ithaca, N.Y.: Cornell University Press, 1975.

Grimm, Jacob and **Wilhelm.** *The Complete Grimm's Fairy Tales.* Trans. Margaret Hunt. New York: Pantheon, 1944.

Jacobs, Joseph. *English Fairy Tales.* 3rd ed. New York: G. P. Putnam's Sons, 1911.

Ong, Walter. *Orality and Literacy.* New York: Metheun, 1982.

Torrence, Jackie. *More Jack Tales.* Columbia, Missouri: Nita, Inc. Recordings, 1980.

Padraic Colum's *The Children's Homer:* The Myth Reborn

by Yancy Barton

Through the stories we now know as "myths," the ancient Greeks provided interesting and meaningful answers to their questions about the workings of the cosmos and of humanity. In this sense, the word "myth" refers to a traditional story dealing with gods and heroes that attempts to explain nature, human origins, our institutions, our customs, or our rituals, in simple human terms. Popularly, a myth has come to mean a story that is untrue; yet we can still gain many insights from the stories of Greek mythology—children in particular, for while they may not be able to articulate such thoughts clearly, they too have questions about themselves and their world. Mythology may not provide the ultimate answers; but at least it offers clear images and ideas to help children understand difficult aspects of the human condition, or realize that they, like the rest of humanity, may never understand at all.

Translations of Homer, the poet of ancient Greece who wrote the *Iliad* and the *Odyssey,* are one of our most important sources of Greek mythology. Since young children often find adult translations of Homer rather difficult, many writers have attempted to adapt the best translations for adults into equally worthwhile texts for children. One who succeeds admirably is Padraic Colum, the Irish poet who wrote three books for children based on Greek mythology. In *The Children's Homer* in particular, Colum achieves a simplicity and quality of style that preserves the same authenticity of Homer as do the best adult translations.

If a literary work originally intended primarily for adults is important enough to be introduced to children, the adaptor must be committed to keeping his abridgement as close as possible to the original, in order to avoid distortions of the elements of plot, character, and philosophy that make the original work compelling. In *The Children's Homer,* Padraic Colum does change the plots of Homer's epics somewhat; he also simplifies character, and he reveals some quite elementary philosophy. Yet there is no serious distortion of any of these elements. Indeed, Colum's clever use of abridgement, his vivid development of character, and his sensitive use of language allowed him to create a surprisingly accurate version for children of the classic epics of Homer—accurate enough to merit its selection as a touchstone.

In *The Children's Homer,* Colum abridges the stories of both the *Iliad* and the *Odyssey,* and masterfully combines them into one volume. Colum follows Homer's *Odyssey* closely until Telemachus is about to return to Ithaca. Then, rather than returning to Ithaca as Homer's Telemachus does, Colum's Telemachus stays in Sparta with Menelaus and Helen, from whom he hears the entire story of the Trojan War, with particular emphasis on Menelaus' account of Achilles' petulance and Hector's universal popularity. After hearing this narrative, Telemachus begins his return trip to Ithaca, and Colum continues the story of the *Odyssey* from Odysseus' release from Calypso to his reclaiming of the kingdom of Ithaca.

Colum carefully plans the transitions between the stories. Since Telemachus is in Sparta with Menelaus, he can logically hear a firsthand description of what happened in Troy from one of the leaders of the Greeks, and from Helen, who was a Greek in Troy during the war. After the tale of Troy is related, Menelaus admits that he knows only that Odysseus is Calypso's captive. So it is appropriate that, as Telemachus disappointedly prepares to return to Ithaca, the story shifts to the story of the *Odyssey*, beginning with Odysseus captive on Calypso's island, but just about to be released. Calypso furnishes Odysseus a boat, and he is shipwrecked in the land of the Phaeacians, where he reveals the story of his wanderings for the previous ten years. Only after Colum's young readers learn the story of the *Odyssey* does the king of the Phaeacians provide Odysseus with a boat and sailors, who deliver him safely to Ithaca for the playing out of Odysseus' destruction of Penelope's suitors, the reuniting of his family, and the regaining of his kingdom.

From his retelling of the works of Homer, Colum omits such characteristic features as the invocation of the Muse, the long catalogues, the epic similes, and the division of the work into twelve books. But these omissions do not distort Colum's retelling, for they appear to be stylistic devices used by Homer rather than important vehicles for revealing plot, character, or philosophy—all of which Colum still conveys. In terms of plot, in fact, Colum combines the two epics so skillfully and creates such natural continuity that it almost seems the two stories were always meant to be one.

Furthermore, by choosing to include certain episodes and actions in his book, Colum gives a quite adequate expression of certain values and mores that are thought to be typically Greek, such as the homage and honor paid to guests and, above all, to the gods. Telemachus, though he felt too young and helpless to overcome Penelope's suitors, is welcoming to strangers: "...he [Telemachus] would never let a stranger stand at the gate without hurrying out to welcome him..." (6). As Telemachus welcomes Athene in the guise of a soldier, so do Nestor and Menelaus receive Telemachus: "And when they saw the two strangers approach, the sons of Nestor rose up to greet them" (32). Furthermore, "A golden cup was put into the hand of each [Telemachus and Athene in the guise of Mentor] and wine was poured into the cups...." And when Telemachus arrives in Sparta at Menelaus' dwelling, and Eteoneus, the steward, asks Menelaus if he should ask the strangers in or bid them enter the Palace, Menelaus' answer further reinforces the Greek habit of welcoming strangers as guests:

> "Why do you ask such a question, Eteoneus?" said Menelaus in anger. "Have we not eaten the bread of other men on our wanderings, and have we not rested ourselves in other men's houses? Knowing this you have no right to ask whether you should bid strangers enter or let them go past the gate of my

dwelling. Go now and bid them enter and feast with us."

(39-40).

Likewise, Telemachus vows, "But for this stranger [Odysseus] I will do what I can," when he first meets his father disguised as an old man, seated in Eumaeus' house (193). Although the suitors to Penelope have taken over Telemachus' own home, he pledges to give the old man clothing, shoes, and a sword with which to defend himself.

Colum clearly shows that, besides being courteous to strangers, the early Greeks also regularly paid homage to their gods. When Telemachus arrives in Pylos, he finds Nestor preparing to make a sacrifice to Poseidon. Forty-five oxen are slain, and the required parts laid on the altar to the god to "bring good to them and to their people" (34). Athene adds another request: "Grant, too, that Telemachus and I may return safely when what we have come in our swift ship to seek has been won" (34). Apparently, when the Greek people forgot their gods, they were punished, as Odysseus was by wandering helplessly for ten years before being allowed to return to Ithaca. Odysseus blinded Polyphemus, a son of Poseidon, and was safe as long as he said "Noman" had done this. When he had gained safety, his vanity made him reveal the truth—Odysseus was the culprit. Thus Polyphemus calls on Poseidon for revenge, and Odysseus must wander. The emphasis on both the honor of guests and the homage to the gods illustrated by Colum's carefully chosen episodes gives his book the flavor of the ancient Greek locales, which are the setting for Homer's poems.

Just as important as careful abridgement to any retelling of a classic for children are vivid character images. Any epic like Homer's *Iliad* shows us a part of ourselves in the characters portrayed. In other words, there is a timelessness to good literature that allows us to see raw human nature as it was in, say, 5000 B.C. in ancient Greece, and to be amazed that it is still much the same. Colum, a superb image-maker, creates characters exemplary of many types of human nature. Nor does he portray characters as totally good or totally evil. Rather, his characters are often torn between good and bad or right and wrong.

Among Colum's strong characterizations of the inhabitants of the Greek mythological world is his Achilles. Although Agamemnon was petty in taking Briseis from Achilles to replace his own slave girl, Achilles, is shown to be tiresome because he is too adamant in his wrath. He vows, "I swear that longing for Achilles' aid shall come upon the host of Agamemnon, but that no Achilles' aid shall come to their help. I swear that I shall let Hector triumph over you" (55). Achilles is so implacable in his bitterness that he is willing to forfeit his loyalty to the Greek forces. Furthermore, he ultimately sends his dearest friend, Patroclus, to his death. Only after Patroclus meets his death does Achilles repent:

> "Straightway then let me die," said Achilles, "since I let my friend die without giving him help. Oh that I had not let my wrath overcome my spirit! Here I stayed, a useless burden on the earth, while my comrades and my own dear friend fought for their country—here I stayed, I who am the best of all the Greeks. But now let me go into the battle and let the Trojans know that Achilles has come back, although he tarried long."
>
> (86)

By his own words, "I who am the best of all the Greeks," we see that Achilles had not changed at all, despite the consequences of his display of wrath. He goes back to the battle not because all is right between him and Agamemnon, but because he is angry at the death of his friend. He still is vain enough to consider himself "the best," and one believes that such vanity will again cause trouble for him. Thus Colum carefully renders the man who is flawed, the man who lets his worst part, vanity, rule his better part, rational thought, and who because of this must live with the consequences of his action: Patroclus' death.

Another Homeric hero that Colum characterizes well is Hector, the leader of the Trojans. Of the three main characters, Achilles, Hector, and Odysseus, Hector seems to be the most perfect, the ideal man. First, he is a brave warrior:

> Then Hector leaped across the gate with two spears in his hands. No warrior could withstand him now. And as the Trojans scaled the walls and poured across the broken gate, the Greeks fled to their ships in horror and dismay.   (72)

Second, Colum shows the young audience that for Astyanax, Hector is a loving father:

> Then he took up his little son and handled him in his arms and prayed, "O Zeus, greatest of the gods, grant that this son of mine may become valiant, and that, like me, he may be protector of the City and thereafter a great king, so that men may say of him as he returns from battle, 'Far greater is he than was Hector his father.'" Saying this he left the child back in his nurse's arms.   (100)

Moreover, Hector takes care to comfort his wife, Andromache:

> Dear one, do not be over sorrowful. You urge me not to go every day into the battle, but some days to stand behind the walls. But my own spirit forbids me to stay away from battle,

> for always I have taught myself to be valiant and to fight in the forefront.   (100)

Hector also has great humility before gods and men:

> Not with words, Achilles, can you affright me. Yet I know that thou art a man of might and a stronger man than I. But the fight between us depends upon the will of the gods. I shall do my best against thee, and my spear before this has been found to have a dangerous edge.   (95)

Last of all, Hector is kind to the captive Helen, who says of him, "Never did Prince Hector speak a hard or harsh word to me in all the years I was in his father's house. And if anyone upbraided me he would come and speak gentle words to me" (97). Such a paragon as the doomed Hector was is clearly portrayed, and he appears even more admirable when juxtaposed to Agamemnon and Achilles, who have many qualities which make a reader dislike them.

Odysseus, too, is a realistically portrayed character. He has made a pact with all other kings of the Greek Provinces to join together to defend Helen if need be, yet he resorts to the trickery of pretending insanity in order to escape the actual service of Agamemnon. Perhaps this is not admirable, but it is certainly understandable, for readers learn that Odysseus has a faithful wife and a baby son whom he hesitates to leave. Colum lets his audience see that Odysseus is torn between his promise and his desire. Moreover, readers must feel sympathy for Odysseus when he is buffeted about for ten years after the Trojan War ends, eventually by what seems to be the whims of the gods. So we rejoice when Odysseus gains victory over the suitors as just revenge for the maltreatment of his family and belongings by these men. The images of the ideal man, Hector, and the flawed men, Agamemnon, Achilles, Odysseus, are clearly portrayed by Colum, and, as vivid images, they speak to young people. Through characters like these, young audiences can learn about human nature in general and about themselves in particular. These images depict men striving for perfection but not always achieving it, so that, through these hero tales of Greek mythology, children may see that perhaps it is not achieving the ultimate goal that makes life worthwhile, but rather, following that goal with loyalty and enthusiasm, and also, realizing and living with one's flaws.

Writing for an audience of children, Colum uses language that is somewhat easier than Homer's. But to eradicate the noble, bardic language so suited to the nobility of the heroic ideals expressed in many of these tales would be to destroy much of their beauty. Colum shows great sensitivity in his use of language, emphasizing rather than omitting the formal language. He was a poet in his own right; his language is more poetic than prosaic, and it is both resonant and beautiful, as in Achilles' speech to Odysseus, who comes to plead with Achilles to return to war:

> Son of Laertes, wisest of men, hearken now to what I shall say to thee. Here I should have stayed and won that imperishable renown that my goddess-mother told me of, even at the cost of my young life, if Agamemnon had not aroused the wrath that now possesses me. Know that my soul is impacable toward him. How often did I watch out sleepless nights, how often did I spend my days in bloody battle for the sake of Agamemnon's and his brother's cause! Why are we here if not because of lovely Helen? And yet one whom I cherished as Menelaus cherished Helen has been taken from me by order of this king! He would let her go her way now! But no, I do not desire to see Briseis ever again, for everything that comes from Agamemnon's hand is hateful to me. Hateful are all the gifts he would bestow upon me, and him and his treasures I hold at a straw's worth. I have chosen.   (62-3)

In this passage, Colum's lavish vocabulary, precise diction, and almost Elizabethan style create a very effective image of Achilles.

Personification, similes, and Homeric epithets abound in Colum's *Homer*, and serve to create very expressive descriptions. One of the finest personifications occurs when Achilles, who is killing many officers of the Trojan army, "came to Skamandos, the river that flows across the plain before the city of Troy. And so many men did he slay in it that the river rose in anger against him for choking its waters with the bodies of men" (96). Agamemnon's act of breaking through the Trojan line is expressed in a strong simile:

> Like fire falling upon a wood and burning up the underwood went King Agamemnon through the Trojan ranks, and when he passed many strong-necked horses rattled empty chariots, leaving on the earth slain warriors that had been in them.   (65)

An Homeric epithet that Colum seems to be most fond of is that of referring to Athene as the "grey-eyed goddess." This reminds adult readers of the original Homer, while it serves to make the goddess visible to Colum's young audience.

An equally important quality of Colum's language is the resonance that comes from alliteration: "The bronze of the spear struck the bronze of his helmet and bronze by bronze was turned" (67). Furthermore, Colum's use of Greek nomenclature, that is, Zeus, Hera, Odysseus rather than the Roman names Jupiter, Juno, Ulysseus, makes his work authentic. Colum's skillful use of language may well prime the imagination of children; it certainly has a better chance of capturing their interest than the more prosaic writing we often find in books for children.

In fact, the most significant books for children are those in which the literary style and tone are beautifully suited to character and situation—as they are in Colum's Homer. The Greek myths are serious stories, explanations of nature both human and external, and as such, dictate the serious tone of Homer rather than the flippant tone that Ovid adopts. Colum accomplishes a serious, earnest style through the use of imagery, rhythm and cadence in sentence structure, and emphasis, thus effectively avoiding distortions of Homer's classic.

Colum's imagery presents readers with the physical world of his book. This world is ancient Greece, peopled by powerful gods and immortals, stalwart heroes, and destructive monsters. The image Colum conjures of the immortal Proteus, the "Ancient One of the Sea" is illustrative of the kind of description that fills his book:

> We rushed upon him with a cry and laid hold on him with all the strength of our hands. But we had no sooner grasped him than his shape changed. He became a lion and faced us. Yet we did not let so of our grasp. He became a serpent, yet still we held him. He became a leopard and then a mighty boar; he became a stream of water and then a flowering tree. Yet still we held to him with all our might and our hearts were not daunted by the shapes he changed to before our eyes. Then, seeing that he could not make us loose our hold, the Ancient One of the Sea, who was called Proteus, ceased in his changes and became as we had seen him first.   (45)

Colum's careful sentence structure and use of repetition here create a rhythm that is almost poetic. He begins with two fairly simple sentences about the capture of Proteus. The next few sentences, each of increasing length, are parallel, in that each describes a shape into which Proteus changes balanced against repetition that emphasizes the extent to which Menelaus and his men persevere in holding on to Proteus. Such patterns of rhythmic recurrence have an order, a cadence to them, which interests discriminating readers as well as creating pleasant modulations of the voice during reading aloud.

As refrain or repetition serves to emphasize an important idea or element, so too do other artistic devices. For example, Colum apparently considers the quest an important element in these stories, for he emphasizes it in Telemachus' search for his father, the Greeks' journey to retrieve Helen, and Odysseus' quest for his homeland. In fact, these are the three major plot lines in *The Children's Homer*.

Colum tells his story in the literary form of a dramatic narrative, rather than as the epic poem of the original. The story is told in action by the characters who are themselves involved, and that makes it more exciting and more immediate. For example, Colum tells the story of the suitors who take over Odysseus' home to waste and destroy his belongings through the character of the young son, Telemachus, and one can glimpse the poignancy of a young man, his mother, and a group of old, faithful retainers trying to fight a larger group of young, vital despoilers. Likewise, the plight of Penelope is pathetic because she tells of the measures to which she has gone in order to avoid remarriage. Readers are also treated to accounts of the Trojan War by Menelaus, who tells of the battle, and Helen, who tells what happened in the city of Troy at the same time. We can follow the chronological events and get a sure sense of immediacy of action through such narratives.

An evaluation of *The Children's Homer* would not be complete without some mention of the illustrator, Will Pogany, whose simple black and white line drawings are reminiscent of the pictures on the vases and amphorae that survive from the time of ancient Greece. Pogany's pictures show Homer's characters to be as beautiful and as heroic as they are depicted to be in the language of Colum's text. Indeed, in *The Children's Homer*, narrative, language and illustration achieve the status of high art.

REFERENCES

Barton, Yancy. *The Shaping of Myth: An Evaluative Study of Selected Versions of Greek Myths for Children.* A thesis 'for Stephen F. Austin University, 1984.

Colum, Padraic. *The Children's Homer.* New York: Macmillan Publishing Co., 1962.

Padraic Colum's *The Golden Fleece:* The Lost Goddesses

by Nancy Huse

> The past is male. But it is all the past we have. We must use it, in order that the future will speak of womanhood, a condition full of risk, and variety, and discovery: in short, human.
>
> (Heilbrun, 212)

Greek myths as children's literature? In a culture which increasingly recognizes women's power to create art, to lay claim to public words and deeds born of private experience and reflection, how shall we share with children a mythology which not only excluded women as recorders and interpreters, but as Lawrence Lipking suggests, quite likely also excluded women as audience for its tragic festivals and recitals of ancient poetry?   (71)

Among people called educated by Western standards, it is a given that a knowledge of the Greek myths is indispensable. Northrop Frye has argued that they, with the Bible, form the structural under-pinnings of story-telling itself (112). His description of the myths underscores both their centrality and their maleness:

> The Classical myths give us, much more clearly than the Bible, the main episodes of the central myth of the hero whose mysterious birth, triumph and marriage, death and betrayal and eventual rebirth follows the rhythm of the sun and the seasons. Hercules and his twelve labours, Theseus emerging from his labyrinth, Perseus with the head of Medusa: these are story-themes that ought to get into the mind as early as possible.

Otto Rank and others have explicated the myth of the hero in detail. These descriptions, available to children's literature professionals in Purves and Monson's *Experiencing Children's Literature* (46-47), dramatize the ubiquity, power, and exclusively masculine focus of the narratives which define the West's ideas of reality.

Classics are said to speak so specifically to the present that they seem specifically designed for each successive era of their survival (Gadamer 257). The life of any classic, however, is a history of retellings and re-interpretations. Recently, Charlene Spretnak, inspired by her studies of archeology and by her need for a myth collection she could unequivocally offer her young daughter, reconstructed certain myths as they existed before the patriarchal eras of such sources as Hesiod, Homer, Apollodorus, and Ovid. In recommending Spretnak's *Lost Goddesses of Ancient Greece*, R. T. Sidwell points out that the "twenty-odd" retellings of the myths now available for children draw from the same written sources; only Spretnak reaches back into times recorded exclusively through artifacts and anthropological evidence. Her retellings, focusing on parthenogenetic motherhood and celebration of the female life cycle, offer a Pandora, a Demeter and Persephone, an Athena and an Aphrodite, who pre-existed the Hellenic writers and who once neither caused the world's misery nor celebrated war and rivalry. "In restoring the Mothers to us, Spretnak has restored a portion of our Western heritage stolen by the Greek mythographers and their patrifocal views" (175).

I, too, admire Spretnak's book and use it in my class on the use of narrative patterns by women writers. But there are pragmatic, scholarly reasons for seeing it mainly as a supplement to Padraic Colum's retelling of the myths. The Hellenic and Roman sources used by Colum are woven, as Frye indicates, throughout subsequent literature and culture. Demeter's partial loss of Persephone to the underworld indicates her subordination to male power in the form of Zeus, and the written sources attribute Persephone's separation to her forcible abduction and acquiescence to rape. Aphrodite's male-defined role functions in John Updike's stories as well as in Homer's epics. Pandora's "box" and Athena's motherless "birth" are taken for granted in Western art and schooling. In fact, knowledge of these myths in their undeniable mysogyny is essential not only to an understanding of literature, but also to all other branches of our culture.

While I hope and believe that work like Spretnak's will continue, and that it will be published in forms accessible to children, I was happy to find that the Children's Literature Association had listed Padraic Colum's versions of the Greek myths as touchstones. Though he is only one of several retellers whose work I value—Edith Hamilton's scholarly account, for example, in contrast to those of Hawthorne and Roger Green, consistently recognizes the pathos and victimization of such females as Medea and Demeter—Colum's poetic vision takes him much closer to the spirit of Spretnak's book than any other reteller has come. At the same time, his work has been praised for its closeness to the original (that is, the original written) sources and for its appropriateness for children.

Colum is linked to my own childhood. I found him in our family's attic, his versions of the *Iliad* and the *Odyssey* having formed the main part of Ginn and Company's Cathedral reader for sixth graders of the thirties. My own readers, in the forties, offered "realistic" stories about helping neighbors caught in floods, or getting lost on camping trips, and I remember staring transfixed before the mysterious text Agnes, Bob, and Ed had presumably managed to decipher when they were my age. The phonetic guide to names like *Tel é ma chus,* and Pogany's illustrations, gave me heart to take the book out of the attic and into my experience. I wept with Achilles, not recognizing the sexual barter at the base of his quarrel with Agamemnon or the male bonding behind his grief for Patroclus. Colum omitted his desecration of Hector's body. But I recognized his moods, his pride, and his potential as my own.

Carolyn Heilbrun suggests that readers today must make "bold acts" of reinterpretation of texts which have carried not only the misogyny of their own eras, but the added and varied forms of misogyny supplied by later commentary (150). Her point, that Freud's discussion of *Oedipus Rex* was a partial one emphasizing what he needed to emphasize, is central to my adult view of Colum. His poetic identity engendered a version of the Golden Fleece narrative unique to him, viewed as remarkably complete by Lionel Trilling in 1956 (Bowen 126), and still capable of vivid life after the watershed of feminist criticism.

The inclusion of the female voice as part of a "fundamental imaginative act" and the ability to perceive women as human beings who create and inspire to worthwhile values has come to be recognized as an aesthetic criterion by which a critic can measure the power of a classic to sustain us now (Booth 66). Colum's narrative—unlike many contemporary retellings of the myths—includes female experience as essential to the human story he tells. In addition to his manner of selecting from the written sources such scenes as the Argonauts' stay on the island of Lemnos (a female utopia)—a scene cut or ridiculed in many modern versions—Colum chooses of his own volition to assign lengthy speeches to women like Jason's mother, Alcimide, who are mentioned only in passing in many ancient sources and entirely omitted from well known children's versions (Hawthorne, Green, Kingsley, Hamilton and others). His inclusion of female experience—of the "lost goddesses"—is intrinsic to his poetic device to unify the myths, thematic motifs often centering on birth, love, and female power. For example, Colum portrays Hera's protection of Jason in detail; she appears to him as maiden, mother, and crone (a trace of the ancient triple goddess of pre-Hellenic times). Colum differs from all modern sources I could locate in showing the power of the goddess; in his account, the crone he meets before going to his uncle's usurped kingdom carries him over a stream. In other versions, he lifts the goddess over the water and loses his sandal that way. Similarly, Colum's versions of Medea, Atalanta, Pandora, Demeter, and even the Harpies differ from other retellings, and help to convey the myths in a way that suggests the interweaving and overlapping of "male" and "female" experience, without the ridicule or fear of female experience that has become a cultural habit in interpreting the ancient stories.

Certain biographical facts help to explain the completeness and beauty of *The Golden Fleece*. Colum was a gifted outsider, somewhat like Hans Christian Andersen in wanting to be a great dramatist. As part of the Irish Renaissance, he wrote plays his colleagues thought too sentimental (feminized?), but which helped to keep the National Theater Society afloat financially (Bowen 62) and are now recognized as tempering effectively the intellectualism and abstraction brought to the movement by Yeats and others. Unlike the other writers—intellectuals with Protestant backgrounds like Yeats, Synge, and AE—and renegade Catholics like Joyce, Colum was a practicing Catholic whose education, after the national schools, was entirely gleaned from a personal program of reading. Alone of his Irish colleagues, he was raised in close touch with rural life, and with its emphasis on folklore and oral traditions that included women as tellers, audience, and characters. He was, and remained, a romantic. The romantic valuing of folklore, and attempts to reconcile culturally perceived oppositions such as male and female, are clear in Colum's Greek myths, where love and marriage are treated uncynically (e.g., the marriage of Atalanta after her race). Many critics have described the relationship of feminist criticism to romantic theories of art; Lipking observes that "Romanticism itself emerged only at that point when women began to play an important role in literature as writers and readers" (81).

Because he was an outsider in terms of education and religion, defining himself as an Irish bard and people's poet empathetic to their struggle against oppression, Colum was predisposed to the lyric completeness of his children's books. But another biographical factor may be just as significant. Colum's wife Mary, a University of Dublin graduate, was a critic and a literature professor. Sources describing their joint seminar on modern literature at Columbia imply a reversal of traditional male/female roles. Mary was analytic and skilled in argument; Padraic tended to be impressionistic and anecdotal (Bowen 21). In fact, Mary was a theorist and Padraic a poet, a poet who deliberately avoided academic conventions in his work. His description of their seminar points to Mary's participation in the historically male modes of discourse common to academe, and his own departure from them:

> I'm not a good teacher...I was never meant to be a teacher because I had no training. Molly was the good teacher. She

had good training in teaching. I would come in and talk to them informally rather than formally. Well, I could always teach them poetry, you know. The business of teaching poetry is to make them interested in it, isn't it? (21)

Colum's tone suggests the ease he felt in addressing a group including, and actually lead by, his wife. Their lifelong devotion, documented in letters, suggests that their literary marriage—unlike others recently discussed in criticism—was free of patterns destructive to the sanity of one partner (the woman). Colum's marriage may reasonably be seen as a factor in the poet's female-inclusive adaptation of Greek myths, an adaptation consistent with the life he and Mary created together.

Keeping his ties to Ireland, Catholicism, and Mary intact, Colum had a tranquillity and humor that set him apart and affected his writing for children. As AE remarked to Frank O'Connor, "Every serious Irish writer has a pain in his belly. Yeats has a pain in his belly. Joyce has a terrible pain in his belly.... Padraic Colum is the only Irish writer who never had a pain at all" (Murphy 143). The lack of rebellion or crisis in Colum's life, which in psychoanalytic terms might be described as failure to mature, might in feminist terms be recognized as evidence of maturity and wisdom (Gilligan). Valuing his bonds with others, and able to see life as process, Colum understood the role of poetry in the development of children, and was proud of his reputation as a writer for the young (Weaver 49). He viewed children as a natural and capable part of his audience, an idea drawn from his understanding of oral tales:

> The story-teller must have respect for the child's mind and the child's conception of the world, knowing it for a complete mind and a complete conception.... If the action be clear and the sentences clear one can use a mature language. Strange words, out-of-the-way words do not bewilder children if there be order in the action and in the sentences. They like to hear such words. (Bowen 123)

Colum's views on poetry in general help to explain his difference from other retellers of the myths. In a passage discussing the rhythm and other sound patterns essential to poetry, he says, "...it builds a bridge between the conscious and the sub-conscious mind, thus affecting the great purpose of art, as Schopenhauer proclaimed it—that is to say, delivering us from our little social selves, and introducing us to a vast range of human emotions" (Campbell 63).

Colum appreciated the myths for their emotive and symbolic power rather than their informative value. This sensitivity to language in and for itself explains why his work meets the needs of educated readers in different eras—ours now as well as the needs of people sixty years ago—and why it can still draw word-enchanted children into literature. Many other versions have worth as sources of information. Hamilton, Asimov, the D'Aulaires, Green and Graves, for example, all communicate in distinctive and interesting ways their extensive knowledge of the myths. These, and other retellers, also shape the myths into various kinds of prose narratives which often have their own intrinsic merit. As a retention of Homeric lyricism, and of the symbolic and ancient verbal power of myth, however, Colum's work excels. The opening pages of several versions, and the stress they place on the myths as history, contrasts with Colum's work and points up his unique achievement in a literature which must hold its readers by the magic of words.

Hawthorne's two collections of myths, *A Wonder Book* (1851) and *Tanglewood Tales* (1852), open with prefaces reminiscent of, though briefer than, the lengthy essay which prefaces *The Scarlet Letter* (1850). The device serves to establish distance from the myths, and the narrative frame is doubled by the introduction of a storyteller, Eustace Bright, an eighteen-year-old on leave from Williams College. These devices impose some of the philosophic and didactic qualities of nineteenth century American literature on the tales. Hawthorne also acknowledges his use of Gothic overtones in telling the tales *(A Wonder Book* ix). Hawthorne treats the myths mainly as fields for the playful erudition of the author and his narrators, and for the pleasant diversion of children.

Robert Graves, true to form as a folklore scholar, begins *Greek Gods and Heroes* (1960) with a description of Olympus, enlivening his informational prose with quips about the foibles of the gods and goddesses. His style is convoluted. While many child readers may find Graves amusing and informative, they will not experience the unity and lyricism of Colum's work in Graves' separate and satiric narratives. The satiric tone limits the emotional range of Graves' stories, and also affects his ability to recognize the validity of female experience; he treats such tales as that of Alcestis with playful cynicism.

Several versions of the myths do a good job of showing the importance of these stories to subsequent art and literature. The didactic intent of a work like H. A. Guerber's *The Myths of Greece and Rome* (1907, 1971) is clear from its preface and expository chapters. The book is a cultural handbook, not—like Colum's—a work of art in itself. The brevity of each retelling removes the psychological and emotional depth of the myths. For example, Thetis' gradual and unwilling loss of her immortality is not mentioned; it is a fully developed theme in Colum—albeit a romanticized one, for Achilles, Thetis, and Peleus become a happy family (218).

Two of the most widely available and respected versions of the myths, Hamilton's *Mythology* (1945) and Green's *Heroes of Greece and Troy* (1960)—each covering in one volume what Colum does in more than the two named as touchstones—can serve as more specific contrasts to Colum's achievement. Hamilton's book is literary history for children; she explains her intent as an effort "to make the reader see some difference between writers who were so different. After all, when one takes up a book like this one does not ask how entertainingly the author has retold the stories, but how close he [sic] has brought the reader to the original" (viii). Hamilton's retelling sustains the excitement of the original versions through skilled plotting and suspenseful tone, and her comments on sources are invaluable introductions to the classic writers. Green's version has the concise movement of an adventure story, but quotations from the classical writers, and good illustrations by Heather Copley and Christopher Chamberlain, add to the authenticity of his account. Both of these versions begin with standard expositions of Olympus, with Green's description of Greece in various seasons—a real place readers can visit—and Hamilton's comment, "With the coming forward of Greece, mankind became the center of the universe, the most important thing in it" (7), serving as expository lure for the reader.

In *The Golden Fleece*, Colum offers no explanation or apology for telling the narrative one way and not another. Instead, the poet commences with a dramatic episode, the entrusting of Jason to the centaur Chiron: "A man in the garb of a slave went up the side of that mountain that is all covered with forest, the Mountain Pelion. He carried in his arms a little child" (3). Within four short paragraphs, Colum creates a mood of high anticipation culminated by the description of Chiron, which Pogany's curly-maned giant supports on the next page. Through occasional but simple departures from conventional word order, Colum implies that this is a solemn moment: "...greater than any horse was Chiron, taller than any man" (3). Simple sentences nonetheless echo epic poetry in their balance and rhythm: "The hair of his head flowed over his horse's chest; in his man's hand he held a great spear" (3). This treatment of the myths is at once more suited for children and less obviously designed for them. Colum achieves exposition through flashback and repetition, intrinsic parts of the stories he is telling. The voice of Orpheus as the Argo sails recounts "The Beginning of Things," the history of the Titans. A single detail suggests the power of Zeus—a description of his first toy: "All of gold was the ball, with a dark-blue spiral around it. When the boy Zeus would play with this ball it would make a track across the sky, flaming like a star" (39). Green, by contrast, omits this detail in favor of the drama of Cronos swallowing his children, highlighted by the idea that readers can go to see the stone at Delphi he swallowed in place of Zeus. Hamilton, too, omits Zeus' childhood in order to convey his cosmic struggle with Cronos. This single example is suggestive of the emphasis each writer uses.

Unique to Colum is the wholeness of his version. Neither Hamilton nor Green pretends to offer this. Colum's use of the journey-quest theme to unify the myths is transformed by the use of female experience as intrinsic to the archetypal pattern of heroic action. Beginning with Jason's birth and finishing with Medea's ascent and Jason's solitary rule of Iolchus as "the greatest of the kings of Greece" (317), Colum constructs the tale to serve his ideas both of poetry and of children's needs. In his book, Jason does betray Medea with Glauce, but Medea does not kill her children. The tale has as happy an ending as Colum's sources will support, and its frame bears other narratives which amplify the ordered whole of the journey. The adventures of the other Argonauts, including Atalanta, Theseus, Heracles, and Orpheus, echo the themes of love, responsibility, labor and glory of the central tale. The death of Orpheus, for example, is an affirmation of love: "Again they were together, Orpheus and Eurydice, and as they went through the place that King Aidoneus ruled over, they had no fear of looking back, one upon the other" (300). Hamilton, instead, ends her account of Orpheus with praise of his songs (142).

The clearest example of Colum's faithfulness to and reinterpretation of his sources is the presentation of Medea. Like Ovid's, Colum's work is replete with details of her prayers and powers; but his tone comes from the largehearted love of magic he learned in Ireland, and from his ability to affirm female power. He introduces Medea as the wise daughter of Aetes, devoted to her sister Chalciope, with a beauty marked by a "secret anger" (127). This rebel daughter of the sun is a worshipper of the moon (Hecate) who undertakes to save not only Jason and his men, but—and this is a persuasive factor for her—the sons of her sister. Torn over betraying her father for her sister and for a stranger who does not know her attraction to him, Medea is anguished until Chalciope quiets her conscience with a plea for her children. When Jason—the "stranger who would sail away without thought of her, without the image of her in his mind" (132)—implores her help, he does so in the names of both Hecate and Zeus. Jason promises that their partnership is to be an honorable one, and her name "will be renowned throughout all of Greece" (135). Colum depicts Medea as willing to help despite her knowledge that her father and Jason will never be at peace. Unlike versions which show Medea entrapping Jason—Green has the "witch-maiden" saying, "I will tell you how to do this thing, and how to take the Fleece, if you will promise to let me sail back to Greece with you and become your wife" (153), with an unwilling Jason assenting for the sake of the Fleece—Colum's Jason claims Medea as part of their mutual triumph in acquiring, through joint efforts, the unjustly held Fleece. Colum's extended description of their work in seizing the prize, and of their strong reciprocal love, contrasts notably with accounts in other children's books. Using Medea's fair hair and dark skin thematically, Colum equates her with the Fleece itself, as the needed component in the life of Jason and of Greece also. Each time the Argonauts hide Medea, they wrap her in the Fleece she helped them win; she and the Fleece offer a fuller view of human possibilities to them, one that includes the magic of the (female) moon as well as the brilliance of the (male) sun. When Jason decides not to return Medea to her brother Apsyrtus, and thus to violate the covenant of the chiefs, he determines that Medea's wish to stay with him, and his own love for her, must override the agreement made without consulting them. Colum's narrator calls this "an ill thing," but the prior account of the lovers suggests that there was cause for them to disobey Medea's father.

Colum shows Jason killing Medea's brother in her presence, a terrible yet understandable crime Circe—Medea's aunt—can help them expiate. No other children's version so elaborates the visit to Circe and the help she recommends from Arete, a wise woman who counsels Medea never to use her magic to kill anyone (160). When Medea departs from this counsel, Colum makes it clear she does so at the request of Jason: "O Medea, help me in this with all thine enchantments and thou wilt be more dear to me than thou ever wert" (301). Jason then turns in disgust from Medea to Glauce, unwilling to live with the results of Medea's actions. "Ah, but if Jason had thought less of his kingdom and less of his triumphing with the Fleece of Gold, Medea would not have had the dragons come to her" (313).

Jason's fate is intertwined with Medea's. Green and Hamilton offer variations which treat the lovers quite differently and create less approving readers for Medea. Green's retelling emphasizes blood-and-guts adventure. Here is his depiction of the death of Apsyrtus: "Then Medea the Witch did a dreadful thing.... She took her brother, the boy prince Apsyrtus, and killed him with a sharp sword in plain view of his father, King Aeetes. Then she cut him in pieces and cast the pieces in the sea, for she knew that Aeetes would stop to gather them up so as to give his son due and honorable burial..." (155). Later, Green's narrative asserts that Jason "had never loved Medea" (164). Green reduces Medea to a temptation which brought Jason ruin—hardly the way she functions in sources like Euripedes. Hamilton's wish to compare sources, and her inherent empathy for female experience, leads her to describe both accounts of the killing of Apsyrtus (174). She states, "All that she did of evil and of good was done for him alone, and in the end, all the reward she got was that he turned traitor to her." (175).

Hamilton's tendency to show the oppression of women occurs in her treatment of Atalanta as well. While Colum has no difficulty with the idea that there were two Atalantas, and has the Argonaut tell the story of her patron the runner, Hamilton disputes even the claim that she sailed on the Argo (247). In describing Atalanta's race with Hippomenes, Hamilton comments on her inevitable subordination in marriage: "Her free days alone in the forest and her athletic victories were over." (251).

Colum's Atalanta has an inherent right to her place on the Argo: "All the heroes welcomed Atalanta as a comrade, and the maiden did all the things that the young men did" (23). (Hawthorne's Atalanta "had grown up in a very wild way, and talked much of the rights of women, and loved hunting and war far better than her needle" [Tanglewood 219].) Colum's version of the hunt parallels the story of the Fleece in depicting a departure from patriarchal claims. Atalanta the hero departs with friends after Meleager pays with his life for killing his mother's brothers when they ridiculed her right to the spoils of the hunt. In narrating the story of the other Atalanta, the huntress and adventurer had shown her predecessor unafraid of love when Hippomenes bested her: "Gladly, gladly do I give up the race..." (89).

Other tales supporting the main narrative demonstrate the unity of Colum's book, and the way his tales use repetitive themes and motifs in the manner of oral narrative. Thus, describing the voyage to Colchis for the Fleece, Colum prepares for the central role of Medea in Jason's quest by the stories of Demeter and Pandora. These tales are related to the heroes' visit to Lemnos, where the queen's ultimate gift of a dove (a symbol of the pre-Hellenic earth goddess) enables them to pass through the Symplegades. The Lemnians insist on hearing stories about female experience, and this cluster of tales enables Colum to prepare for the final part of the book, when the accounts of individual Argonauts are shown to be related to the fates of the women they encounter. Though many children's books tell of Heracles' labours, few are like Colum's in showing the importance of his marriages to his character and destiny.

Colum's treatment of the Demeter myth is important because it introduces child readers to the mother/daughter theme, too often overlooked in literary studies. Not only powerful, Colum's Demeter is loving; and though she wins Persephone back for only part of the year, Persephone in the underworld "has joy, too, knowing of the seasons she may walk with Demeter" (81).

Like the retelling of Demeter's love for her daughter, Colum's story of Pandora is much closer than other children's versions to the positive powers of the "lost goddesses." Colum sets the story into his narrative as the means Castor and Polydeuces take to remind the Argonauts of the quest they have undertaken and may forget in Lemnos. Far more complex than the Hamilton or Green versions, Colum's is not a single-minded condemnation of Pandora. The Golden Maid brings with her a clay jar, not a treasure chest (an important point in the Spretnak version as well). The clay jar is buried, and plants cover it while Epimetheus and Pandora enjoy pastoral happiness. On the journey to the home of Epimetheus, "Epimetheus may have knocked the jar about, for the lid that had been tight upon it now fitted very loosely" (96). The inevitable opening of the jar comes not through Pandora, but through the desire of other women to share her beauty and grace. Self-thought, Sickness and War escape, but another woman releases Hope from the clay as well.

The theme of female beauty and fecundity is lost from the other retellings, which depict Pandora as idly curious. The Argonauts must tear themselves away from the Lemnians, for each male/female pair is accompanied by the jar which can make journeying impossible. Despite this recognition of male/female limitation through fecundity and the problems generativity brings, the final note in Colum's account is one of trust. Jason keeps his promise to Hipsipyle, waiting until morning to sail from Lemnos, and she therefore brings him the dove which makes possible the heroic quest.

The Lemnos interlude—compressed into a paragraph in Hamilton and a line or two in Green—allows Colum to develop his archetypal theme of a human journey that includes love, and the loss and regaining of love, as intrinsic to identity, adventure, and freedom. His confidence in the theme permits another important dimension, the acknowledgement of betrayal, rage and despair within the romantic quest. It is important, for example, that he and Pogany present the Harpies as female (55); child readers thus are prepared for a fuller understanding of Greek mysogyny after their initiation into the myths' power and truth. The Harpies, the Furies, the Amazons and other depictions of female rage in the myths represent the Greeks' understanding of the suppression of women after the discovery of paternity. This interpretation, common

among classicists and discussed in such sources as Philip Slater's
The Glory of Hera, is also related to Mary Daly's language in
Gyn/Ecology, where she validates women's identity as Hags,
Crones, Harpies and Furies (Furious Women) by showing how
etymology and reinterpretation can give women access to our
powers to create authentic culture. The origin of such names for
women offers a part of human history children need to
understand and to feel.

Though Colum's romantic view may sound like Blarney to
some readers (who may prefer Hamilton's open acknowledge-
ments about women's status) it is important that his version
incorporates the beauty and hope of Homeric song. Moreover,
the "facts" are there: Medea and Jason part irrevocably; Meleager
dies for challenging the existing order; The Lemnians and
Argonauts have conflicting desires. The Golden Fleece itself is the
magic remnant of a mother's love; she was able to protect her son,
but not her daughter (Helle). The reader of Colum is initiated into
a culture in need of change, as well as into "the glory that was
Greece." As Ann Murphy suggests, Colum's idea of poetry
recognized its dependence on the structure of the society it
incarnates (64). His selections from sources, and creation of tone,
demonstrate his trust in poetic power to reshape the world out of
the riches and shames of the past. *The Golden Fleece and the
Heroes Who Lived Before Achilles* offers that kind of opportunity
to new generations of readers.

REFERENCES

Asimov, Isaac. *Words from the Myths.* New York: Houghton, 1961.

Booth, Wayne C. "Freedom of Interpretation: Bakhtin and the
Challenge of Feminist Criticism." *Critical Inquiry* 9 (September
1982): 45-76.

Bowen, Zack. *Padraic Colum: A Biographical-Critical Introduction.* Southern Illinois University Press: Carbondale and Edwards-
ville, 1970.

Campbell, Douglas, "Padraic Colum's Celebration of Littleness."
Journal of Irish Studies 9, 3 (1974): 60-68.

Colum, Padraic. *The Golden Fleece and the Heroes Who Lived
Before Achilles.* New York: The Macmillan Company, 1962. (1921)

Daly, Mary. *Gyn/Ecology: The Metaethics of Radical Feminism.*
Boston: Beacon Press, 1968.

D'Aulaire, Ingri and **Edgar Parin.** *D'Aulaires' Book of Greek Myths.*
New York: Doubleday, 1962.

Frye, Northrop. *The Educated Imagination.* Indiana University Press: Bloomington, 1964.

Gadamer, Hans-Georg. *Truth and Method.* 1960; New York: Continuum, 1975.

Gilligan, Carol. *In a Different Voice.* Cambridge: Harvard University Press, 1982.

Graves, Robert. *Greek Gods and Heroes.* New York: Doubleday, 1960.

Green, Roger Lancelyn. *Heroes of Greece and Troy.* New York: Henry Z. Walck, Inc., 1961. (1958)

Guerber, H. A., rev. Dorothy Stuart. *The Myths of Greece and Rome.* London: The British Book Centre, 1971. (1907)

Hamilton, Edith. *Mythology.* Boston: Little, Brown, 1945.

Hawthorne, Nathaniel. *A Wonder Book.* New York: Dutton, 1949. (1850)

_____. *Tanglewood Tales.* New York: Dutton, 1950. (1851)

Heilbrun, Carolyn. *Reinventing Womanhood* New York: W. W. Norton, 1979.

Hunt, Kellogg W. "Early Blooming and Late Blooming Syntactic Structures." in Charles R. Cooper and Lee Odell. *Evaluating Writing.* NCTE, 1977.

Kingsley, Charles. *The Heroes.* New York: Macmillan, 1954.

Lipking, Lawrence. "Aristotle's Sister: A Poetics of Abandonment." *Critical Inquiry* 10 (September 1983): 61-81.

Murphy, Ann. "Appreciation of Padraic Colum." *Journal of Irish Studies* 17, 4 (1980): 128-147.

Purves, Alan C. and **Dianne L. Monson,** *Experiencing Children's Literature.* Glenview, Illinois: Scott, Foresman, 1984.

Sidwell, Robert T. "Rhea Was A Broad: Pre-Hellenic Children." *Children's Literature in Education* 12, 4 (1981): 171-76.

Slater, Philip E. *The Glory of Hera: Greek Mythology and the Greek Family.* Boston: Beacon Press, 1968.

Spretnak, Charlene. *Lost Goddesses of Ancient Greece.* Boston: Beacon, 1981.

Weaver, Jack. "The Padraic Colum I Knew." *Journal of Irish Literature* 3, 3 (1974): 49-50.

The Norse Myths and the D'Aulaires' *Norse Gods and Giants:* Patterns of Paradox

by Caroline R. Goforth

Where does Norse mythology fit in the constellation of children's literature? In his preface to *George MacDonald: An Anthology,* C. S. Lewis questions whether any myth should be classified as literature, because the power of myth lies in its pattern of events, not in its words. "What really delights and nourishes me is a particular pattern of events," Lewis writes, "which would equally delight and nourish if it had reached me by some medium which involved no words at all—say by a mime, or a film" (xxvi-xxvii). Northrop Frye provides a powerful denial of Lewis' assertion that myth is not literature with his system of literary criticism based on myth patterns, a system which suggests how powerful a part myth plays in our enjoyment of literature. But that merely replaces my original question with a slightly different one: do the patterns of Norse mythology delight and nourish child readers?

Carl G. Jung's theory of the collective unconscious offers one general answer. The patterns of myth are the archetypal patterns of the psyche, and the reflection of inner conflicts in stories where the conflicts are explored and resolved offers the reader or listener the delight (or at least relief) of recognition and the nourishment of belonging to the human family. Myth in children's literature becomes especially significant in light of Jung's assertion that the individual human mind progresses through psychological stages of development similar to those the human species experienced in prehistory (Jung 98). Since traditional myths reflect those stages of development, it would seem that children have a psychological need for them, perhaps even a natural affinity.

Bruno Bettelheim, however, distinguishes between myth and fairy tale when he asserts in *The Uses of Enchantment* that, from the human viewpoint, fairy tales are optimistic while myths are pessimistic. Fairy tales are more suitable for children, he concludes, because ordinary human characters overcome obstacles to success and live happily ever after here in the concrete world. These happy endings reassure children that the psychological conflicts enacted in the fairy tales—the same ones they are themselves experiencing—will be satisfactorily resolved as they grow up. Myth, on the other hand, emphasizes the inferiority and powerlessness of humans, who always suffer in their dealings with gods, even if they try to follow orders. Human mythical heroes don't serve as effective models either, because they are so unreachable they're discouraging. Besides, any reward comes after death in another world, a reward so abstract that it is meaningless to a child (Bettelheim 35-41).

Other writers, however, view myths from different vantage points and see, in addition to the psychological models, more positive models of the relationship between the individual and the universe. Although Jane Yolen, in "How Basic Is SHAZAM?" includes as one of her four functions of myth for children its value as "a tool of therapy" for gaining psychological insight, she also lists three other functions that are oriented outward: "landscape of allusion," "knowledge of ancestral culture," and "a model for belief" (186-191). All three focus on connectedness—either between the individual and the society or between the individual and the cosmos.

Cosmic order is also the center of John S. Morris' functions of myth for primitive man in "Fantasy in a Mythless Age." According to Morris,

> (1) Myth was the verbal declaration of the Act in which order is established over chaos.
> (2) Myth was the verbal declaration of the Act that sustains order.
> (3) Participation in the declaration of the myth enabled the individual to participate in its creative and sustaining power as he lived his life as a journey towards the achievement of an end. (80)

Participation in myth, then, becomes participation in creation, in order, and in power, while in real, everyday life, chaos and helplessness often predominate. Even the happiest children have little control over their inner or outer world. Even the most carefully cared for children live in a world where they have to learn to suspect people they don't know, where violence screams out of televisions and radios, where they find out the nuclear threat is real before they discover the tooth fairy isn't. How can any twentieth-century child participate in myth? How can he find any delight and nourishment in story patterns that invite him to believe in an order that doesn't seem to exist in his real world?

Paradoxically, it is this apparent weakness of the myths that gives them their strength and earns them an essential role in literature for children. Like many other myth researchers, Penelope Farmer found parallels in myths of many cultures and discovered one essential similarity she calls the "cosmic agreement": life comes out of death, creation out of destruction

(179). Myth never denies the existence or the power of disorder, of violence and destruction. What myth does is embrace disorder by integrating it as paradox into the cosmic pattern. To participate in myth is to free oneself from chaos. John S. Morris contends that "The power of Evil is not the power of a counter world, but the power of no-order in this world" (82). Myth as imposition of order is the individual's most effective weapon against fear and despair.

The Norse myths are filled with the paradoxes of reality. The gods themselves—the Aesir, as they are collectively called—have paradoxical personalities, they act paradoxically, and they experience paradox. Creation grows out of destruction, and the broad sweep of the Aesir's story from Ginungagap to Ragnarokk is toward the bad end that literally *turns* good in a cycle, what J. R. R. Tolkien called *eucatastrophe,* "a fleeting glimpse of Joy, Joy beyond the walls of the world, poignant as grief" (68).

At the heart of paradox in Norse mythology are the Aesir, the gods themselves. They are neither immortal nor omnipotent. Subject to aging, they must eat Idunn's apples of youth to stay young and beautiful. From the beginning, their destinies lie in the power of the Norns, who weave the threads of human lives. Ragnarokk, the Twilight of the Gods, bears down inexorably. Odin is the wise All-Father, visiting earth as a wanderer to advise his human children. But he is also the fierce god of war, demanding bloody sacrifice in battle. Thor, god of thunder, protector of the Aesir, is a glutton with a fiery temper. Although Freya, goddess of love, is desired by gods and giants alike, although she hosts lavish feasts for Odin's warriors in Asgard, she weeps tears of gold for her lost husband Od. Most paradoxical of the gods is Loki— handsome, charming, smart, yet mean-spirited and envious. Although he is an incorrigible trickster, he also gets the Aesir out of numerous scrapes—sometimes under pressure, sometimes on his own.

The gods are often called the "kind" Aesir while the giants are called evil, but their relationships with one another shift. The gods prepare for the creation of the earth by decimating the giants, with little justification except that Ymir, progenitor of the giant race, "had always been wild, and old age had made him worse" (D'Aulaire 18). Yet Odin has several children by giantesses, and Frey gives up his magic sword to marry Gerd, a giant maiden. The giantess Grid saves Thor from the giant Geirrod by lending him weapons. When the gods can't move Balder's funeral ship, they call on the ogress Hyrrokkin for help. Loki and Bragi are both giants who are accepted into the Aesir. Loki is loyal to no one, playing tricks on the gods, yet joining them in their exploits against giants, and finally turning against them and leading the giants' attack at Ragnarokk.

As Nicholas Tucker has pointed out, child readers need a universe that makes moral sense. They want to be able to tell the good guys from the bad, and they want to see goodness rewarded and evil punished (180-181). For this reason myths are probably better suited to older children who are coming to grips with the reality of moral ambiguity, the children who expect immediate redress when they say, "It isn't fair," and who are enraged, frustrated, and betrayed when their claim—though it may be true—effects no change in their situation. For such children, the Norse myths provide a way to reconcile justice and reality. The gods and all the other inhabitants of the nine worlds may not be clearcut heroes and villains, but the overall movement of the myths affirms a child's sense of moral order. The Twilight of the Gods is a direct result of the gods' failure to keep their own code of honor. For example, they bind the wolf Fenris after they have promised not to, and they trick a giant mason out of taking Freya away as his fee for building a wall around Asgard. In these and other cases, their dishonorable behavior averts a disaster, but in a child's and the myths' rigid moral system, the breaching of the code has consequences, whatever the cause. There are two messages here. First, nobody is all good or all bad—not children themselves, not their parents or their friends or their teachers or anybody else they know. Second, we all suffer the consequences of our imperfections, but there are also new beginnings. After Ragnarokk a new universe comes into being.

The gods also experience paradox beyond their control. Odin, the All-Father, must build his power through conscious effort, and the greatest powers aren't earned by conquering an enemy or competing against other gods to show them who's boss. Instead, Odin must conquer himself through suffering and sacrifice. He gains the magic of the runic letters (that is, literacy) by hanging for nine nights and nine days on Yggdrasil, the World Tree. He humbles himself before the giant Mimir to get a drink from his well of wisdom. When Mimir offers a trade, one of Odin's all-seeing eyes for the water that will give him the inner sight of wisdom, Odin acquiesces.

Loki, too, discovers the limits of his power. His tricks don't always turn out as he plans. When he cuts off the lovely golden hair of Thor's wife Sif, he is forced to make restitution—a new head of real gold hair made by the dwarfs. At the same time he has gifts made for several other gods. Two of these prove crucial to the survival of the gods and men: Odin's spear Gungnir, which never misses, and Thor's hammer, Mjolnir, which becomes the Aesir's principal weapon against the giants.

Perhaps the most paradoxical of the gods' adventures is the story of Thor's visit to the giant Utgardsloki, undertaken specifically to challenge him to a contest of physical strength. Thor takes Loki along because Utgardsloki has a reputation for cunning as well as muscle, and they pick up a servant along the way, Tjalfi, apparently a giant. Before the trio reaches Utgard, the paradoxical context is set. On the road they sleep in what they think is a strange cabin. When it turns out to be the giant Skrymir's glove, the reader gets a mental image of an absurdly tiny Thor. The superman of the gods shrinks to midget proportions. From this point, the adventure becomes more and more humiliating. Skrymir ties up the travelers' food in his bag for the day's journey; but when they stop for the night, he goes to sleep without eating or unfastening the bag. Thor tries desperately to untie the bag, but he fails and realizes that Skrymir is mocking his famous strength. Enraged, Thor takes his giant-smashing hammer to the sleeping Skrymir three times during the night. Skrymir barely stirs, wondering whether a leaf, an acorn, or finally, with Thor's hardest blow, a branch has fallen on his head.

At Utgard Thor's party fails miserably at every challenge. Loki loses an eating contest, Tjalfi loses a race, and Thor fails to empty a drinking horn, to pick up Utgardsloki's cat from the floor, and to throw old Granny Elle in a wrestling contest. As they leave, however, Utgardsloki accompanies them outside the city. He explains that he has fooled them by illusion. Posing as Skrymir, he bound the food bag with a troll knot and moved a mountain between himself and Thor when Thor used his hammer. Loki competed against wild-fire in his eating contest; Tjalfi, against Thought in his footrace. Because the end of Thor's drinking horn reached to the sea, he would have had to drink the ocean to empty it. Utgardsloki's cat was really the Midgard's Serpent, and Granny Elle was Old Age itself. Utgardsloki compliments his visitors on their performances, considering who their opponents were, but the humiliation stings Thor to the quick. He raises his hammer only to find Utgard and Utgardsloki have disappeared.

In this adventure, a tiny Thor is hoodwinked by magic. His strength fails, and his rage is futile. The master deceiver Loki is deceived. Natural forces—fire, the sea, old age—are stronger than the gods. The evil Midgard's Serpent is more than a match for the protector of the Aesir. The threat of Evil as no-order surfaces in this myth, and it is not resolved. Thor is unable to restore the order imposed by the Aesir over the giants in this particular case. The implications would be frightening if they were indeed a manifestation of no-order. Instead, the gods' failure is part of the order, which demands that the Aesir fall. No-order is contained within order, and thereby controlled. For child readers, there is the reassurance that unavoidable chaos (illness, death, divorce, personal failure), when it is accepted, becomes part of the pattern of life. Only if the disordering factor becomes the individual's ordering principle does chaos take over. Thor never throws in his hammer, not even at Ragnarokk. He acts in spite of the paradox to make a larger meaning.

No-order is even a part of the pattern of ordering itself in Norse mythology. Creation almost always grows out of the disordering of destruction. Life begins out of nothing in the great void Ginungagap. There, sparks from the fires of Muspelheim whirl together with ice crystals from the frozen fog of Niflheim (the opposites of fire and water). Out of this mixture the shapes of Ymir, the first frost giant, and a cow emerge. The ice cow licks the salty frost around Ginungagap for nourishment; and, as she warms the place where she licks, a third creature takes form, Buri, who is the grandfather of the first three gods, Odin, Hoenir, and Lodur. When these three undertake the creation of the world, they begin by killing Ymir, whose flowing blood drowns all but two of the giant race. Ymir's body, pushed into Ginungagap, provides raw material for the earth: his flesh becomes soil; his bones, mountains; his teeth, rocks; his skull, the dome of the sky; his eyebrows, a wall to separate the world of men, Midgard, from the world of the giants, Jotunheim.

More complex and more directly paradoxical is the story of how poetry came into the world. It begins in violence, the war between the Aesir gods and the Vanir gods. When the adversaries agree to stop fighting, they seal their pact by chewing berries and spitting the juice into a vat. Out of the liquid comes Kvasir, the spirit of knowledge. Two dwarfs kill Kvasir. The D'Aulaire edition of the myths, the one named by the ChLA Committee on its list of touchstones, says the dwarfs steal his essence of knowledge and add honey and magic herbs to make mead (64); some other editions, like H. R. Ellis Davidson's *Scandinavian Mythology*, specifically state that the dwarfs take Kvasir's blood to make the mead (46), a more graphically violent image. In the hands of the dwarfs, the mead itself leads to more violence. They feel so heady under its influence that they kill a giant and his wife.

When Suttung, son of the giant couple, comes to avenge them, he spares the dwarfs' lives in exchange for the mead. Odin, sitting on his throne in Asgard, sees the hidden kettles of mead, guarded by Gunnlod, Suttung's daughter. As a snake he crawls into the mountain chamber where the mead is, then changes into a handsome young man and woos Gunnlod. She allows him to take a sip from each kettle, but instead he empties all three of them, changes into an eagle and flies away. Suttung almost catches him, but he manages to get to Asgard and spit out the mead. From then on Odin speaks in verse, sharing the mead with other gods and with gifted men. Odin regrets his betrayal of Gunnlod and brings her son Bragi to live as his son in Asgard. He becomes the bard of the gods.

Disorder runs through this story—the Aesir-Vanir war, the murder of Kvasir, the murder of the giants, Odin's betrayal of Gunnlod. Yet the result is poetry, the most ordered language. Paradox is again the basis of pattern: beauty from death, truth from betrayal, creativity from violence.

Just as the personalities, actions, and individual adventures of the gods are patterned in paradox, the broad sweep of the myth cycle is paradoxical. In the beginning destruction begets creation. The creation, unable to escape the disorder of imperfection, hurtles toward Ragnarokk, where the creation is destroyed. But the cycle doesn't end in chaos; death gives way again to life when the new day dawns after the Twilight of the Gods.

The end begins with Balder, god of light, the only perfect one of the Aesir. As lawgiver and judge, he, more than any other god, represents order. Paradoxically, he must succumb to disorder to play out his key role in the cyclical order. It is his destiny to die. Despite the gods' recognition of their own impotence in the face of destiny, the Aesir love Balder so much that they try to prevent his death. His mother Frigg travels the whole world extracting promises of every organic and inorganic thing not to harm Balder. But Loki is jealous, and in his effort to destroy the order of the Aesir by killing Balder, he sets in motion the new order of Ragnarokk. Posing as an old crone, Loki finds out from Frigg that the only thing she didn't make promise not to harm Balder was the weak, harmless mistletoe. Loki makes an arrow of mistletoe and persuades Balder's blind brother Hod to shoot it at Balder to celebrate his invulnerability. Balder dies and goes to Hel.

Loki foils the Aesir one last time when they try to rescue Balder and his wife Nanna from Hel by insuring that everything, living and nonliving, weeps in mourning for them. Disguised again as an old crone, Loki refuses to weep, and Balder and Nanna must remain in Hel. This is Loki's last trick because Odin finally agrees to banish him, despite their vows to one another as blood brothers.

When the day of Ragnarokk comes, Loki bursts his chains and leads the enemies of the Aesir against them. Odin is swallowed by Fenris, the wolf, as Thor fights the Midgard's Serpent. Vidar, Odin's son, kills Fenris. Thor smashes the serpent's head with his hammer, but he dies from the monster's venom. Heimdall, watchman of the gods, and Loki kill one another. Frey dies at the hands of a fire-demon. Odin's warriors and the giants and monsters battle until none are left living. The sun and moon are eaten by the wolves that have chased them since the beginning of time.

Finally, the only gods of the Aesir left are Magni and Modi, Thor's sons; Vidar and Vali, youngest of Odin's sons; Hoenir; and Balder, who, when the world splits open, leads Hod out of Hel. A man and a woman survive also, Lif and Lifthrasir. When the daughter of the old sun shines on the new day, the earth is recreated, and an era more ordered and peaceful than the first begins.

This is Tolkien's *eucatastrophe*—the good containing bad, the order enfolding disorder, the pattern embracing paradox. Although the old gods must die, they do not die meaningless deaths. Their destruction of Loki, his children (Fenris and the Midgard's Serpent), and the giant race makes possible the creation of the new day. From the beginning the Aesir know they must act within their destiny. They recognize also that even if their destiny must be the disorder of Ragnarokk, they are still acting within a larger order. To impose order as far as they can, to act honorably, and to keep trying when they fail at both order and honor—these are the guiding principles of the Aesir and their gift to twentieth-century children.

Describing her personal experience of the "cosmic agreement" in myth, Penelope Farmer writes: "...we must be comforted by the notion that even if in spite of myth, we do end up blowing our earth to smithereens, we may set another universe to spin thereby" (185). This may sound like grim consolation to children trying to cope with the paradox of reality, but it is the only consolation humanity has ever had: that human life and death might mean something because they hold some unique place in a pattern comprehensible only to the imagination. This consolation, this mythology of paradox, does nourish and delight child readers because it connects them to the whole of humankind and of the cosmos. Myth makes the universe a shared wonder, a delightful adventure precisely because it refuses to submit to the disorder of ordinary experience by setting it in the larger order of the "cosmic agreement."

REFERENCES

Bettelheim, Bruno. *The Uses of Enchantment: The Meaning and Importance of Fairy Tales.* New York: Knopf, 1976.

D'Aulaire, Ingri and **Edgar.** *Norse Gods and Giants.* Garden City, N.Y.: Doubleday, 1967.

Davidson, H. R. Ellis. *Scandinavian Mythology.* London: Paul Hamlyn, 1969.

Farmer, Penelope. "On the Effects of Collecting Myth for Children and Others." *Children's Literature in Education* 8(1977):176-85.

Jung, Carl G. et al. *Man and His Symbols.* Garden City, N.Y.: Doubleday, 1964.

Lewis, C. S., ed. *George MacDonald: An Anthology.* New York: Macmillan, 1947.

Morris, John S. "Fantasy in a Mythless Age." *Children's Literature* 2(1973):77-86.

Tolkien, J. R. R. *Tree and Leaf.* Boston: Houghton Mifflin, 1965.

Tucker, Nicholas. "How Children Respond to Fiction." *Writers, Critics and Children.* Ed. Geoff Fox et al. New York: Agathon Press, 1976. 177-88.

Yolen, Jane. "How Basic Is SHAZAM?" *Childhood Education* 53(Feb. 1977):186-91.

The Poetry of Walter de la Mare: Sweet-tongued Words

by Norma Bagnall

Children may come naturally to poetry; it is certainly present in the cadence of their first sounds, and it is borne on the rhythm of the way they learn to speak. The first sounds we use with our children include lullabies, our first play with them is the rhythm and rhyme of finger and toe games, and the first reading we do with them is nursery rhymes. Then children themselves continue their speech growth with chants, riddles, and rhymes as they play with words and learn the magic of language. After that, if their growth in language is not impeded, they may extend their exploration of language by experiencing the pleasures of poetry written for them. One sure place they can go to continue their enjoyment of rhythm and alliteration, rhyme and metaphor is to the poetry of Walter de la Mare, the English poet whose work began before the turn of this century and continued until his death in 1956.

More than any other, Walter de la Mare is the poet of childhood. He has the unusual ability to see the world through a child's eye, and yet speak to children through his own experience in a lyrical way that makes his poetry appealing to all of us. His language is precisely on the mark, so that he describes the commonplace in fresh, crisp language as he writes about death and fears, joy and movement. He invents nonsense, plays with rhythm and sound, and describes the mystical and the mysterious in a way that can evoke wonder in his young audience. He does so consistently throughout his *Collected Rhymes and Verses,* a rich volume that includes over two hundred of his poems and incorporates children's poetry from more than ten of his earlier published works.

De la Mare's unique vision is the most distinguishing mark of his work. In one poem after another, he scrutinizes an object closely, so that we are peering with him directly—at a snowflake, for example; and then he backs off, taking us with him, so that we are forced to see the scene from another point of view.

"Snow" is a good example. This poem describes a snowfall, as the snow "Whirls softly down—/. . . All in an icy/Quiet, forlorn./ Whispering, rustling,/Through the air,/On sill and stone,/Roof— everywhere". Through imagery of sound and sight, de la Mare achieves a sense of hush and beauty; "No breath of wind,/No gleam of sun" disturbs the scene until

> At shut of day,
> Stoops from the West
> One wintry ray.
> And, feathered in fire,
> Where ghosts the moon,
> A robin shrills
> Her lonely tune.   (185-6)

The flaming color of the sun's ray and the brilliance of the lone robin at the end of this picture of whirling snow adds a dimension of sound and color and loneliness that the poem without it would not achieve. The surprise of sound and color alerts reader/listener to look for the unusual not only in de la Mare but in their own world also.

The unusual and the beautiful abound in our world, but de la Mare warns us that we must be careful observers in order not to miss either. In "The Snowflake," de la Mare offers yet another way of looking at snow (and snow remains one of children's lasting delights); this time he invites close inspection of the intricate design one flake makes as well as of the loveliness of the accumulation of many such flakes:

> Before I melt,
> Come, look at me!
> This lovely icy filigree!
> Of a great forest
> In one night
> I make a wilderness

Of white:
By skyey cold
Of crystals made,
All softly, on
Your finger laid,
I pause, that you
My beauty see:
Breathe, and I vanish
Instantly.   (193-94)

Here the snowflake is the speaker, pleading for examination of that which may otherwise be ignored. It invites intimacy; the snowflake is viewed so closely that a breath can destroy its beauty. But the snowflake also expresses itself, not as a single snowflake, but as representative of the snowfall that covered the entire forest and made it a wilderness overnight. By giving to a single snowflake the characteristics of an entire snowfall, de la Mare gives unexpected magnitude to what otherwise would be perceived as a small, perfect specimen of beauty and fascination. The firm implication is that loveliness and wonder are waiting for us to discover them, and that we must look and appreciate before they disappear.

Looking at things close up in order to see them thoroughly, and then backing off from them so as to see a larger view; this is a common device of de la Mare. "The Magnifying Glass" (245-46) expresses the magic one can find in an inch of moss or a drop of water; it reports the delicious fearfulness of the "tigerish claws" of a spider. Then the last stanza proposes that if one could look at the universe in like manner, the moon would be but an afternoon's walk away. This refocusing from close up to a grand view gives the audience a feeling of both perspective and wonder. "All But Blind" (96) takes the device of changing perspective to show the oneness of humankind with all of earth's creatures. As the mole is almost blind in its chambered home underground, and the bat and the owl are near blind in the light of day, so, says de la Mare, must we be to someone greater than we.

Thus, de la Mare invests our humanness with a sense of the mysterious; in contrast, when he writes about death, one of life's greatest mysteries, he grants it the status of the commonplace. For example, "The Funeral" (291-92) never loses its matter-of-fact tone nor the perspective of its young narrator:

They dressed us up in black,
Susan and Tom and me;
And, walking through the fields
All beautiful to see,
With branches high in the air

And daisy and buttercup,
We heard the lark in the clouds,—
In black dressed up...

This reporting of the commonplace in the face of the death of someone close to the three children involved in the narrative, gives the poem an unusually unsentimental view of both death and of childhood. Faced with death children (as perhaps all of us) may be overcome by the immensity and finality of it; but these children respond by becoming keenly observant of life as they see, hear and smell it around them and as they feel it course through them, making its ordinary demands.

De la Mare affirms that what the children see, what they hear, and what they feel is not death but life. Virtually every sense is evoked in this poem, from the contrast of the black clothing the children are wearing to the brilliance of daisy and buttercup, to the sounds of lark and thrushes and the smell and taste of their tea which are described in later stanzas. The poem tells of Susan's hair blowing in the wind, of the length of grasses in the field, and of Tom's fatigue; all create a mood appropriate to death, and to the innocence of children when they must encounter it. The children in the poem are spectators at the funeral, but their vitality, humanity and innocence separate them from it.

Here de la Mare writes about death prosaically, so that this poem has an air of matter-of-fact reporting; he writes about children's fears in quite another way. "Hark" (250-51) is a brief narrative of young Charles, put to bed at evening. He is alone and afraid of the dark, and he pleads with his parent to listen to hear the noises he hears. He is comforted by being told that what he hears are only the most ordinary noises: the wind, a mouse, or an owl. But the words used to comfort him are also those which frighten; the "door ajar," the "wind at the keyhole," and the "moon looking into the house" all suggest that something is watching and trying to get to him. If Charles were to try as hard as he could, the narrator tells him, "You still wouldn't hear what you think you hear;/There's nothing to fear in what you fear." But Charles is not comforted and, because of de la Mare's imagery, we understand his misery and fear.

We also understand Ann's fear in "The Phantom" (159-62). She is asked by her grandmother to go up the stairs to a large closet and bring down a Bible; it is evening, grandmother's house has dark corners, and Ann has only a candle to light her way. The images of "Vast shadows on the heedless walls [which] Gigantic loom, stoop low" are caused by Ann's wavering candle flame which seems "to languish small and blue." "Around her loom the vacant rooms" and the walls are "Gloomy with night." This imagery depicts exactly the fears that bedevil children, even in the homes of their beloved grandmothers. The poem also speaks to the bravery of Ann who, in spite of almost overwhelming fear, "climbs on into a loneliness."

"The Old Stone House" (164) also expresses that which children fear. In this poem, the child narrator tiptoes past "the nettles, porch, and weedy well" of a house long empty because he knows full well that "A friendless face is peering" out, watching as he silently passes by.

That de la Mare knew the fears of childhood is evident; those he tells of are universal and timeless. But he also knew how to soothe children. His lullabies are serene journeys into the magic of evening. The best known of these, or at least the most anthologized, is "Silver" (256), which paints a silvery vision of evening beginning with "Slowly, silently, now the moon/Walks the night in her silver shoon." The entire poem is a tribute to the vision of soothing magic brought on by the moon's power. "Lully" (252), another lullaby, calms a fretful child through telling of the commonplace by recounting soothing images: the robin which is abed, the snow which covers the fields, and the safety provided by the fire warming his own home. The child is urged to "rest then, pretty soul,/Safe on thy mother's arm." "Lullaby" (253) opens and closes each of its three seven-line stanzas with "Sleep, sleep, thou lovely one," and it is filled with imagery—a little mouse, a nightingale, both singing "in darkness, lonely, sweet"—that can lull a child to sleep. Even the sea in this soft lullaby is whispering "Peace."

In the imaginative "House of Dream" (258), de la Mare invents a magic place where children in sleep can go, a place of dreams where they will be soothed and entertained:

Candle, candle, burning clear,
Now the House of Dream draws near;
See what shadowy flowers move
The solitary porch above,
Hark, how still it is within,
Though so many guests go in.

No faint voice will answer make
While thy tapering flame's awake.
Candle, candle, burning low,
It is time for me to go.
Music, faint and distant, wells
From those far-off dales and dells.

Now in shoes of silence I
Stand by the walls of witchery;

89

> Out then, earthly flame, for see,
> Sleep's unlatched her door to me.

Dream becomes a house that beckons through an unlatched door to the stillness of night and sleep. The scene is shadowy, and the music is the "faint and distant" serenity we almost always hear in de la Mare's lullabies.

In contrast to this misty serenity, de la Mare's poems about the joys of childhood are celebrations meant to be read aloud, sung, or shouted.

"Silly Sallie" (44) begins rhythmically in a childhood chant: *"Silly Sallie! Silly Sallie!/Called the boys down Blind Man's Alley,"* and we are swept up into the rhythm and chant of this poem. It entices us even though we learn little about Sallie except that she ignores the boys by smiling and looking "Some other place, not out, but in"—the eternal best response to teasing boys as they insensitively continue their exuberant shout.

"Then" (37) opens with the steady rhythm of "Twenty, forty, sixty, eighty,/A hundred years ago" to tell about the times when little boys could awaken in the middle of the night to the "shout" of the Watch calling out the hour or to the "scream" of a northeast gale.

De la Mare constantly uses noise to speak to the energy of children. In "Missel Thrush" (122), the thrush "shrills" and "shouts wild." "The Song of Soldiers" (60) reports the "shouting and the shattering of the sea" as well as the ringing of the "trumpets of the sea." "Thunder" (29) begins and ends with the shout "Call the cows home!/Call the cows home," in a chant that makes a game of movement and sound to bring the animals in from a storm that threatens with "Louring storm clouds" and "whistling wind."

The vigor of childhood is also evident and joyous in "No Bed" (33). "No bed! no bed! we shouted" opens this poem of children enjoying their last minutes before being called in to go to bed. The green and golden woods cry to them to come, and they yodel "loud and shrill"; they laugh and quarrel. Even the creatures join in their revelry; the owl calls, and the evening birds sing wildly in this rollicking paean to childhood sound and fury.

Not only sound, but movement was also important to de la Mare. Poems like his "Away Go We" testify to the spontaneous movement of children:

> One, two, three,
> And away go we!
> Shingle, starfish,
> Sand, and sea!
> Wind on cheek,

clear sun on skin;
The tumbling waves
Sweep out, sweep in.

A magic, broken
Music calls
In the water
As it falls;
Voices, a sigh,
A long-drawn hush,
As back—in myriad
Bubbles—gush
The green-grey ripples,
Flecked with snow—
A music solemn
Sweet, and low.   (31)

The first stanza and the first four lines of the second plead to be chanted. The switch in line thirteen is abrupt and decisive; the sibilants in "voices" and "sigh" insist that the reader slow down, and the mood of the poem changes as we move from the sensation of touch (wind on cheek, sun on skin) to the sense of sounds that are magic, broken music.

De la Mare's nonsense poems are less magical, perhaps; but they have the same vitality of sound. Many readers are familiar with the frequently anthologized "Miss T" (272), who has the uncanny ability to transform everything that she eats into herself. They may be less familiar with the equally rich "Tillie" (214-15). Old Tillie Turveycombe yawned wide, swallowed a seed and disappeared. However, "when the mist do sigh,/Old Tillie Turveycombe's/Floating by."

The idea of an adult being transformed or of growing smaller while the child grows bigger is a recurring and often expressed thought of early childhood. So, while Tillie Turveycombe disappears altogether, "Old Mister Jones,/Once all but bones" grows younger in stages in "The Corner" (212-13). His long white beard changes to jet black, his trousers into short breeches, until at the end of this rollicking nonsense, he is an infant in a cradle, still growing "Younger, younger, younger."

"Full Circle" (285), a brief twelve lines, considers the same theme, that of the child growing big while the adult diminishes, but the tone is altered. The child narrator assures his mother that he will lovingly care for her when she has grown young and he old. He promises to sing her a lullaby to soothe her fears, and to supply milk and honey to soothe her hunger, so that the poem moves from a nonsensical theme to a song of praise for the way the child himself has been cared for.

"Sam's Three Wishes" (215-21) is a long story on the same theme of the adult growing younger, but unlike the two mentioned above, the theme is developed into a lengthy narrative that speaks seriously to the inevitability of growing old. In this narrative, Sam has grown old; his only company is a mouse. Late at night he hears the tapping of a fairy on his door. Fairies live round about his farm, and this one tells him, "A friend is a friend, Sam, and wonderful pleasant." Because he is such a good man (even his cow is exemplary; it "Never crops over the fairy-knowes"), Sam is allowed three wishes. He asks for a fat goose for the fire, and his mother to share it with him. He then asks for her to be healthy and young again and himself a youngster happy in her care, for "There's none can compare with the joy of one's youth." But because "time is a river for ever in flow,/The weeks went by as the weeks must go", and we see the futility of Sam's wishes; he has his youth and his mother for a while, but he must also go through the heartache of losing both again.

The mouse appears several times in this poem; at the beginning it is Sam's only companion, and when the goose is sputtering on the fire, the mouse and his family squeak in joy at the thought of a feast. By the end of the tale, the mouse is sitting on top of Sam's cheese, and he is talking with it when there is yet another knock at his door.

De la Mare often included mice in the telling of his tales; they appear in lullaby, narrative and nonsense as peripheral characters, and in some poems they become the main focus.

"Supper" (102) pictures for readers the very real fear that a tiny mouse has when she must venture from her doorway if her family is to be fed, yet fears the cat which she knows awaits and watches. Grimalkin has already dispatched the mouse's mate, as we assume from line two where she is clad "in widow's fur." The poor widow, "stark with fear" and with "pinched grey body," can see the crumbs in the last of evening's light while she must remain within the safety of the walls because Grimalkin is "like a tiger"— as indeed he must appear to a mouse.

The rhyme in this poem is regular on the even lines, and the poem itself is one long sentence in twelve lines. De la Mare keeps the poem from being sentimental by altering his point of view. The poem begins with a close-up view of the mouse at her small doorway; but the last two lines have moved the viewpoint so that we view the crumbs just beyond safety, and with the coming of dusk, we get yet a much larger view which encompasses all of night. Ms. Mouse's dilemma is not solved, and we leave her as frightened and as hungry as we found her.

"The Prince" (111-12) is quite another mouse; the cat does not frighten him at all. When Grimalkin is asleep, Peridarchus, the prince of mouses, "Steals up and gnaws away her claws,/And plucks out all her whiskers." He has a flair that will not be denied; he

Fandangoed in the attics and
From basement on to basement.

His eyes like bits of rubies shone;
His coat, as sleek as satin,
With teeth as sharp as needle-points
He kept to keep him fat in.

He'd gut a Cheshire cheese with ease,
Plum cake devoured in slices,
Lard, haggis, suet, sausages,
And everything that nice is.

We follow this dapper fellow's escapades, which include his dangling his tail into a bottle to get the oil therein, dancing on a pianoforte "to listen how it sounded," and stealing into the bedroom of the bailiff where he danced on his nose, nibbled the toes of the bailiff's wife, and kissed the squalling baby.

It will probably come as no surprise to the reader/listener that Peridarchus comes to an early demise. His end comes from taking on a bully, a rat three times his size, but he dies a hero, and it is typical of de la Mare that the death is not sentimentalized:

O Mouseland, mourn for him that's gone,
Our noble Peridarchus!
In valiant fight but yesternight,
And now, alas, a carcass.

Surely the rhyming of "Peridarchus" to "carcass" was carefully shaped by de la Mare, and it at once puts the story into perspective and adds humor that cannot be denied.

There is a large section of poems about animals in this collection, many of them about small animals seen in a fresh way. In "Chicken" (116), chickens come like "feathers blown in a great wind" in response to the clapping of Bess' platter calling them to eat. "Master Rabbit" (103) appeals to the sense of smell with "Thyme sweet to my nose" and turf that is "sweet to nostril," while it iterates a repeated theme of de la Mare's—we are intruders in the forest, and we are foes to the gentle rabbit.

De la Mare speaks often in his poetry about his aversion to hunting. In "Quack-Hunting" (115), he hunts through the darkening evening to find ducks so he can listen to them "Squeak and chuckle, sup and suck," throw crumbs to them and watch them feed. He says that not for him is "the dismal fowling-piece,/The *living* duck for me."

"Tit for Tat" (104-05) speaks directly to young readers about hunting, asking them if they have "gunned a poor bunny,/Or a blinded bird of the air," making them consider how it would be if some ogre were hunting them. De la Mare is explicit with his imagery of "your bent knees strung round his old iron gun/And your head dan-dangling by." This is strong stuff, certain to give any of us pause about hunting; but for the most part de la Mare is not so didactic. His "March Hares" speaks to his abhorrence of hunting, but the rhyme is almost music as it ends every line with "you know" in a decided singsong, until the young hunters sight a hare; then the music changes as de la Mare includes dashes between each word in order to slow down the reader. The change in rhythm alerts the reader that the meaning may change as well, and we are prepared for the hare escaping to live another day.

That change in rhythm is only one of the ways in which de la Mare alerts readers to pay close attention to his words. He may send us scurrying to the encyclopedia to discover what kind of a chicken a "Dorking" or a "Cochin China" is in "Chicken" (116). We may have to check our dictionaries to find out what the "haggis" is that Peridarchus eats in "The Prince" (111-12). We may also be curious about the Cheshire cheese consumed by Peridarchus in this same poem, and wonder if it is only coincidence that we are reminded of Lewis Carroll's Cheshire cat. This sort of word play is the mark of a careful poet, one who gives to the child audience only the very best, and de la Mare insisted that "only the rarest kind of best in anything is good enough for the young."

De la Mare was a distinguished poet. His sense of rhyme and rhythm, his precise use of words, and his imagery that calls into play all of our senses, allowed him to create priceless works for all of us.

But de la Mare's poetry is especially for the young. The poet Norma Farber once said that when we deny our children poetry, we deny them their second language—a language that comes to them as naturally, perhaps more naturally, than their first language. De la Mare's poems bear this out repeatedly—and never with more verve than with "Words," a poem that sums up the effect of much of his poetry:

How I love the rhymes that I can dance to, sing to—
Sing to, dance to, and echoing with birds!
Rhymes that, like bells, the mind may chime and ring to,
Elf-bells, steeple bells—sweet-tongued words.   (29)

REFERENCES

De la Mare, Walter. *Collected Rhymes and Verses.* London: Faber, 1970.

Dunning, Lueders, and Smith's *Reflections on a Gift of Watermelon Pickle:* A Watershed in Poetry for the Young

by Alethea K. Helbig

"It's the only time I've ever really liked reading poems," enthusiastically asserted a student as she walked into my classroom about fifteen years ago, the first semester I used Stephen Dunning, Edward Lueders and Hugh Smith's *Reflections on a Gift of Watermelon Pickle* as a text in my children's literature classes. "It's the first time I've been able to understand what poets are trying to say," she went on, "and really enjoyed what I was reading." As the class gathered, other students pitched in with their reactions to the book, and added their own reasons for finding it attractive and pleasurable.

Those students told me that they liked the book because it reflects late twentieth century concerns—their own concerns—because it uses the language, speech rhythms, and varied forms of our time, and because it comes in an attractive, modern format. They sang the praises of the collection with an obvious appreciation for the new insights it gave them, both into life and into a literary form about which they had reservations for themselves and for the young. This led us to a discussion of individual poems and their quality as poetry, an informal, sometimes heated, but always lively exchange that the students seemed to relish and which they noted was unique for them in their experience with this kind of literature.

At one point I pressed them. I asked, "Are you really serious about what you're saying? Is this enthusiasm for real? Hasn't there ever been any other book of poems that you've felt this way about?" After all, these were college students, most of them upperclassmen, almost all of them preparing to be teachers, and all of them presumably receptive to the written word and to literature in general.

Some replied that there were indeed some poets, like Frost, whose work they enjoyed and whom they found themselves compatible with; but they insisted, and some of them rather testily, that most of the poems that their elementary teachers had read to them, or asked them to read—and their high school and college teachers, too—were poems whose subject matter they simply did not care for. They asserted that in most instances the poems dealt with things they just were not much interested in and that these poems always seemed to be intended to teach them something, if only the elements of prosody. And the language was so different from their own—a language appropriate to an earlier era but foreign to their ears. Evidently, poetry had been for them a burdensome chore, something they read because it was assigned and they felt obligated to read it. But here was a book that appeared intended purely for pleasure and, what's more, gave it.

They were "hooked on the book"—what I had hoped would happen when I chose it as a text, since an adverse reaction to poetry was not unique to my experience with college students. So I decided to pose the crunch question.

"If you like this book so much—and you're college age—do you think children will, too? Can anybody here say whether or not children might like this book?" The irony hit them then. This book was intended for readers a good deal younger than they. They had been talking about its appeal for themselves. Could it serve both audiences? Could it appeal to children as well as college students?

"How about finding some children and trying the poems with them?" I suggested. They agreed, and we set a date for them to report on their findings.

The second scene of this story took place about two weeks later. All the students had found at least one child of elementary or junior high age, or one teenager, with whom to share the book. Some had read the poems with youths of different ages, and so brought a broader perspective to their research. The response was decidedly the same, general approval and enthusiasm, and for essentially the same reasons. Middle and later elementary graders, junior and senior high students, all enjoyed the poems—some more than others, of course, and of course some poems appealed more to the younger ones than to the older, and the other way around. But the consensus was that the children enjoyed them just as much as did my students. The children felt the poets talked to them about matters they themselves knew about and could respond to, and spoke in diction that used not only today's terminology but also today's rhythms. My students had discovered that *Reflections* had a double barreled appeal. They learned that such poetry could be enjoyed by children, by adults, by both together.

That experience and subsequent years have confirmed that Dunning, Lueders, and Smith, three college professors of English and English education, accomplished their purpose in compiling *Reflections*. They say in a note at the beginning of the hardcover edition that the three of them had been discussing together "how hard it was to find a collection of good poems for young readers—

readers who had had their fill of verse about galoshes, bunny rabbits, and 'what I want to be when I grow up.'" So they decided to make one themselves. They found twelve hundred poems they liked, discarded nine hundred of them, and from the remaining three hundred selected 114, half of which were chosen by children themselves, all with subjects and language that "came from the world they [the children] know through their own experience."

The book met with immediate approval from critics. Thomas Lask of the *New York Times Book Review* said that the poems have an "explosive and reverberating quality," and that there is "a solidity to the poetry that is bound to leave a mark on the reader's mind," while Paul Heins of *Horn Book* remarked that this is a "book for a browsing experience that could change a looker at pictures to a lover of poetry." The collection immediately became popular with its intended audience of later elementary and junior high students, too. Senior high students and adults enjoyed it also, and some libraries placed copies in adult and youth departments as well as in their juvenile divisions.

In other words, *Reflections* was a hit. It was issued in paperback by Scholastic and by Scott, Foresman, was put out in another hardcover edition by Lothrop, was used as a text in high school, middle school, and elementaries, and came out as a phonograph recording, also by Scholastic, that also remains popular today. Librarians attest that *Reflections* is still one of their most checked-out books of poems, and my students of today recall it fondly from their childhood. The Scott, Foresman edition alone has gone to fourteen printings and is still currently in print. As many as a million copies of the various editions have been sold. *Reflections* has quite a track record for an anthology in what has traditionally been the least popular of genres.

It is true, of course, that poetry generally enjoyed a renaissance in the sixties; but there had been other books of poetry published for the young that did not catch on as this one did, and others that caught on but did not remain read. The felicitous publication of soft cover and recording undoubtedly helped to popularize it. But it does seem that *Reflections* offered something the others did not, something that made it special.

That special quality lies in the excellence of the poems themselves. Many of them are by little known or unknown poets, but here and there appear ones by such familiar older poets as de la Mare, Pound, and Millay. Well-known modern writers like Swenson, Hillyer, and Justice are well represented, too. The subjects they talk about cover a broad range from the sensory joys of the changing seasons, as in the spring poems "in Just" by E. E. Cummings and "April" by Marcia Masters, to the marvels of animal behavior and appearance, as in "Catalogue" by Rosalie

Moore, whose mysterious, inscrutable cats "condense," "sing on a major scale," and "sleep fat and walk thin," while in "Unsatisfied Yearning" by Richard Kendall Munkittrick, a fickle, scatterheaded dog amusingly scampers to go out and once out straightway yowls to get back in.

There are poems about a seal, bats, the lion at the zoo, the giraffe, crows, and sparrows, even everyday sights like an apartment house, which Gerald Raftery likens to "a filing cabinet of human lives," hitchhikers, and a garden hose, seen sinuously by Beatrice Janosco as a "long green serpent" that

> ...lies in loops across the grass
> And drinks softly at the faucet.

Ordinary actions like shaving take on a new meaning in "Gone Forever" by Barriss Mills:

> Halfway through shaving, it came—
> the word for a poem...
> But now it's gone with the whiskers
> down the drain...,

like the girls the speaker knew but never kissed. Freda Quenneville's "Mother's Biscuits" presents a remembered picture, rich with imagery of smell, taste, and touch as well as sight, that vividly describes the baked goods for which mother became famous in her time and town:

> Cooked high, crusty, with succulent middles
> That took attention
> At company dinners...

and "were finest/Soaked with pot liquor or gravy."

Some poems are about hunting, some about fishing, organized sports, unusual people, swift things, loneliness, dreams, even poetry itself—the book presents a generous offering of different subjects. Some poems deal with war, arguments, and resentments, matters which were not generally at that time considered suitable matters in poetry for so young an audience. Some look at startling contemporary phenomena, like sonic booms, fireworks, and space shots. Taken together, all support the book's theme that poetry can be about anything, anything at all in the world about one, as well as about things one carries in one's heart or wonders about in one's head.

Among the poems that tell stories is "Fifteen" by William Stafford, in which "I" ("I was fifteen") describes finding an overturned motorcycle on the road and its bloodied rider lying in the ditch, helps the owner back to his machine, and stands bewildered and silent while the fellow in brazen patronage terms him "good man" and roars off down the road. "Rebecca" by Hilaire Belloc tells of a child "Who slammed Doors for Fun and Perished Miserably" in order to spoof the old time didactic verse once thought the only proper reading fare for children, while Maxine Kumin's "The Microscope" offers a lighthearted explanation for the invention of that instrument.

Most poems describe or reflect upon memorable moments. "Foul Shot" by Edwin A. Hoey graphically recreates the last two seconds' game winning throw, and in a cleverly arranged series of gradually lengthening verbs filled with dentals and sibilants succeeds in approximating the almost unbearable tension that accompanies it:

> The ball
> Slides up and out,
> Lands,
> Leans,
> Wobbles,
> Wavers,
> Hesitates,
> Exasperates,
> Plays it coy...

until the poem explodes in a climax of sound and emotion as "Right before ROAR-UP" the ball "Dives down and through" the basket and the game is won.

Moods vary. "Foul Shot" pulsates with excitement; "Rebecca" raucously pokes fun; "Fifteen" quietly ponders. Wry comment occurs, mild protest on the times and on the ways and attitudes of human beings. Sy Kahn's "Boy with Frogs" jabs at youth's propensity to collect even living things, such as small frogs that

> ...hop
> And pulse in their
> Suddenly glass world...

while the boy plays "a game for a God." "The Forecast" by Don Jaffe comments on the plasticity of modern life, how people seem to take pains to avoid the real experience and choose to get even the weather secondhand from the TV screen. Train passengers in Donald Hall's "Transcontinent" know they've arrived at a city when they see "cars and shacks," and notice that

> dumps grow the oil-can shacks from
> Portland, Maine
> to Seattle....

Irony forms the core of many poems: people cheer the space shots but ignore the marvel of seeds bursting into life; a hunter allows a rabbit to lie snug by his door on a cold night; husbands and wives sit in stony, isolated silence on the subway, "with children between them," so near, yet so far in spirit from one another they cannot even converse. This and some other poems present adults in a light unusual for children's literature prior to the sixties, as people with problems, foibles, and glaring imperfections.

Some poems haunt, like Sandburg's "Lost," Roethke's "The Bat," and Monro's "Overheard on a Saltmarsh," some tease, like Ciardi's "Why Nobody Pets the Lion at the Zoo," and some tickle, like McGinley's "Reflections Dental":

> How pure, how beautiful, how fine
> Do teeth on television shine!...
> With miles of smiles the airwaves teem,
> And each an orthodontist's dream.

Some poems parody well-known rhymes for topical protest that is, unfortunately, only superficially humorous:

> Hey diddle diddle
> The physicists fiddle...(Paul Dehn).

And Little Miss Muffet collects her shell-shocked wits in another poem by the same writer. Sara Henderson Hay's "The Builders" has the third pig tell the story of "The Three Little Pigs" and by his words condemn himself as an insufferable, self-righteous prig—symbolic, incidentally, of those human beings who always know best.

Effective metaphor abounds, occasionally in brief similitudes. William Jay Smith likens the toaster to "A silver-scaled Dragon with jaws flaming red" in a poem of the same name, and Charles Malam says steam shovels remind him that

> ...dinosaurs are not all dead.
> I saw one raise its iron head...
> Its jaws were dripping with a load
> Of earth and grass that it had cropped.

Some poems are intensely serious, others tender or poignant, some nonsensical. Many employ wordplay, like Philip Booth's "Crossing," which recreates the sound and sense of a train speeding down the track by numbering and naming the cars as they pass by:

> eight-nine-ten
> Erie and Wabash,

Seaboard, U.P.,
Pennsy tankcar,...

Eve Merriam's "Oz." is a lighthearted, witty poem that talks about two kinds of ounces simultaneously, one the unit of weight, the other

This jungle ounce [that]
will jounce
you out of complacency...
P.S. Better not take a chounce.

A few poems are fantasy, but most are realistic, solidly concrete writings that talk about the changed life of the Indians, about nuclear holocaust, about the futility of suicide, about gray November, about canoes slipping silently toward beckoning shores, about baseball, all things that are on children's minds, expressed in language with which they can connect, language that pulls and draws but does not intimidate.

Forms vary, too, from couplets to tidy three liners to quatrains and combinations thereof, but most of the poems are free and flow across the page according to the poets' peculiar inclinations and purposes. A few have regular rhythm and end rhyme, like Lew Sarett's tender "Four Little Foxes":

Speak gently, Spring, and make no sudden sound;
For in my windy valley, yesterday I found
New-born foxes squirming on the ground—
    Speak gently.

But most employ more subtle rhythms and internal chimes and echoes, like "The Base Stealer" by Robert Francis, which skillfully combines vowels and consonants to create tension and anticipation both in base runner and spectators:

Poised between going on and back, pulled
Both ways taut like a tightrope-walker,
Fingertips pointing the opposites,
Now bouncing tiptoe like a cropped ball....

Many poems sound prosy and lack melody, not unusual in modern poetry. Sandburg's "Arithmetic" is a good example. But Sarett's fox poem and "Swift Things Are Beautiful" by Elizabeth Coatsworth stand out for their musical quality:

Swift things are beautiful:
Swallows and deer,
And lightning that falls
Bright-veined and clear,...

Language is predominantly contemporary, straightforward, and casually conversational, employing the diction and idioms of our time:

Today they cut down the oak.
Strong men climbed with ropes
in the brittle tree.
("The Stump," Donald Hall)
With two 60's stuck on the scoreboard
And two seconds hanging on the clock,....
("Foul Shot," Edwin A. Hoey)
Gangway for violets,
Old snow in the corner.
("The Child's Morning," Winfield Townley Scott)
A tourist came in from Orbitville,
parked in the air, and said:...
the hard bodies—are they
their guts or in their brains?
("Southbound on the Freeway," May Swenson)
"Hush, babe. Some pilot we equip,
Giving the speed of sound the slip,
Has cracked the air like a penny whip."
("Sonic Boom," John Updike)

Contemporary subject matter, language, and tone produce a strongly realistic effect, an overall air of tangibility and concreteness, yes, even toughness, quite different from preceding collections for this age group. Earlier anthologies tended to project an aura of politeness, of "suitability," and seemed inclined to teach and protect while providing antiseptic amusement. Dunning, Lueders, and Smith treat their readers as intelligent, knowledgeable peers who are capable of handling the profundities as well as the trivia of life.

The poems are not all of high quality. Nonsensical poems, very short poems, and in particular, poems of topical comment tend not to hold up under repeated readings. Yet these weaker poems do not weaken the book. What keeps it from seeming uneven is, first, the editors' talent for choosing poems that though topical would retain their immediacy, and, second, their skill at arranging them for maximum appeal and impact. Poems which give the same or even opposing views of the same subject are often paired, like those by Herschberger and Roethke on bats, and sometimes even tripled or quadrupled. Raffel's poem about watching the construction of a skyscraper leads to Raftery's on the apartment house, which is followed by Hay's "The Builders." Neither of these three poems has much enduring substance in itself, but taken together they offer exciting potential for extending the imagination and the intellect.

The same is true about many other poems, which considered singly seem weak and ineffectual but which, enjoyed in their groups, expand the reader's and listener's horizons. Lechlitner's "Kansas Boy," who "walks through the young corn rippling at his knee," a quite pensive piece, is followed by "Wonder Wander" by Lenore Kandel, a briskly active poem, jerky with movement, that gives the effect of children walking about busy city streets feasting their eyes on city sights and filling their ears with its sounds. The contrast points up the poems and makes each more vivid and memorable.

The poems are further enhanced by imaginatively designed pages, on which sharp, definitive, tastefully selected black and white photographs perfectly catch and extend the meaning and mood of the poems. Even the publisher's choice of typography was felicitous. Crisp, modern print captures the atmosphere and seems as appropriate today as it did when the book first came out.

Reflections on a Gift of Watermelon Pickle represents a watershed in poetry for the young. It paved the way for other collections of its kind. Though not the very first of its type—for example, Hannum and Reed's *Lean Out of the Window* (Atheneum, 1965) preceded it—*Reflections* caught on. Its popularity made possible books like Larrick's *Room for You and Me and a Mountain Lion* (Evans, 1974), *Straight on Till Morning* (Crowell, 1977) by Hill, Perkins, and Helbig, and those by Peck, McCullough, and Hannum and Chase, among others that came later.

While today's critical standards call for a tighter theme and more cohesive arrangement, *Reflections* works well as it is and succeeds in making its point. Uneven though they may be in quality, all of its poems are accessible to the young. Through *Reflections,* children can see that poetry is to be enjoyed, that it can be about familiar as well as unfamiliar things, that the poet's eyes and ears can be extensions of their own, and that poems do not have to be long or complicated or filled with layers of suggestion and couched in old-time language. It was the first collection of modern poems that appealed over a wide age range. It showed young people that they and their elders can find pleasure in the same poems. It was—and still is—a book that adults and youth can enjoy together, and do.

Dunning, Lueders, and Smith published another book of modern poems, *Some Haystacks Don't Even Have Any Needle* (Lothrop, 1969), for an older audience and also popular. But it was with the perennial favorite, their watershed anthology, *Reflections on a Gift of Watermelon Pickle* that they earned themselves a permanent place in literature for the young.

REFERENCES

Dunning, Stephen, Edward Lueders and **Hugh Smith.** *Reflections on a Gift of Watermelon Pickle.* Scott, Foresman, 1966.

The Tales of the Brothers Grimm: In the Black Forest

by Joyce Thomas

As the great-grandparent of children's literature, fairy tales occupy a privileged place as touchstones for that literature. Basic as the peasant's crusty black bread, they nourish us upon essential sustenance—the fare of elemental story. Especially do the *volksmarchen* or folk fairy tales—those stories that were once part of an oral tradition of storytelling—lay the foundation for many, if not most, classics of children's literature. The works of such beneficiaries as Charles Kingsley, Lewis Carroll, George MacDonald, L. Frank Baum, Kenneth Grahame, C. S. Lewis, J. R. R. Tolkien and Ursula Le Guin, among others, would be unrecognizably altered—if not rendered non-existent—without that essential cornerstone of "faerie."

Ironically, this elder genre is frequently regarded as something children grow out of—if, indeed, they are accorded the direct experience of the tales in the first place. Fairy tales too often are diminished, if not openly denigrated, by our society, which tends to view them as "mere" fare for young children. The very term "fairy tale," like its cousin "myth," is employed as a synonym for what is devalued—for fantastic lies, absurd exaggerations, all manner of escapes from the "real world." Probably more than any other type of children's literature, fairy tales have suffered from the tamperings of well-intentioned adults. They have been rewritten and censored, withheld from children or temperately spoon-fed to them as cautionary tales. These adults only find faerie palatable if it offers an obvious, cookie-cutter moral or "nice," "safe," innocuous fantasy. They would vouchsafe "Little Red-Cap" to children since its moral appears to be that a child should heed her mother and not tarry on the way to grandmother's house. They would rewrite "Hansel and Gretel" so as to make its action less horrific. They would discard "The Almond Tree" and "The Robber Bridegroom," fearing their gruesome matter would fuel a child's worst nightmares.

Perhaps as the logical extension of such tampering, no other genre of children's literature has been subjected to so many different interpretive approaches. Beginning with the nineteenth century mythologists, fairy tales have been alternately viewed as masquerading nature and solar myths; as folkloristic fossils upon which are etched early man's rites, customs and superstitions; as psychodramas wherein are played out the traumas of birth and sexual discovery, oedipal struggles, sibling rivalry, conflicts between the pleasure and reality principles, conflicts among the id, ego, and super-ego; as archetypal creations depicting the process of individuation and assimilation of one's shadow, anima or animus; as cosmogonic scenarios wherein the hero traverses the cyclic round of trials and tests, helpers and foes, to descend into the underworld and emerge with a boon for all mankind; as socio-historical documents recording the survival concerns and wish-fulfillments of a beleaguered lower class; as poetic metaphors in which are clothed life's profoundest truths. All such intellectual, theoretical translations—always interesting, frequently illuminating—can, however, never replace the tales' own, most eloquent voice. That the humble *volksmarchen* should spark so many and such divergent responses suggests something of their eternal mystery and appeal. Despite all tamperings and interpretations, the tales survive, reminding us, as Marie von Franz says, that "the interpretation of the dream is always less good than the dream itself" (26), always less than the tale from which it trails. In the midst of our cacophonous babble, the tales speak on, as they have for countless centuries, in their own simple yet symbolic tongue.

Precisely what fairy tales mean is far less significant than the obvious fact that the tales *are*. Fairy tales have survived as an art form in their own right because their value transcends whatever meaning with which we tag them. There are the lost children, the confectionary hut in the woods, the cackling witch, the twilight landscape of the Black Forest: play with them as we will, analyze them as we choose, there is always something else, some other thing, coyly peeping behind the folds of that bent crone's black skirts, tantalizingly lurking just beyond the far conifer at the edge of our scrutinizing vision. No wealth of words can ever squarely fix that shadowly presence nor properly articulate exactly what pulses at the magical heart of the fairy tale.

Yet fairy tales are an art, and can be examined as such on the basis of the experience they give us, both children and adults. As Isabelle Jan notes in writing of children's literature, the person who first reads of Babar the elephant experiences something just as singular and absorbing as does the person who reads *The Brothers Karamazov* for the first time (143); in terms of the experience literature or any art offers, a reader's age seems scarcely significant. And, of course, the *volksmarchen* were originally intended for an adult audience. Though their audience has grown younger over succeeding centuries, the tales continue to speak in a non-discriminating manner to an audience basically undefined on the basis of age or sex or race. Certainly the aspects of "faerie" which J. R. R. Tolkien describes (46)—Fantasy, Recovery, Escape, and Consolation—indicate part of the tales' age-less and time-less appeal. If anything, the latter three aspects seem especially suited to adults: to anyone seeking to recover the potency and wonder of simple, basic things; to escape from life's imposed restrictions and from one's own mortality (what Tolkien calls "the oldest and deepest desire, the Great Escape: the Escape from Death" [67]); to find consolation in communion with other species, in happy endings, in a truly democratic justice. Paradoxically, the tales offer a simultaneous experience of both escape and initiation; perhaps the former speaks strongest to adults while the latter speaks best to the children, though that is a relatively moot distinction. What does concern us is the nature and value of the tales.

First and foremost, fairy tales provide an experience of pure story. Especially is this true of folk collections like those compiled by the Brothers Grimm. Despite literary alterations on the part of Jacob and Wilhelm—their stylistic embellishments, simplifications, fusions of tales and their variants, all done in keeping with their era of romanticism and *Biedermeier* culture, yet as Luthi suggests (28), always with an eye toward what they felt was best in the tales—these tales exist as narrative in an elemental and elementary form. The distinction between Grimms' best and usually most popular tales and more decoratively literary ones is readily apparent if one compares their "Little Briar-Rose" to Charles Perrault's "The Sleeping Beauty," the latter an embroidered tapestry, weighed down by the narrator's intrusive voice, appliqued moralisms, and a second, quite obviously tacked-on story. It is no accident that Grimms' tales comprise the most popular collection in our culture, nor that certain of their tales—"Little Briar-Rose," "Hansel and Gretel," "The Frog Prince," "Snow-White," "Rumpelstiltskin," "Rapunzel," among others—exemplify *the* fairy tale in the minds of most people. Yet other collections contain the same plots, same bits and pieces of physical matter, same stock of familiar characters, same resonating archetypes. Perhaps the Grimms' tales are so often equated with all fairy tales because they succeed best in communicating those plots, characters and archetypes via their initiation into what is an abbreviated yet complete experience of story, of literature. Flowing through time, honed to essentials, the best of these tales smoothly move from beginning to middle to end, presenting in clearly recognizable forms the basic literary elements of plot, character, setting, style, point of view, theme and symbolism. Having experienced a mere handful of these tales, the reader or listener has in essence experienced all story—has witnessed the bare bones of narrative which writers from Charles Perrault to Charles Dickens, from Mary Shelley to Ursula Le Guin, from William Shakespeare to Franz Kafka, flesh out and garb in their respective colored cloths.

All of literature waits within the simple fairy tale. Recall Grimms' "Little Briar-Rose" as it opens upon the simple declarative statement, "A long time ago there was a King and Queen who said every day: 'Ah, if only we had a child!' but they never had one." The setting is timeless, placeless, yet regal, the characters mere nouns yet real human beings; even Briar-Rose is there, conspicuous by her absence, by the importance accorded her in the parents' voiced wish. In fact, the situation, that of recognizable, unrealized desires, is ordinary enough. Only with the second sentence does the extraordinary, the faerie, enter the story, in the form of a prophesying frog: "But it happened that once when the Queen was bathing, a frog crept out of the water on to the land, and said to her: 'Your wish shall be fulfilled; before a year has gone by, you shall have a daughter.'" A rather complete drama has already unfolded in just these two understated lines: a human couple desires a child but has none; a magical amphibian foretells the birth of their daughter. Out of this brief drama, all the tale's ensuing action evolves. What has been set in motion is the dynamic tension of desire and its fulfillment, of prophecy and its realization, of the magical enacted upon and within the human sphere. Likewise, the tale's thematic strains of life and its absence are first sounded, to reverberate until the final chord's happy ending.

What a marvelous, logical chain of causality is drawn out, link by soldered link, before our eyes. Briar-Rose is born, and the King celebrates his desire's actualization with a birth-feast; there we hear the thirteenth Wise Woman pronounce her death curse, hear the twelfth Wise Woman mediate it to a hundred years' sleep, witness the King's vain, fiery purge of all the spindles in his land, watch as Briar-Rose grows to one day ascend the tower's winding stair and greet her fate poised at the tip of the unfamiliar spindle...tick off those hundred lotus years, to witness the prophecy's completion and maiden's awakening. In terms of plot, the prince's arrival is but an ancillary action: he simply happens to be in the right place at the right time, unlike his less fortunate, bramble-impaled predecessors. He holds no place in the prophecies of any of the supernatural characters; like the King who cannot prevent his daughter's fate, the prince cannot break its bonds, and he neither rescues nor disenchants Briar-Rose. It is all a matter of timing. His coincidental arrival does, however, provide for the happy ending's union of prince and princess, man and woman, and thus brings the tale full circle, and makes it a completed narrative.

Protagonist and antagonist, a dramatic plot of crisis and climax, a denouement tying-off the story with a tight love-knot: all the basic narrative elements are there. Told in the third-person narrative voice, lacking detailed characterization, a complex plot and any superfluous stylistic embroidery, the tale communicates the very essence of story. As to symbolism and theme, they, too, are communicated simply, via the picture-language of precisely drawn images. Through such imagery one apprehends a wealth of relations as richly woven as a medieval tapestry: there are the prophesying frog and Wise Women, all clear incarnations of Fate; there is the alien spindle upon which Briar-Rose pricks her finger to fall into a deathlike sleep, and there are the bramble-thorns upon which a host of premature suitors fall into the eternal sleep of death; there are the blooming briar-roses which herald their namesake's awakening and return to life; there is as well that other, less easily articulated relationship between prophecy and act, the voice and the world it defines, so crucial to the taleteller's own creation. And there is the richly detailed, thrice-repeated description of the sleep itself, in which all elements—Briar-Rose, King and Queen, the entire court, horses in the stable, dogs in the yard, pigeons on the roof, flies on the wall, flaming hearth fire and roasting meat, the very wind and even leaves on the trees—are wrapped within the princess's soporific cloak. This lengthy description is given first as Briar-Rose falls into sleep, again while she is sleeping, again as she awakens. Admittedly, it is a type of stylistic embroidery, but one perfectly suited to the tale. The richly detailed texture and repetition serve to reinforce the sleep and its mesmerizing spell, while also underscoring one's sense of the interconnectedness of all things—the individual and the world, the microcosm and the macrocosm. Further, it functions as a melodic litany offering reassurance and solace in the face of that malevolent Wise Woman and the fact of one hundred somnolent years.

According to Jane Yolen, "The gift of words is magic" (89). It is this gift that fairy tales proffer both child and adult. The tales constitute a primary experience of literature and thus set the stage for all later experiences. Not only do we participate in story; we also necessarily participate in that story's language. As with nursery verse, a child acquires a sense of how language functions, of how it defines and shapes the world, through the tale's varied voices of the third-person narrator, dialogue and monologue, verse and rhyme. Different happenings demand different voices, reality turns upon verbalization (as heard in each crucial prophecy's direct quotation in "Little Briar-Rose")—two valuable truths the tale bestows as part of its word-gift. The fairy tale's simple opening suggests infinite possibilities, infinite dramas sprung from that one fertile seed: "Hard by a forest dwelt a poor woodcutter with his wife and his two children" ("Hansel and Gretel") "There was once upon a time an old king who was ill, and thought to himself: 'I am lying on what must be my death-bed'" ("Faithful John"); "Once upon a time in the middle of winter, when the flakes of snow were falling like feathers from the sky, a Queen sat at a window sewing, and the frame of the window was made of black ebony" ("Little Snow White"); "There was once a man whose wife died, and a woman whose husband died..." ("The Three Little Men in the Wood"). One need merely begin, "Once upon a time there was a person," to read oneself into the oldest story, the one we title "Life."

From the incantatory "once upon a time" to that solacing amen of "happy-ever-after," the tales unwind, weaving a verbal spell by which one is, as Yolen says, "caught up in the centrifugal force of the spinning story" (42). Anything is possible, given the word and its mastery, as Rumpelstiltskin regrettably learned. While this is a truth any literature might impart, it is one particularly transmitted by the *volksmarchen* collected by the Brothers Grimm because of those tales' honed narratives. Few unnecessary elements intrude between the word and the world it creates, between that word, that world, and the audience. Since fairy tales often constitute the first or one of the first experiences children have of literature as a sustained and complete narrative, the value of that experience cannot be over-estimated.

As a prototypical experience, the tales gracefully lend themselves to another crucial experience, that of the shared experience of story. They were, after all, oral narratives originally, and the varied voices in which any one tale speaks almost demand to be spoken aloud again. As Yolen has written, "the tale apprehended by the ear is different from the one taken in by the eye," for eye and ear "are different listeners" (42). We need both faculties to fully experience the tales. In hearing a story, one returns to that charmed inner circle delimited by the sound of the taleteller's voice. A special sphere is created in the intimate relationship between story-teller and audience, whether the audience consists of one child, one adult, or many. The spoken tale is different from the tale read silently, in part because in hearing it one is vouchsafed the auditory experience of his own language, of its full potency and melodious musicality. Just as nursery rhymes for younger children provide them with an experience in their language whereby they develop a sense of that language's functions—how it structures the universe and imitates the rhythms of life—so do the tales' spoken words provide us with a message in themselves. Furthermore, the shared, spoken tale extends the sphere of relationship open to the child. Whereas silent reading comprises a smaller relationship of reader and tale, recounting a story aloud automatically brings a third party into that relationship. One participates in a humanly shared experience, shared between the taleteller and individual child and also shared among children if the audience is multiplied. If no one bothers to share stories in this manner, the message conveyed is that the tales—or any literature, for that matter—simply are not worth the effort; omission, neglect, indifference, silence, are themselves evaluations which are not lost on children who likewise suffer in their own measure of self-esteem. Again, as honed, brief, originally oral narratives, fairy tales lend themselves especially well to such sharing.

As Nietzsche said of myth, the tales represent a mode of thought which presents an idea of the universe through the sequence of events, actions, and sufferings (Zimmer 310). Those who have fundamental story, have experienced the *volksmarchen*, are better able to integrate life itself as story—to read themselves into that oldest tale. Depth psychologist James Hillman has noted that such a "reading into" is crucial if one is to perceive life as a coherent and meaningful experience rather than chaos of isolated characters and inexplicable occurrences. Through basic story we acquire the experience of "imaginative meaning," which can then be applied to our own life as a means of understanding and integrating it. Story-awareness provides us with the awareness to come to terms with our own case history and encourages the synthesis of material that is ugly, cruel, obscene, socially or personally unacceptable. According to Hillman, both myths and fairy tales present such material in a safe, accepting, even joyful package. They tell us there is a place for things we might otherwise deny or repress—that child-eating witch, that robber bridegroom—and thus encourage us to accept even the worst aspects of our lives and selves: "the more attuned and experienced is the imaginative side of personality the less threatening the irrational, the less necessity for repression, and therefore the less actual pathology acted out in literal, daily events (9).

Hillman terms literalism "sickness" because it denies the imagination, the metaphorical, the fantastic, all of which are not only aspects of our minds and world, but together represent the more dominant forces in them. We are, each one of us, continually reading ourselves into now one story, now another.

The psychological activities of identification and empathy comprise a large, healthy measure of what makes us human; lacking such "readings," we would be cut off from our own human kind and culture and history. Chaos rather than cosmos, that sense of an ordered and meaningful universe, would result. Disconnected from the world without and within, we might all the more readily destroy ourselves, destroy the very planet to which we cannot relate. That marvelous causal chain in "Little Briar-Rose" fairly sings of the interconnectedness of all things. Snap its links, experience the isolated curse of the thirteenth Wise Woman or Briar-Rose's inexplicable coma, the seemingly senseless deaths of all those early suitors—and cosmos shatters; the mirror of story and what it reflects becomes no more than scattered shards. All reassurance dissolves, and we lose the tale's consoling insight into how "the human creature was blessed with all birthday gifts, yet cursed with death; and how death also may be softened to a sleep" (Chesterton 177).

To deny fairy tales to children, or to allow only those with "acceptable" morals and innocuous fantasy, is to retard their psychological and imaginative growth and expression. Fairy tales stand independently of the adults who select books for children as if selecting the right food for them to consume. Indeed, the tales may constitute the fullest, most nutritionally complete diet, unlike the "junk books" (equivalent to fast-food fries) that Paula Fox cites: such books, devoid of fantastic play and imaginings, "dull the hunger of a child's mind, stuff it with unearned certainties, those straws, Henry James wrote, that 'we chew to cheat our appetites'" (30). Characteristic of such literature is its tendency to "promote and vindicate adult predispositions toward children and childhood"; further, it absolves us of responsibility, "the effort of self-knowledge without which we cannot really think about and understand children, who are not a race apart but ourselves when new."

We should not forget that fairy tales are moral literature, in the fullest sense of the word. Though few posit precise morals, virtually all the tales convey a fundamental esthetic which may be gleaned within their predominant theme, the seeming disparity between appearances and reality. This theme, manifested in almost every classic tale, aptly represents the core of a genre that treats the fantastic and the real as existing on the same plane of human experience. Typically the tales portray the least likely thing, creature or human as the most likely to confer rewards or punishments, to conceal a prince, to be the hero. Apparently ordinary, mundane physical things are revealed to be extraordinary and magical upon a closer look. In Grimms' "The Table, the Ass and the Stick," for instance, the three possessions are markedly mundane—and markedly marvelous. The little table is "nothing much to look at, and made of common wood; but it had one great quality": upon command, it spreads itself with a sumptuous repast. Similarly, the dumb beast of burden can spit gold nuggets and the stick, surely one of the unlikeliest things to contain the faerie, can beat anything or anyone upon command.

Animals and all manner of magical beings also are portrayed as least likely creatures. From the helpful ants, ducks and bees in "The Queen Bee" to the little old grey man in "The Golden Goose," the lowly, all-too familiar creature is found to be the magical aide, provider and advisor. Almost always, it is the most ordinary and unexceptional animal that proves to be just as extremely exceptional—so exceptional, that the hero usually would not survive or succeed without it. Tales of helpful animals tend to portray the hero as one who acts out of a perceptive, usually compassionate response to nature. Coincidentally, the hero often is depicted in contrast to other humans who either do not see the natural world they have become habituated to, or view it in a selfish, destructive manner. Kindness is repaid in kind, as is unkindness. That obvious moral, however, is far less important than what has preceded it: the hero's seeing and responding to nature as valuable in itself. Frequently this is the true test of the hero, and whatever other tasks face him are accomplished by the creatures he treated well. A mutual relationship and reciprocal exchange is established between man and animal which extends to embrace all of nature; nature metamorphoses to the supernatural, and, again, the world proves ecologically wonder-full.

At times, the least likely is decidedly noticeable, though in a negative manner, as seen in countless tales of animal-grooms and brides. As in "The Frog Prince," insight into the creature's true self is gleaned after an initial period of repulsion or fear that limits one's vision to the animal's outer, physical shell. Thematically, the groom's enchantment is more the result of others' negative perceptions than it is of any supernatural spell; usually the spell ceases the moment the heroine sees truly. Conversely, tales treating a physically human groom who possesses a bestial nature depict a process whereby initially positive or accepting responses to him are replaced with genuine loathing and horror once his true self is discovered. Interestingly, no disenchantment is possible, for the human is always human and the sole solution to his inner, vile nature is that of his death. In the nightmare world of "The Robber Bridegroom," accurate perception assumes a life or death significance.

Surely the most common portrayal of the disparity between appearances and reality is found in the fairy tale's own heroes and heroines. Wherever there is a youngest son or daughter, an abused, neglected, poverty-stricken Simpleton or Cinderella, little tailors and Tom Thumbs and abandoned children, the least likely figure emerges as the most likely to be the hero. It is the Cinderella human, female or male, who stands as the typical fairy tale hero, who stands as the fleshy incarnation of the tales' recurrent theme—in John Buchan's words, "survival of the unfittest" (8-9). As Max Luthi has noted, Cinderella represents the perfect "riddle princess" (132); that riddling aspect may be extended to include almost all fairy tale protagonists, who pose a riddle in the apparent disparity between what they appear to be and what they are in actuality. "Apparent" is the clue, for accurate perception reveals that Cinderella is both raggedy *and* regal, just as the groom is both animal *and* human, the crone ordinary *and* extraordinary, the creature natural *and* supernatural, the stick mundane *and* magical. One state or characteristic need not contradict the other, for it is the combination of the two which makes the entity what it is. Cinderella would not be the heroine were she solely an ash-covered maiden or solely a glass-shoed princess. The marvel of the food-spreading table would be meaningless were the table not both common and capable of its meal-time conjurings. We tend to perceive the ash-maiden who attends the ball in glass or golden shoes as being the regal girl who is belied by her ashy state. But over and over again, the tales point to a far more complex and realistic perspective: the ash-maiden and regal girl are one and the same, appearance is reality, and one must learn to see truly.

All manner of messages, essential and profound, reveal themselves in the fairy tale's simple silhouettes of physical objects, animals, humans and super-natural beings. Legions of wicked stepmothers demonstrate in their antagonism and hatred toward the child how the past continues to live on in the present and how tenuous is the relationship between parent and child. The dangers of self-worship and of failing to see one's self in another resound through "Little Snow-White," while many a "fee fie foe fum"-chanting giant demonstrates the dangers of uncurbed appetite and how anyone of us might topple under the weight of our own gravity. All those least likely heroes and heroines enact a scenario whereby success is attained within before it is attained without, in the world of men and daylight deeds. Accurate perception, compassion, and proper use of intellect comprise the touchstones of most heroism in tales that span the distance between "a day dream which stays in control, a nightmare which plunges into horror" (Fiedler xv). In the manner of a primer, fairy tales speak to us in simple terms and stark images whose language, says Bruno Bettelheim, is the only one "which permits understanding before intellectual maturity has been achieved" (161). Rose and thorn, life and death, ash and gold, frog and prince, sight and insight, blood and bone, Red Cap and the wolf, the lost children and the waiting witch—fairy tales expertly choreograph life's polar possibilities.

This fine balancing act is itself one with human existence. We should never forget that fairy tales are but another times' reflection of basic human concerns—that, as Joseph Campbell writes in *Hero with a Thousand Faces*, "The latest incarnation of Oedipus, the continued romance of Beauty and the Beast, stand this afternoon on the corner of Forty-second Street and Fifth Avenue, waiting for the traffic light to change" (4). We should always remember that the "lie" of art, of fiction and the faerie, exists as a deliberate distortion by which one can experience the truth; that

> The debutante combing her hair before the glass, the mother pondering the future of a son, the laborer in the mines...the ambassador with portfolio, the soldier in the field of war—all are working in order that the ungainsayable specifications of effective fantasy, the permanent patterns of the tale of wonder, shall be clothed in flesh and known as life. (Campbell, "Folkloristic Commentary" 863)

How truly realistic the tales are, translating for us the best and basest of human emotions and strivings: Love, Trust, Compassion, Honor, Friendship, Fidelity, Courage, Fear, Greed, Lust, Betrayal, Hatred—they are all there.

One could go on and on, reciting the multifarious messages the tales communicate, each one of which is yet another part of their value for us. As a mode of entertainment, says Campbell in his "Folkloristic Commentary," they exist "not simply to fill the vacant hour, but to fill it with symbolic fare" (862). Their messages are multiple, imaginatively playful yet seriously speculative. Deceptively simple, the *volksmarchen* have often been dismissed on the basis of their appearance, as was Cinderella, the frog prince, the wooden table, and virtually every bit of common matter, comman man, within the tales. We know the danger in that dismissal, know that the playful and serious, fantasy and reality, natural and supernatural, can exist side by side, exist even as one entity. It is true the tales can shift in a protean manner between blessing and curse, daydream and nightmare, but they nonetheless offer an ongoing reassurance long before their (almost always) happy ending is attained. It is true the human characters, like their real-life counterparts, often appear to be at the mercy of strange and stronger forces upon which their fate rests, just as they frequently experience a state of disequilibrium and disruption not unlike that experienced in today's own protean world. What is absent in our contemporary response is the second part of the story: not necessarily the state of being "happy until their days' end," but the realization that disequilibrium, disruption, are with us always, and may even represent a disguised boon. Fairy tales accept the very disturbances they create, and do so in a joyful manner. Their heroes, too, demonstrate a sensitive awareness and acceptance of the extraordinary; indeed, no hero's fate would be heroic were he to balk at the supernatural forces he experiences. This is not a passive acquiescence in matters beyond one's control; rather, it is an almost appreciative recognition of things as they are, which is then acted upon. The hero is he or she who takes "the road less travelled by."

How reassuring it is to see that the disturbing supernatural is but the super-natural; that it has been a part of one's world all along and is simply manifested when the ordinary is experienced as extra-ordinary. The Coleridgean conceit that all existence is comprised of the wondrously strange murmurs in the tales: if we had but the eyes to see, we would perceive the latent form of the unfamiliar asleep within the familiar, the magical housed within the shell of the mundane. This realization of the fantastic as the realistic represents yet another esthetic of fairy tales; it is one of the most precious gifts they offer us. Again, it speaks to the interconnectedness of all things, and thus again affirms the patterned web of life and all spun story. This casual affirmation paradoxically presents the real as yielding the fantastic while simultaneously the fantastic is shown to be essentially non-fantastic and real. In contrast to the unreassuring fantasy of Lewis Carroll's *Alice* books, fairy tales impart an idea of existence which views all matter as both mundane and magical. Their casual portrayal is in itself a comfort: this is the world, the tales say, and it is truly marvelous, mysterious, wonder-full. The tales matter-of-factly embrace all apparent disparities, polarities, and resolve them in that embrace, leaving us with a single impression, familiar as any common briar-rose.

As Selma Lanes suggests (94) there is a magic to existence that defies charting, just as there is a defiant meaning. In the most fundamental sense, everything in our lives is older than we are, and always there is something there, some thing winking just at the edge of our peripheral vision. Like all good art, like our own imaginings and dreams, fairy tales function as a sort of incantation by which is called forth the things we but half-glimpse. Just what we witness cannot ultimately be defined, though certainly part of the experience we gain is one with a sense of pure, elemental wonder, without which we remain fixed, dull and ignorant as stone; as Iona and Peter Opie say,

The magic sets us wondering...this is the merit of the tales, that by going beyond possibility they enlarge our daily horizon. For a man not given to speculation might as well walk on four legs as on two. A child who does not feel wonder is but an inlet for apple pie. (16)

It is true that a story which depicts life solely as a study in meanness, in a reality devoid of joy and wonder, is more fantastic and incredible than any fairy tale. John Buchan appropriately quotes Robert Louis Stevenson's words, "To miss the joy is to miss all" (15).

To deny anyone the experience of such tales as "Little Briar-Rose," "Hansel and Gretel," "Little Snow-White," "Rapunzel," "Rumpelstiltskin," "The Goose Girl," "The Robber Bridegroom," "The Frog Prince," "Cinderella," "Little Red-Cap," "The Bremen Town Musicians," "The Queen Bee," "Snow-White and Rose-Red"—the list spools out in one silken strand—is to deny him his own inheritance of story. Ultimately, as Jane Yolen claims, it is to deny him his own humanity. We are, each one of us, the individual hero of one story, our own life. Lacking the sense of story which fairy tales provide at an early age—that cohesive beginning, middle, and end; that commingling of the ordinary and extraordinary, mundane and magical; that sense of a patterned cosmos wherein all polarities are but interconnected filaments— we exist as little more than animated clods. Like the best of literature and art, fairy tales remind us of who we were and are and yet might be. They are not "escapist" fare, unless, of course, the escape is into our very selves, our deepest desires and fears. The tales tell us, not that life isn't fraught with perils, but that its story can be lived in a joyful manner, even when the crumb trail has been picked clean and one is lost inside the very heart of the Black Forest. Perhaps that is why fairy tales have survived so long, and perhaps the Brothers Grimm's "Household Stories" remain so popular and so exemplary of the genre because they do best what all fairy tales strive for. Perhaps not. But what a full experience those tales give us; their value is inestimable yet need not be spelled out like some chemical formula. Quite simply put, fairy tales *are*; the Black Forest yet rises in our fondest dreams and darkest nightmares. That is, finally, all we need to know.

REFERENCES

Bettelheim, Bruno. *The Uses of Enchantment: The Meaning and Importance of Fairy Tales.* New York: Knopf, 1976.

Buchan, John. *The Novel and the Fairy Tales.* Pamphlet No. 79. Great Britain: The English Association, July, 1931.

Campbell, Joseph. "Folkloristic Commentary." Grimm, *Complete Grimm's Fairy Tales.*

Chesterton, G. K. *A Selection from His Non-Fictional Prose.* Selected by W. H. Auden. London: Faber & Faber, 1970.

Fiedler, Leslie. "Introduction." *Beyond the Looking Glass: Extraordinary Works of Fairy Tale and Fantasy.* Ed. Jonathan Cott. New York: Stonehill, 1973.

Fox, Paula. "Some Thoughts on Imagination in Children's Literature." *Celebrating Children's Books: Essays on Children's Literature in Honor of Zena Sutherland.* Ed. Betsy Hearne and Marilyn Kaye. New York: Lothrop, Lee & Shepherd, 1981.

Grimm, Jacob and **Wilhelm.** *The Complete Grimm's Fairy Tales.* Trans. Margaret Hunt, revised by James Stern. New York: Pantheon, 1972.

Hillman, James. "A Note on Story." *Children's Literature* 3 (1972).

Jan, Isabelle. *On Children's Literature.* London: Allen Lane, 1973.

Lanes, Selma G. *Down the Rabbit Hole: Adventures and Misadventures on the Realm of Children's Literature.* New York: Atheneum, 1971.

Luthi, Max. *Once Upon a Time: On the Nature of Fairy Tales.* Trans. Lee Chadeayne and Paul Gottwald. New York: Ungar, 1970.

Opie, Iona and **Peter.** *The Classic Fairy Tales.* New York: Oxford U Press, 1974.

Tolkien, J. R. R. "On Fairy Stories." *The Tolkien Reader.* New York: Balantine, 1966.

von Franz, Marie-Louise. *Interpretation of Fairy Tales: An Introduction to the Psychology of Fairy Tales.* Zurich: Spring, 1973.

Yolen, Jane. *Touch Magic: Fantasy, Faerie and Folklore in the Literature of Childhood.* New York: Philomel, 1981.

Zimmer, Heinrich. *The King and the Corpse: Tales of the Soul's Conquest of Evil.* Ed. Joseph Campbell. Princeton: Princeton University Press, 1970.

Joel Chandler Harris' *Tales of Uncle Remus:* For Mixed Audiences

by Hugh Keenan

In 1955, the folklorist Richard Chase compiled a rich anthology entitled *The Complete Tales of Uncle Remus,* a collection of 185 tales taken from the nine books of Uncle Remus tales written by Joel Chandler Harris. Three of those books were published posthumously, an indication of the wide popularity that Harris' stories had for adults and children in the late nineteenth and early twentieth centuries. Chase's anthology was intended to be the capstone and memorial of Harris' literary achievement.

Since 1955, however, the popularity of the tales has wavered, quite often under inaccurate and biased criticism. Uncle Remus has been called an "Uncle Tom." The dialect of the stories has fallen out of fashion. Even Brer Rabbit has been suspected of revolutionary tactics. In the most extreme, erroneous, and influential of these attacks, "Uncle Remus and the Malevolent Rabbit," Bernard Wolfe almost did what Harris' literary creation could not do—put an end to Brer Rabbit. The sentimentality and the postwar propaganda of Disney's *Song of the South* (1946), which was thinly based on a miniscule portion of the tales (only six out of the 185) did nothing to rectify matters.

But times are changing. Uncle Remus has been rehabilitated by scholars. Recently, Raymond Hedin has even argued that Remus was putting on the Little Boy. Southern dialect has become more acceptable, as evidenced by recent popular books such as Alice Walker's *The Color Purple* and Mark Childress' *A World Made of Fire.* Toni Morrison has even drawn on Brer Rabbit's most famous encounter, as the title of her novel *Tar Baby* and its contents bear witness.

Through it all, the *Complete Tales* has remained in print, and in continued use by parents, teachers, folktellers, folklorists, and children. This mixture of audiences is appropriate. The main body of Afro-American tales that Harris drew on and re-told had originally been communal lore; that is, tales told by adults to adults and to which children were allowed to listen. He changed the situation by making a little boy the primary audience in the first book. But in *Nights With Uncle Remus* (xv-xvi) he described the normal adult audience situation, and he recreated such a circle of adults telling stories to each other and to the little boy in the latter portion of the book.

Harris' first collection *Uncle Remus: His Songs and Sayings: The Folklore of the Old Plantation,* was published by D. Appleton and Co. in 1880; it was listed in their catalog of humorous publications for a general audience. Yet in his introduction to the book, Harris maintained "that however humorous it may be in effect, its intention is perfectly serious." And commenting on the dialect in which the tales were written, he added that this would give it "solemn, not to say melancholy, features" (3). Partly, of course, Harris is pulling the legs of those who read the introduction. But he did see the tales more as folklore than just simple entertainment, as the rest of the introduction and the subtitle of the book make clear. Indeed *Folklore of the Old Plantation* had been his choice for the main title.

As Paul M. Cousins suggests, this first book succeeded beyond anyone's expectation, selling 10,000 copies in four months (115). It has never gone out of print, and today it is available both in hardcover and in a paper back edition. Its complete contents clearly show that Harris' intended audience was not just children. Besides the thirty-four tales, there are plantation proverbs, nine poems in dialect on adult themes, a sentimental love story, and twenty-one stories of Uncle Remus' experiences in Atlanta and his observations on city life. All these are forgotten today, though to the scholar they suggest the range of creative writing that Harris would attempt and repeat in his career. It is the thirty-four tales that have survived and become the common property of children and adults, along with the others collected in Chase's *Complete Tales.*

Today these tales are even more valuable for this mixed audience. Since they remain in dialect, it is necessary that adults continue to act as the transmitters. To do this, they will have to choose whether to reproduce the dialect, to simplify it, to paraphrase the material, or otherwise to translate the Black dialect in which the tales were printed. Some educators find that dialect unacceptable; William Faulkner chooses to retell in standard English stories he first heard in dialect because "I am opposed to allowing children, black or white, to use dialectical speech in school, and I would not want this book to encourage such language patterns" (7). Indeed, the kind of speech represented by Harris has mainly disappeared, as the nation has become more linguistically sophisticated, better educated, and prone to think that the standard language of printed books reflects a standard speech spoken across the nation. But adults who deal wisely and effectively with the problems of the language of the tales will find their efforts amply rewarded. The tales are humorous, full of a shrewd yet compassionate view of mankind, and didactic without imposing a narrow standard of conduct.

In short, *The Complete Tales* is an excellent anthology for parents to read, and to introduce to children as part of their mutually difficult nurturing, sharing, and rearing process. It is no fanciful revery. It has a great deal to say about real life.

This anthology is also an excellent resource for the professional storyteller, as many can testify, and for the teacher in upper grades as well. For such professionals involved with instructing and entertaining children, it offers rich materials—and also guides to effective oral communication. Only a little study will reveal Uncle Remus' techniques, as he engages and retains the wavering interest of the Little Boy. He piques the boy's curiosity, withholds additional information and the conclusions of stories, and reproduces the sounds and actions of the animal characters like any skilled story-teller.

The anthology also provides an opportunity for older students to compare variants of tales, especially those taken from the second collection *Nights With Uncle Remus* (1883). In this book Daddy Jack, 'Tildy, Uncle Remus, and Aunt Tempy compete as story-tellers with variants of the same tale. Thus numbers 31 and 32; 39, 40, and 41; 47 and 50; 50, 55, and 56 are their respective versions of the same tale. Older students can also compare the different oral styles of the narrators. African Jack tells nine tales in all; Aunt Tempy tells the golden arm ghost story that Mark Twain had suggested to Harris as good material. Throughout the whole collection there are variants, as Harris tends to retell favorite stories with different emphases and details. One such is the story of the animal whose pride leads to its asking that its head be cut off; viz., "How Old Craney-Crow Lost His Head," "Brother Bear Learns to Comb His Head" and "Brother Tiger and Daddy Sheep." This story had meaning in Harris' personal life; he stressed modesty and humility, to the point of being old-fashioned in dress and reclusive towards his public. He refused ever to make a public speech. Harris also published three different versions of his most famous tale—the tar baby story; each has a different message and varying details.

Students may also wish to compare tales in the anthology with the use of similar materials in other collections or adaptations, such as Susan Feldman's *African Myths and Tales* (1963), Gail E. Haley's *A Story A Story* (1970), which was a Caldecott winner, or more recently, Priscilla Jacquith's *Bo Rabbit Smart for True: Folktales from the Gullah* (1981). The closest parallel in content and frame is William J. Faulkner's *The Days When the Animals Talked* (1977), in which both real life reminiscences and Brer Rabbit tales are told by the Black narrator and ex-slave Simon Brown to a young black boy. Simon Brown had told these stories to the author between 1900 and 1907 in Society Hill, South

Carolina. Harris' tales also bear comparison to two classics of children's literature: Grimm's *Fairy Tales* and the *Arabian Nights*. He admired both of these classics as a child; as an adult, he reflected the violence and retribution commonly found in Grimm's stories, and he imitated the style and structure, especially that of the interrupted tale of the *Arabian Nights,* in his 1880 book. In "Mr. Rabbit Grossly Deceives Mr. Fox," Harris overtly compares Uncle Remus' tales to "those Arabian ones."

The scholar and critic will perhaps wish to delve more closely into the literary craftsmanship of the tales, their reflections of changing values in late nineteenth century American society, and their continuing value as folklore. For insight into such matters, the three recent books by R. Bruce Bickley, Jr. and Florence Baer's *Sources and Analogues of the Uncle Remus Tales* (1980) are essential. In her comprehensive analysis of the sources of *The Complete Tales,* Baer claims for Harris that "His is the first serious attempt to record the folktales, songs, and sayings of the southern Negroes in the exact language and style in which they existed" (24). Her study points out the accuracy of Harris' tales in both content and oral styles as recognized by modern collectors of African materials.

Harris' contribution to folklore has been long recognized and often debated. Perhaps far too little credit has been given as well to the literary craftsmanship of Harris: this may be due to his inaccurate, modest disclaimers that he was only a collector of folktales, or, in the later portion of his career, a dull old reporter and only a simple entertainer of young children. But *The Complete Tales* and Harris' artistry are both more complex and varied than they appear to the casual reader. Certainly anyone in this book's mixed audience of adults and children soon realizes their superiority to the watered down versions in Walt Disney's *Song of the South* (1946), which is heavy on post World War II propaganda. More than any other popularization, this film distorted the realistic values and ambiguous contents of Harris' tales. But reading and studying the originals of the six tales that Disney did use can provide a useful starting point of comparison for parent, child, folk-teller, teacher, scholar, and critic. Overall, Disney's film presents a world where conflicts are resolved; troubles, eased; and where people and animals harmonize in its most famous song: "Zip-a-dee-do-dah, zip-a-dee-ay, My oh my what a wonderful day." Not even when he was at his most sentimental and optimistic in his adult novels and essays was Harris' vision of the real world so false and simple. And this optimism certainly does not represent the tales.

In *The Complete Tales,* Harris juxtaposes the violent and highly competitive world of the animals with the relatively cooperative and benign one of Uncle Remus and the Little Boy. Harris avoids any easy or sentimental resolution of the competing values of each world. For example, in the first book *Uncle Remus: His Songs and Sayings,* Harris has Brer Rabbit kill his three antagonists: Brer Wolf, Brer Bear, and Brer Fox. After having scalded the Wolf and gotten the Bear stung to death, Brer Rabbit gets Brer Fox killed by Mister Man in the last tale, "The Sad Fate of Mr. Fox." He then carries the head to the fox's family for their dinner, is captured in turn, and then escapes. Remus caps this violent denouement to the first book by the outrageous suggestion that some say that Brer Rabbit then married the widowed Mrs. Fox. Doubtless, if Harris had known of the success the first book would have, he would not have killed off the rabbit's three chief antagonists. In subsequent books, Remus has to explain that the stories in which they are alive belong to an earlier period. But the Little Boy is not always quite convinced.

Throughout the whole collection, and especially in the first book, the animals of the tales steal food from each other, lie, cheat, trick each other, and occasionally even maim or kill each other. All the time, they scrupulously observe the rules of sociality—speaking politely when they meet, sharing or exchanging dinners, starting communal projects such as a crop, a well, or a house, and even going courting together when they visit "Miss Meadows and the gals." Struggles for power, food and sex are very evident, as reflections of the concerns of the adult world in the imaginary one of the tales.

But in the frame of the stories, Uncle Remus and the Little Boy are honest with each other, share food, and exchange ideas. And while Remus is telling tales, he is also showing the boy how such useful articles as horsecollars, fishbaskets, or ax handles are made, and how to sew a coat, to sharpen a knife or to half-sole shoes. Uncle Remus himself is a complex figure: teacher, companion, father substitute, upholder of social mores, anti-social critic, and occasionally a manipulator and trickster like Brer Rabbit. Early on he establishes the condition of the story-telling sessions: he is to have independent control of the material and the Little Boy can only accept, not question or change the stories. Remus even deliberately frightens the boy by a series of ghost stories, and then relents to walk the child home ("A Plantation Witch"). On the other hand, Remus shows more often how the excessive trickery and over-confidence of the animals is punished in the tales. And in the main, the world of the Little Boy and Uncle Remus is benign, whereas in the tales, competitiveness, aggressiveness, voraciousness, and chicanery are only masked by a thin social veneer. When the frame and the tales are considered together, this dual view of life that Harris presents is more realistic than many other children's books, and accounts in part for the tales remaining classics.

On the other hand, one has to recognize the limitations of the collection. The earlier portions (drawn from the first two books) are more memorable than the later tales. Harris soon ran out of material and solicited tales from friends, his children, family servants, newspaper correspondents, and others. He even recast a few French or English tales into Black dialect, and more and more he repeated materials, while the later collections of tales were severely reduced in contents. Also, the sexual component of the tales and the frame is played down for the 19th century audience. For example, in his most famous tale "The Wonderful Tar-Baby Story," the conflict of the rabbit and the tar figure suggests a sexual assault. The tar figure accosted and beaten is female (see the pronouns in the text). But most readers are unaware of this implication. Harris also allowed an early illustrator (Frederick S. Church) to bowdlerize "Miss Meadows" as "Mother Nature," but the text belies such puritan interpretation. In "Brother Rabbit and the Mosquitoes" in Nights With Uncle Remus, the rabbit even courts the wolf's daughter. The frame story of this book concerns in large part the elderly Daddy Jack's courtship of young 'Tildy and ends with their marriage. See also "Brother Rabbit's Courtship" in the Daddy Jake volume (1889). And Remus becomes a less interesting character in the minimal frames of later collections, being reduced to little more than a mouth piece in the last ones.

Still the stories, on the whole, are realistic and convincing, for the innocent are not immune from suffering and death. In "Mr. Rabbit Nibbles up the Butter," the possum is framed by the rabbit, and burns to death in a trial by fire. And in "The Sad Fate of Mr. Fox," the cow Bookay is deliberately killed by Brer Rabbit and the fox is blamed. Overall, however, the greedy or wicked are punished and the young and innocent are saved, as in "A Story About the Little Rabbits," "Why Brother Wolf Didn't Eat the Little Rabbits," or "Mrs. Partridge Has a Fit."

There are other flaws also. The tales touch only slightly on racial matters, as in "Why the Negro is Black." And established religious beliefs are seldom questioned. Prominent exceptions are the alternate flood story in "The Story of the Deluge, and How It Came About," and "The Origin of the Ocean." Some stories of the supernatural may be a bit frightening for very young children, making "Taily-po" and "How a Witch Was Caught" seem unsuitable to some parents. Some tales deal with superstitions, as in "Brother Rabbit's Love-Charm." Others seem very adult, such as "The Hard-Headed Woman," which may offend feminists, for it describes how a husband gets magical revenge on a slothful wife. Supernatural and marriage tests occur also in "The Adventures of

Simon and Susanna," and changeling panther-women confront a teenaged boy in "The Little Boy and His Dogs." But despite these exceptions the coverage of sexual, satiric, and social commentary in the *Complete Tales* may seem to be limited—especially in comparison to other collections of African folktales.

In the main, in fact, Harris' stories concentrate on the theme of the trickster tricked, as in episode after episode Brer Rabbit, Wolf, Fox, Bear, Lion, or Dog get their comeuppance. A number of stories are etiological, as their titles bear witness:

"Why the Alligator's Back is Rough"
"Why Brother Bear Has No Tail"
"Why the Guinea-Fowls Are Speckled"
"Where the Harrycans Comes From"
"Why Brother Fox's Legs Are Black"
"Why Mr. Cricket Has Elbows on His Legs"

But besides explaining matters of nature of interest especially to a child, these changes almost always also involve moral causes.

No discussion of the contents of *The Complete Tales of Uncle Remus* can overlook two ways in which the title is a misnomer. Not all these tales are told by Uncle Remus. Tales told by Crazy Sue (from *Daddy Jake*) and by African Jack, 'Tildy, and Aunt Tempy *(Nights With Uncle Remus)* round out their number. The collection by Richard Chase, however, omits similar tales told by Aunt Minerva. In *Plantation Pageants* (1889), she tells two Brer Rabbit tales. She also tells eight tales in *The Chronicles of Aunt Minervy Ann* published the same year. There is more reason for Chase's excluding the tales in *The Tar-Baby and Other Rhymes* (1904) as these are in verse and he limits his *Complete Tales* to those in prose. But this editorial policy deprives the reader of two stories found nowhere else.

The Complete Tales is uneven, as obviously not all of Harris' tales are of equal quality. Chase included some that were printed posthumously, and that Harris had chosen to pass over. Of *The Complete Tales*, the thirty-four from the first book *Uncle Remus: His Songs and Sayings* are the most familiar and are presented in the simplest manner. Those from the next book *Nights With Uncle Remus* are the most complex, varied, and extensive (seventy-one in number). The frame for this is also the most difficult, sophisticated, and complex that Harris ever attempted. Remus has to tell five tales on each of the first three nights, and later in the book, there are frequently two tales a night. The time span in the frame ranges from fall to Christmas, and from rain to harvest. The frame also includes the lengthy illness and recovery of the Little Boy, the courtship and marriage of Jack and 'Tildy, and a general movement from sorrow to consolation, from small and conflicting groups to a larger and harmonious community. Harris never attempted so much again. Instead, he imitated the far simpler structure of his first book. And he gave up most of the claims to be a folklorist and linguist of Black literature and language and culture to be found in *Nights With Uncle Remus.*

The thinnest tales are perhaps those taken from his last book, *Uncle Remus and Brer Rabbit* (1907). By this time Harris had long since tired of being restricted in the public's mind to the persona of Uncle Remus. He had even threatened to have Uncle Remus die. The later volumes of tales emphasize entertainment rather than instruction, and are less indebted to African sources. Even by the second book, Harris had begun to run out of first hand material. Increasingly for subsequent books, he had to rely on material garnered from family servants, friends of his own children, correspondents who replied to Harris' newspaper advertisements for material or those who volunteered such tales, and finally, on published collections of folktales. At the last, he resorted to putting any folktale into Black dialect to satisfy the public's and his publishers' demands. For example, "The Story of Teenchy-Tiny Duck" as found in *Uncle Remus and the Little Boy* (1910) is retold in Black dialect from a French book of folktales *(Evening Tales)* that Harris or his wife translated and that was published in 1893. There are other examples in his last years of Harris publishing the same tale both in standard English and Black dialect.

Their percentage is small, however, as the first two books contained the bulk of his Uncle Remus tales and these mainly have African or Afro-American sources. Florence Baer concludes from her study of the 184 tales in *The Complete Collection* that "there is evidence that the immediate source of 122 (66.3%) is Africa. Twenty-eight (15.2%) probably came from Europe (this includes the British Isles); seventeen (9.2%) seem to have arisen in the New World . . ." (168). Only sixteen cannot be positively identified as to origin. North American Indian lore is also presented, but in a very minor degree. This mixing of the folktales of different countries and cultures can be found in other collectors and popularizers of the nineteenth century, in the colored fairy books of Andrew Lang, for example.

Critics have sometimes faulted Harris for not giving a more comprehensive survey of Black folktales. But he never claimed to do this. He concentrated on the animal tales. The majority of his tales—eighty-nine of them—are such stories. He shaved the truth by saying that all were Black folktales, but Harris was trained as a journalist and not a folklorist. And even for professional folklorists, that study was in its infancy. Harris himself was a charter member of the first folklore society in America, though he soon left it. Perhaps he felt that his vision of a split society and the divided nature of man could best be conveyed by animal stories which allegorize man at his competitive worst, and by an optimistic frame which showed the narrator and the hearer in harmonious cooperation.

In that regard, the significance of the title of the first story "Uncle Remus Initiates the Little Boy" is too often overlooked. The teller's role is to instruct the boy as to the worst man can do in the animal stories and also to the highest ideals of family love, honesty, and devotion that man may aspire to. This purpose is reaffirmed later in the collection in "Brother Rabbit Ties Mr. Lion," when Remus takes issue with Aunt Tempy over the reason for telling stories. She wants only to amuse the boy and is disappointed at his solemn face. Remus replies,

> "Well, I tell you dis, Sis Tempy," said Uncle Remus, with unusual emphasis, "ef deze yer tales wuz des fun, fun, fun, en giggle, giggle, giggle, I let you know I'd a-done drapt um long ago. Yasser, w'en it come down ter gigglin' you kin des count ole Remus out."

Remus tells the stories to show how the weak in body and inferior in power (like the child and others) can use their wits to overcome their enemies and their subservient condition. Remus did not believe that one could expect fairy godmothers or like creatures from outside to solve an individual's problems. In "Brother Rabbit and the Chickens" (Told by Uncle Remus, 1905), he asks the boy to give an example of the kind of story he likes. The boy tells "Cinderella." Remus responds, after having pretended to find it new and interesting: "'It's a mighty purty tale,' he said. 'It's so purty dat you dunner whedder ter b'lieve it er not.'" He guesses the odds are probably "one time in forty'-lev'm hundred." The animals of his stories have to make their way in a more realistic world.

Tales which for a hundred years have refreshed readers and listeners with their acute perceptions of the real and the ideal can properly be considered a touchstone for children's literature. For Harris' mixed audience of adults and children, parents, teachers, and story-tellers, The Complete Tales of Uncle Remus still remain valid and well worth reading, retelling, and passing on to subsequent generations. Not only are they literature based on folklore, but also, they have more to say about the naturalistic view of the world and about the fine art of survival than many have fully realized, though all readers have probably gotten part of this message along with a great deal of enjoyment. That is all that can be expected of any piece of literature, whether for adults or children, or as with Harris' tales, for both at the same time.

REFERENCES

Baer, Florence E. *Sources and Analogues of the Uncle Remus Tales.* Helsinki: Suomalainen Tiedeakatemia, Academia Scientiarum Fennica, 1980.

Bickley, R. Bruce, Jr. *Joel Chandler Harris.* Boston: Twayne Publishers, 1978.

_____. *Joel Chandler Harris: A Reference Guide.* Boston: G. K. Hall & Co., 1978.

_____. ed. *Critical Essays on Joel Chandler Harris.* Boston: G. K. Hall & Co., 1981.

Brookes, Stella Brewer. *Joel Chandler Harris—Folklorist.* Athens: University of Georgia Press, 1950.

Cousins, Paul M. *Joel Chandler Harris: A Life.* Baton Rouge: Louisiana State University Press, 1968.

Faulkner, William J. *The Days When the Animals Talked.* Chicago: Follett Publishing Co., 1977.

Harris, Joel Chandler. *Uncle Remus: His Songs and Sayings: The Folklore of the Old Plantation.* New York: D. Appleton and Co., 1880.

_____. *The Complete Tales of Uncle Remus.* Intro. Richard Chase. Boston: Houghton Mifflin, 1955.

Hedin, Raymond. "Uncle Remus: Puttin' on Ole Massa's Son." *Southern Literary Journal,* 15 (Fall 1982): 83-90.

Keenan, Hugh T. "Joel Chandler Harris." *American Writers for Children Before 1900.* Vol. 42 of *DLB.* Ed. Glenn E. Estes. Detroit: Gale Research Co., 1985. 222-240.

_____. "Twisted Tales: Propaganda in the Tar-Baby Stories." *The Southern Quarterly,* 22(Winter 1984): 54-69.

Mikkelson, Nina. "When the Animals Talked—A Hundred Years of Uncle Remus." *ChLAQ,* 8(Spring 1983): 3-5, 31.

Stafford, John. "Patterns of Meaning in *Nights With Uncle Remus.*" *American Literature* 18(May 1946): 89-108.

Wolfe, Bernard. "Uncle Remus and the Malevolent Rabbit." *Commentary* 8(July 1949): 31-41.

Joseph Jacobs' English Fairy Tales: A Legacy for Today

by John Warren Stewig

In 1890, a former Australian with impressive credentials as a Jewish historian and researcher published a collection of forty-three folk tales that was destined to have significant impact on the study of folklore in general. Then only thirty-six years old, Joseph Jacobs published *English Fairy Tales,* and followed it in less than five years with three other volumes of folk literature. These and other books for children firmly established him as the person most responsible for preserving the body of British folk tales.

Jacobs' collection presents people, animals, giants, and ogres, in stories long and short. "Jack and His Golden Snuff-Box" runs to fourteen pages, while four of the tales are miniatures of only two pages each. Outcomes are happy and sad, conflicts are major and inconsequential, and throughout the collection runs the sprightly good humor which distinguishes English tales in general.

Actually, the term "English" must be taken a bit loosely, for as Briggs and Tongue tell us, Jacobs "slipped across the border to lowland Scotland for selections, roamed to the United States and Australia, and even adapted ballad stories into tales" (xii). So, "Henny Penny" actually came from his native Australia and "Nix Nought Nothing" from Scotland, while "The Johnny Cake" came from America.

The collection's greatest significance is that it recorded old tales at a critical time when they were in danger of being lost—and did it so well. As Eloise Ramsey says, Jacobs "rescued the fast-disappearing English tales from a threatened oblivion and rekindled interest in them by the success with which he realized his ambition 'to write them as a good old nurse will speak' in telling them to children" (17). In the process, he provided a rich source of visual and language images which have influenced both literature and popular culture, in forms such as advertisements and plays, and also in allusions in everyday language.

Though the tales are often considered as a group, folklore scholars point out that Jacobs' book includes many different kinds of tales. Katherine M. Briggs identifies five different kinds of folk narratives in Jacobs' collection:

1. *Fables and Exempla* (animal stories which satirize human frailties), of which "Belling the Cat" is an example. Briggs distinguishes between fables and exempla quite clearly,

but chooses to lump them into one category for some reason.

2. *Fairy Tales* (which include a state of enchantment, though not necessarily a fairy person, per se). "Jack and the Beanstalk" is an example.

3. *Jocular Tales* (drolls, noodle stories and bawdy tales which are social commentary, scorning undesirable behavior), of which "Master of all Masters" is an example.

4. *Novelle* (which include no explicitly supernatural elements) of which "Cap O'Rushes" is an example. Written down earlier than the fairy tales, when accuracy was less prized, these as a group are more tampered with than other types.

5. *Nursery Tales,* like "Henny Penny," "Mr. Vinegar," and "Three Bears."

The best known of Jacobs' tales have been exceptionally popular with young listeners. The collection is full of clear, direct stories of inherent interest; some tales, like the "Three Bears," have enthralled boys and girls of every generation, and they are equally popular with the television-image saturated children of today. Though children seldom stop to analyze the reasons for their responses to literature, the undeniable pleasure they take in stories like Jacobs' makes these stories an important part of their literary experience—particularly in classrooms. As a teacher, it is the latter that most interests me, and that I would like to say more about.

Many authorities in education have analyzed the reasons fairy tales should be part of the literary experiences of children in the elementary school. Schwartz points out that the tales take children far from their everyday environments, to lands in which they encounter fantastic events and rather abstract hero figures, and in which they can learn of basic human situations and relationships in disguised form. Huck speaks of the pure entertainment I mentioned earlier, and also of the insights into modern tales which children derive from acquaintance with the older tales.

But these general reasons for including fairy tales as essential in the literary experience of young children apply to tales from many lands. There are some more specific reasons which are particularly pertinent to the English tales—especially their value as literature. Several authorities have commented on the intrinsic literary quality of the British variants of the tales; Stith Thompson says, "Several tales have their most distinctive form in England— Jack and the Beanstalk... Tom Tit Tot..."

We can speak generally, as Thompson does, of "distinctive literary forms," or we can take on the task of trying to identify what makes a piece of literature distinctive. Two aspects of Jacobs' tales make them distinctive in ways that are of concern to adults who share literature with children—especially classroom teachers.

First, we share the tales with children for the rich load of vocabulary they bring, far richer than the homogenized language too common in much modern literature for young readers. As youngsters read, or listen to the tales, they encounter such words as "deliverance," "clitter-clatter," "deceived," "cautiously," "possession," "gatless," and "address" (as a manner of speech). Such language is far more diverse than what students meet in instructional materials, and in many modern stories.

Second, in addition to vocabulary, students can also absorb from these stories syntax more involved than they usually read. An example:

> Well, Jack was not content, and it wasn't very long before he determined to have another try at his luck up there at the top of the beanstalk.

Sentences of such length are not uncommon in Jacobs' work, but because these alternate with much shorter sentences, the tales do not appear wordy.

We need to share both this mature kind of syntax and these expanded lexical resources, for the enriching effect they have on children's own language. Schmidt tells teachers that we must consciously choose such language-rich material, for the language environment of home, peers, and mass electronic media is generally too similar to the child's own language to provide the necessary stimulation and modeling needed for continuing language development.

Teachers and children can benefit from this rich language because of Jacobs' belief that children would enjoy it:

> In general, then, I eschew obscurity and like precision. But as you well know, context can supply meaning and children do like the sound of unusual words. (Trustees 43)

In the process of collecting and editing, Jacobs did freely change words (as well as make more significant editorial changes). But despite this, he did not share the too common American compulsion for shortening syntax and controlling the diversity of vocabulary, a compulsion which is exemplified in all American textbooks, and indeed, too often in trade books also.

As teachers, then, we can share these tales with students because of the extraordinary language richness that they provide. But there are also psychological reasons that suggest why boys and girls could benefit from encountering these tales.

A point often made, which applies equally to the English fairy tales, is that folk literature in general can be used to further children's ability to work through problems and fears. In the process students come to greater self-awareness, as they move from dependence to autonomy. That point of view is fully presented, with extensive analysis of over a dozen tales and detailed recommendations about how children use them, by Bettelheim. His book *The Uses of Enchantment*, though long and in some places fairly opaque to read, has been responsible for alerting many teachers to this potential use of fairy tales.

Bettelheim's work has served an important purpose, even though some critics, notably Jack Zipes, raise doubts about this work. Zipes says, ". . . assuming that there is some validity to using folk tales therapeutically in educating children, one must still question the manner in which Bettelheim imposes meaning on the tales as well as his indiscriminate application of their meaning to children of all ages, sexes, and class backgrounds" (169). Zipes concludes, "The imminent meaning of the tales has little to do with providing suitable direction for a contemporary child's life" (170).

Yet Zipes' criticism applies only to the specific Freudian ideas Bettelheim finds in the tales. The same general point about the uses of fairy tales for self-realization is made, but without Bettelheim's heavily Freudian underpinning, by John Weiser and others, who believe that "Often the child. . .is locked into one view, and by embedding the problem in the rich imagery of a fairy tale, a different perspective can be gained." Their analysis of tales found in text books recommended by an Ontario government publication shows that, while such textbooks do indeed include tales which could be used for the type of self-realization the authors advocate, few of the accompanying teacher's guides actually bring out in any apparent way this potential. In addition to group discussion to highlight the problem and ways a character deals with it, the authors recommend informal drama activities to further illuminate alternate ways of perceiving and dealing with problems. They feel students could assume the roles of the characters, and create "dialogues between characters where the desired quality is being expressed" in order to resolve the protagonist's difficulties. They suggest using "What if. . ." questions so children can enact mini-plays and thus explore alternative solutions to problems.

These suggestions are valuable, and might well apply to Jacobs' tales. Indeed, teachers at various grade levels could choose to work from Jacobs' book itself, reading stories from it on a regular basis, so that by the time students left sixth grade, they would have heard all of the tales. That in itself would be a useful curriculum plan, as most children are unfortunately exposed to only a small number of the best known tales. Probably all students encounter "Johnny-Cake" and "The Story of the Three Bears"; few, if any, hear or read "Jack Hannaford" or "Mr. Miacca." If, for example, teachers wanted to share this body of forty-three tales with students, apportioning them out in the seven years (kindergarten through sixth grade) of elementary school, they would be establishing a firm groundwork on which further study of English and other folk literature could be based in the high school. In the process, we would be enriching our students' knowledge of their literary heritage, knowledge which at this time is notable for its tenuousness.

Beyond that overly simple curriculum plan, however, the Jacobs tales offer an additional opportunity. Because they have been so popular, many of them have appeared in numerous different versions. This variety of versions allows teachers to search out different versions of these tales in varying book formats and plan specific classroom exercises to involve students with the books. Such experiences can sensitize children to both visual and verbal variation.

In terms of variation, one of the most interesting of the stories in the Jacobs collection is "Tom Tit Tot." The tale comes from Norfolk, where the dialect spoken was East Anglian, and Briggs and Tongue feel the story is "the flower" of those which have been accurately told in their local dialect. In discussing this tale, author Macleod Yearsley identifies it as responsible for spawning a large cycle of Rumplestiltskin and related tales. He comments on the fascination variants of this tale held for readers: "...to obtain a man's name meant to the primitive mind the possession of something which...gives power over him, and may be used for the working of very potent magic" (152).

To introduce this tale, teachers might use the version with which Jacobs opens his collection, allowing children to respond first to hearing this tale read or told aloud. Having done that, it is important to share the story in the most distinguished context in which this tale has been presented: the picture book version illustrated in woodcut by Evaline Ness (Scribner's, 1965). This book is a paradigm of the ways in which a gifted illustrator can take the word story and extend it, adding detail and deepening appreciation by creating an accompanying expanded visual story.

Children should experience this book because of the exceptional success Ness had with this often attempted and less often accomplished task. The rough angularity intrinsic to woodcut clearly echoes the clarity and spareness of the book's language. Beyond that, two other characteristics make this an edition not to be missed. First, Ness has chosen an unexpected palette, which draws our visual attention. Eschewing the now-commonplace but sometimes irrelevant four-color palette which dominates children's book illustration today, Ness chooses three colors which interact strongly: each competes with the other, none of the three dominating, so an invigorating tension between colors develops. Ness's black, pale blue, and brown (actually tan and brown) create a more vibrant effect than the more expectable, and more placid, three color combinations found in other children's books. Second, the juxtaposition of various patterns, an enduring trademark in Ness's work, here again creates an active, vigorous effect. Stripes bump up against stars, circles run into (and sometimes over) chevrons. On the title page, patterns of bricks of the oven, pie crust, and four designs on the mother's dress juxtapose intently. Because of the flatness of the patterns, we read them as visual symbols, not as realistic representations.

Using color and textures, Ness has done visually what composers do aurally with dissonance and differing time meters: she creates intensity and vivacity. It is not exaggerating to say that she has achieved, in admittedly smaller format, what avant garde American composer Charles Ives accomplished in his "Variations on America", a work which astonished listeners when first performed in 1891. In Ives' work, instrumentalists play in different keys (colors) and time signatures (patterns) at the same time! So too, with Ness. But as Ives was not immediately popular with his listeners, so children will not intuitively appreciate Ness. She is, in fact, an acquired taste, developed after extended exposure to this and other of her work.

A softer, more pastoral version of this tale by Jacqueline Ayer (Harcourt, 1967) will introduce students to the German variant, "Rumplestiltskin." Also in three colors, pictures in this edition are rounder, more elegant, more expectable. It is no less appealing because of this more easily "readable" visual language.

The Cornish version of this important droll tale, first published in 1865, is "Duffy and the Devil." It is most effectively presented with Rabelasian good humor in the context of Margo Zemach's picture book (Farrar, 1973), with ebullient watercolors by this accomplished illustrator. Zemach creates her usual lumpy peasant people, in this case depicting Squire Lovel of Trove with the potato nose and ample belly; Duffy, the lazy bufflehead," and the scraggly-bearded, horned devil. Zemach's distinguishing gift is her energetic, scratchy black line, which she uses to prevent her soft pastels from turning saccharine. The robustness of her illustrations is visual reinforcement of the word descriptions of Duffy, in no way a stereotypic ladylike heroine.

Obviously, these different artists interpret similar stories in quite different ways.

Classroom teachers can select a pair of variants of this, or of some other of Jacobs' tales, and encourage students to observe visual differences and similarities. After careful scrutiny, students can use verbal or written language to record their responses. An in-class recording of verbal responses from children comparing and contrasting the visuals and story structure of the versions of "Tom Tit Tot" by Ness and Ayer are included in "Literature and Young Children: Classroom Approaches," an audio tape (stock number 72636R) available from the National Council of Teachers of English.

One of the things we want children to notice is the way language varies with different editions of the same tale. For example, we might focus on the verse the creature chants in "Tom Tit Tot" and its variations. In Jacobs' book, the creature says:

Duffy, my lady, you'll never know—what?
That my name is Terrytop-top.

By contrast, in Zemach's version, the "devil-creature" sings:

Tomorrow! Tomorrow! Tomorrow's the day!
I'll take her! I'll take her! I'll take her away!
Let her weep, let her cry, let her beg, let her pray—
She'll never guess my name is Tarraway!

And in a Scots' version, the creature says:

Little kens our guid dame at hame
that Whuppity Stoorie is my name.

In addition to these variants easily available in formats for children, Yearsley points out that variations of this tale also come from Lower Austria, the Tyrol, France, Hungary, Italy, Iceland, Mongolia, Nigeria, and Spain, among other countries. It is interesting to note the American Negro variant of this chant:

To-day I was buried,
To-morrow I was brew.
And then for de queen chil'
I shall take.
I'm so glad then she do not know
That my name is Tambutoe.   (Parsons 198)

Consciousness of variants can lead to creativity; one of the most useful ways to link folk literature to children's own language is to have students create their own version of a favorite tale. In the process of moving from literary language to their own language, children: 1) think more deeply about the original; 2) bring to conscious level their previously unarticulated notions of story structure; and 3) become involved in the challenging task of creating their own stories within an organizing structure. From the Jacobs book, we might use "The Story of the Three Little Pigs." Recently I read this to a class of third graders, and then the teacher discussed it with her students. Following this, children were encouraged to write their own version. These are some of the stories which resulted:

Once upon a time there were ten pigs and they didn't have a big enough room in their home so they had to make their own house. So they left their house. One pig saw a man with some grass and he said, "Man, can I have some of that grass to make me a home?" The man gave him some. He made a home. The second little pig saw a man with some candy. He said, "Man, can I have some candy to build a home?" The man gave him some candy. The third little pig saw a pile of mud so he made a home of mud. The fourth pig made a straw home. A man gave the fifth pig some sticks. He made a home of that. Another man gave the sixth pig some fruit to build a house with. Another man gave the seventh pig some vegetables. He made a home of vegetables. Another man gave the eighth pig some cement. He made a cement home. Another man gave the ninth pig some bricks. He made a home of bricks. Another man gave the tenth pig some steel. He made a home of steel.

The wolf went to the first house and said, "Little pig, let me come in." "No, no." So the wolf smashed the window and got in and ate the pig. Two other pigs were on a walk. The wolf saw them and ate them up. Five others were playing hide and seek. The wolf ate them for a snack. Two others were sleeping. The wolf ate them for dinner. Then the wolf went out to the tenth pig's house and said, "Little pig, little pig, let me in," and he said, "No, I can't." Then the wolf said, "I know a place where there are pool tables and we can play." "Ok, what time?" "6:00 o'clock." So the pig woke up at 5:45 and went. The pig got there at 6:00 o'clock. At the end of the game, the pig threw the ball at the wolf and ran home. Then the wolf went to the pig's house and went down the chimney and landed in a pot of hot water. The pig threw the water away and the pig never saw him again and he lived happily ever after.

by Nicky

Once there was three little pigs. The first one was Jabba. The second one was Marbles, and the third one was El Chico. One day Mrs. Labels (their mother) said: "I won't be able to take care of you any more (Sadly). You will have to move to Canada where it gets very cold and sometimes warm and it's good for your skin." So the three little pigs went to Canada where the cold is good for their skin. One day when Jabba was walking he found some animal fur, and so he decided to make his house out of fur. Now El Chico was even dumber than Jabba. He wanted to build a house out of grass. Now Marbles is the smart one, he's the one that wants to build a house out of candy. (Now the wolf comes.) "Fee, Fi, Foe, Fome, I smell three little pigs! Ah, ah, a house. A pig! Little pig, little pig, let me come in." "Not by the hair of my little, little head." "Then I'll huff and I'll puff and I'll blow your house down." (Now since this pig was dumb, he stayed in the pile of fur.) And the wolf ate him up. And the same thing happened to El Chico. Now Marbles was smart. But the wolf was smarter. Marbles made his house out of candy and so the wolf ate, and ate, and ate the house up. And Marbles got eaten up. The mother still doesn't know about this yet. And a few days later she forgot all about them and she lived happily ever after!

by Renee

One summer day in Seattle, Washington at about 6:45, 3 pigs were going to have breakfast, but while the mother was fixing breakfast she had a heart attack and died. In the meantime the 1st little pig went to Milwaukee, Wisconsin. He met a boy named Danny. The little pig said, "Will you please give me those leaves you're raking? You see, My mother died and I need those leaves to make a house and I'll be your friend if you give me them" Danny said, "Well... O..., and I'll give you this horn if you need me." "How do you use it?", said the little pig. "All you have to do is blow in that little hole," Danny said. "O.K.", said the little pig. So, the little pig walked a mile or two, and by the time the little pig got to the place he wanted to build his house, he was so tired he went to sleep.

Two hours later the 2nd little pig was on his way to Topeka, Kansas. When he got there he met a boy named Stephen. The little pig said, "Will you please give me those sticks to make a house? You see my mother went up with the angels." Stephen said, "Well...O..., here is a whistle in case you need me."

Meanwhile, the 1st little pig was watching T.V. in his leaf house when suddenly there was a thump on the door. It was a wolf! The wolf said, "Little pig, let me eat you up!" The little pig thought to say "No," but instead he blew the horn. Danny came and shot the wolf, and the piggle pig could have a happy life.

Meanwhile the second little pig was just finished gluing the last two sticks to his house. When he was resting, a bobcat came to the door and said, "Let me eat you up!" Just like the 1st pig, he blew the whistle. In a second Stephen came and shot the bobcat, and both pigs had a happy life.

by Donny

After students have composed their own versions, and read them aloud in class, teachers may be interested in expanding this experience, using the variants included in Briggs' A Dictionary of British Folk-Tales. Though this book for adults is without illustrations, children are likely to be fascinated with at least two variants she includes. The one taken from Andrew Lang's The Green Fairy Book tells of Browny (a very dirty little pig) who chooses a mud house; his greedy sister Whitey who chooses a cabbage house; and Blacky (who had nice dainty ways [for a pig], who chooses a brick house). Mother pig, before her death, has the houses built for her children. It is Blacky who is able to release his two less-sensible siblings from their imprisonment in the fox's cave.

In the other variation, taken by Hamish Henderson from a Scottish source, Dennis, Biddy, and Rex have been sent from home on a stormy day, because Dennis had inadvertently trod on one of mother pig's younger family. After building a straw and a slat house, both Dennis and Biddy must flee the fox, seeking refuge with Rex, who wisely built of brick. The fox is incinerated in the chimney and afterwards the three pigs "hooked him down the chimney and cut him up into collops...for their dinner."

There are many ways to use these and other variations of Jacobs' story about the pigs for educational purposes. I recently used a trio of books: the versions by Erik Blegvad (Atheneum, 1980); by Lorinda Cauley (Putnam's, 1980); and by Edda Reinl (Neugebauer Press USA, 1983). The Blegvad edition is the most traditional visually. Very precise black ink pen line details unify the pastel color, in fairly small and restrained illustrations. Cauley's full page illustrations, also in watercolor and ink, nonetheless create a very different visual effect as they push toward the constraining borders which encompass them. Reinl's batik illustrations are the most exuberant of all, bleeding off the pages' edges and leading to a massive double page explosion of the wolf!

Each of these versions was read to a third grade class on succeeding days, and then left on the reading table so children could examine them further in their spare time. Following this, during a group discussion, children commented on what they had observed about the illustrations and told which version they preferred. Those students who commented about the Blegvad version made these remarks:

137

The third pig ate up his brothers, inside the wolf.
That pig was dumb: there might not have been an apple tree.
Most books I've heard have the pigs stay alive.
This is too long. I like the shorter one better.
There is so much detail in the background.
I like the way the pictures only take up part of the page.

About the Cauley version, children commented:

I liked this one because the wolf is dressed in clothes. You
don't usually see that.
The pig used his bag as a headband.
Those pigs look like bums.
These are more colorful than the other pictures.

Comments about the Reinl version included:

That's a very small house.
They don't go to a man for hay.
That wolf looks like a porcupine, not like the other wolves.
That's a very nice house they have. Where did the tables and
chairs come from?
This is the only book in which he burst.
There's no trip to the apple tree and turnip garden in this one.

At another time, or with older students, the teacher might—
instead of leading an oral discussion—ask each student to write
their observations and then make a value statement. Putting into
words an answer to the question: "Which one do you prefer, and
why?" is a useful linguistic challenge for children.

For example, a fifth grade class of gifted students recently
studied the Blegvad, Cauley and Reinl versions of this story. After
group discussions about each, children wrote individual responses. David wrote:

I preferred the Blegvad because of the pictures. They
were much more realistic, not in what's drawn, but in how it's
drawn. The pictures aren't exaggerated either, like the
elephant-like ears in the Reinl. Blegvad was done in
watercolors, and they looked better than the batik. There is
probably a limit to realism and accuracy in such a time-
consuming process (like batik). Cauley was more colorful, but
the pictures were not very realistic and were more like
cartoons.
The story was also better as Cauley and Reinl were more
like young children's versions. Having episodes was better
than having a wolf just burst and it's a little odd to hear about
pigs reading picture books. Also, in Cauley, there were less
words and more pictures, so it was somewhat less exacting and
detailed.

As these examples show, children still have much to learn from the tales Jacobs collected. For pure enjoyment, literary heritage reasons, intrinsic language reasons, visual awareness, and for the effect on students' own language, the Jacobs tales deserve an important place in the elementary curriculum. Beginning with the tales in his book itself, teachers can branch out into a variety of activities based on the most significant modern day variants of these old tales. The life in these tales can still vivify language arts programs today.

REFERENCES

Bettelheim, Bruno. *The Uses of Enchantment.* New York: Vantage Books, 1975.

Briggs, Katharine. *A Dictionary of British Folktales in the English Language.* London: Routledge and Kegan Paul, 1970.

Briggs, Katharine and **Ruth Tongue.** *Folktales of England.* London: Routledge and Kegan Paul, 1965.

Huck, Charlotte S. *Children's Literature in the Elementary School.* New York: Holt, 1979. 158-9.

Parsons, Elsie Crews. "Tales from Guilford County, NC." *Journal of American Folklore* 30 (1917).

Ramsey, Eloise. *Folklore for Children and Young People.* Philadelphia: American Folklore Society, 1952.

Schmidt, Sheldon. "Language Development in Intermediate Classrooms," *Insights into Open Education* (May, 1977):2-9.

Schwarcz, Joseph H. *Ways of the Illustrator.* Chicago: American Library Association, 1982. 106-7.

Thompson, Stith. *The Folktale.* New York: Dryden Press, 1951.

Trustees of the Public Library of the City of Boston. *Proceedings of Children's Books International 4.* Boston: The Library, 1979.

Weiser, John, et al. "Fairy Tales in the Elementary School Curriculum," *Orbit* (June, 1981):18-21.

Yearsley, Macleod. *The Folklore of the Fairytale.* London: Watts and Co., 1924.

Zipes, Jack. *Breaking the Magic Spell: Radical Theories of Folk and Fairy Tales.* Austin: University of Texas Press, 1979.

Andrew Lang's *The Blue Fairy Book:* Changing the Course of History

by Glenn S. Burne

There have been only a few individual books that have changed the course of literary tradition. Andrew Lang's *The Blue Fairy Book* was one of them—at least in the realm of children's literature. The controversy between the two factions of realism and romance, and "the battle of the fairy tale," were still going strong in 1889 when Lang's book appeared; and despite the success of such children's works as Thackeray's "The Rose and the Ring," Lewis Carroll's *Alice* books, and the fantasies of George Macdonald, romances in general and fairy tales in particular were losing ground to the advancing forces of realism. Early in 1889, Mrs. E. M. Field wrote in her *The Child and His Book* that "At the present moment the fairy tale seems to have given way entirely in popularity to the child's story of real life, the novel of childhood, in which no effort is spared to make children appear as they are" (177). And in *Andrew Lang, A Critical Biography*, Roger Lancelyn Green says that in mid-Victorian England fairy tales had "almost ceased to be read in British nurseries, and the novel of child life, the stories of Mrs. Ewing, Mrs. Molesworth, and L. L. Meade, were the only fare" (82). Just before her book was published, however, Mrs. Field added this footnote: "Since the above was written eighteen months ago, the tide of popularity seems to have set strongly in the direction of the old fairy tales." Green believes that "it would probably be no exaggeration to say that Lang was entirely responsible for this change in the public taste" (82).

Interestingly enough, the book that effected the change was seen as an experiment, both by Lang and his publishers, who were not at all sure there would be a market for a volume of fairy tales—this in spite of the fact that Lang was a well known author with an impressive list of successful titles to his credit, works for both adults and children. As it turned out, of course, *The Blue Fairy Book* was enormously popular, so much so that Lang hastened to collect and publish a sequel, *The Red Fairy Book,* in time for the Christmas trade the next year. Then followed ten more volumes of "color fairy books," almost annually, all of them receiving a warm welcome.

Almost everything in Lang's life up to 1889 prepared him to edit fairy books. He was born and raised on the Scottish border, a land rich in local legends, ghost stories and superstitions, and populated, beyond a doubt, by fairies, elves, and bogies. The young Lang was steeped in fairy lore, and he added to the local stories and "border ballads" by his avid reading of the fairy tales of Perrault, Grimm, Mme. d'Aulnoy, *The Arabian Nights,* and Sir George Dasent's popular *Tales from the Norse.* These early imaginative experiences were later to develop into intellectual and scholarly interests. His classical training at Oxford was reflected in his translations (in collaboration) of the *Iliad* (1883) and the *Odyssey* (1879), but while a don at Oxford he shifted his attentions to the emerging science of anthropology, and soon earned a very respectable reputation as a folklorist. Lang thrived on controversy, engaging in spirited anthropological debates with eminent figures like Max Muller, and he "vastly enlarged the concept of folklore" by rejecting the current tendency to restrict that concept to European peasant traditions and by emphasizing the more inclusive oral inheritance of all races in all parts of the world. Lang was fascinated by the "universality" of fairy tales, "the correspondence, the recurrence," their *mythic* tendencies (Dorson 212).

To support his theories of the independent origins of similar stories, Lang began collecting examples from all over the world— written tales, oral accounts reported by travelers and explorers, missionaries, any and all sources. His belief in independent invention and universality did not prevent him from occasionally focussing on national cultures, as in his "The Folk-Lore of France" (1878); but in 1896 he restated the basic article of his creed: "All peoples notoriously tell the same myths, fairy tales, fables, and improper stories, repeat the same proverbs, are amused by the same riddles or devinettes, and practice the same, or closely analogous, religious rites and mysteries." This credo will be echoed in his various prefaces to his collections of stories, and is reflected in his choice of fairy tales in *The Blue Fairy Book* and its sequels. The "color fairy books" include original tales, many of them published for the first time, from such widespread sources as India, Brazil, Hungary, Australia, Africa, Japan, China, Egypt, the Iberian peninsula, the South Sea Islands, and one of Lang's favorites, the "Red Indian" of the Americas, as well as western Europe. In his prefaces, Lang often invites his readers to note similarities in the basic plots of the diverse stories.

In *The Blue Fairy Book,* however, Lang tends to stick rather close to home: of the thirty-seven stories, only four are of "exotic" origins—"The Bronze Ring" from Asia Minor, and three tales from the *Arabian Nights* which were sometimes omitted from subsequent editions. He chose his stories for this volume largely from the traditional and familiar of western Europe and justified doing so in his preface: "the tales in this volume are intended for children, who will like, it is hoped, the old stories that have pleased so many generations." And elsewhere he expressed his conviction that children enjoy hearing their favorite stories re-told. In a long introduction that appears only in the first edition (it is omitted even from the Dover reprint of that edition), Lang explains that some of the stories are presented in existing translations (but usually modified somewhat), while others are freshly translated, or adapted, by persons he names in his preface. Lang himself did very few translations: his job was to collect the stories, select those to be included in the volume, and supervise the translating, with the aid of his wife, who was especially concerned that the vocabularies and sentence-structures were appropriate for young readers.

As a good folklorist, Lang often preferred the rough, "savage" versions of tales as they are found in oral forms among the world's peoples, yet in his first two color fairy books he included many of the sophisticated "court fairy tales" from France. Charles Perrault is represented by seven tales—just about all of his elegant, gently satirical stories, which were written as much for the court of Louis XIV as for the children of the time—and for these Lang chose the "old English version of the eighteenth century" (apparently that of Robert Samber, 1729). Lang explains that he preferred Perrault's "Cinderella or the Little Glass Slipper," with its fairy godmother and benign ending to those involving the "helpful animals" and bloody revenge on the evil sisters.

He also included several tales by the refined ladies of the French court: five by Madame d'Aulnoy ("The Yellow Dwarf," "Felicia and the Pot of Pinks," "The White Cat," "Pretty Goldilocks," and "The Wonderful Sheep"), and one each by Mme. Leprince de Beaumont ("Prince Hyacinth and the Dear Little Princess") and Mme. de Villeneuve ("Beauty and the Beast"). For the latter, Lang chose an adaptation and condensation of Villeneuve's original and very long (over three hundred pages) story rather than Mme. de Beaumont's later and more familiar short version.

Lang's decision to include so many of these polished French stories might have been influenced by his having published, in the previous year, his *Perrault's Popular Tales,* along with "Johnny Nut and the Golden Goose," translated from the French of Charles Deulin (1887). Also, he had just published his own fairy tales, written in an urbane style with strong tones of parody and burlesque: "The Princess Nobody" (1884), in which he drew on a number of familiar fairy-tale devices; "The Gold of Fairnilee" (1888), which is based on tales, legends, and his personal experiences of the Scottish border; and "Prince Prigio" (1889), which, combined with "Prince Ricardo of "Pantouflia" (1893), would later be published as *Chronicles of Pantouflia*. In the volumes following the first two fairy books, however, Lang's selections draw mainly from the "savage" folk-tales, with a few taken from the French *Cabinet des Fees* and Hans Christian Andersen as the only more sophisticated stories admitted.

Lang chose seven tales from the Brothers Grimm for *The Blue Fairy Book*, most of them familiar ("Hansel and Gretel," "Rumpelstiltskin," "The Youth Who Learned What Fear Was," "Snow White and Rose Red," "The Goose Girl," "Trusty John," and "The Brave Little Tailor"); and he chose four tales from Scandinavia ("East of the Sun and West of the Moon," "The Master-Maid," "Why the Sea is Salt," "The Princess on the Glass Hill"). Lang considered the northland—with its dark forests, enclosing caves and deep tarns, its woodcutters, wolves, and trolls—to be an especially suitable setting for fairy stories, and he comments on the relative paucity of children's stories from the southern regions. He explains that his borrowings from Sir George Dasent's *Tales from the Norse* differ from other stories in *The Blue Fairy Book* "by a certain largeness of treatment; the clear, cold air of the north, a healthy fragrance of pine forests, blows through them, borne by the strong north wind (xx).

Lang also provides one tale of his own invention, adapted from ancient Greece. "The Terrible Head" is his re-telling of the story of Perseus and Medusa, in which he draws from the accounts of Pindar, Simonides, and Apollodorus. He suppressed all local references and proper names, replacing them with "the King," "the Prince," "a beautiful girl"—even the frightful Greek kraken becomes merely "a monstrous beast out of the sea." In this way Lang transforms the story into an ordinary folktale, like something out of Grimm. Lang believed that the Greek scene, "by literary association, was no longer sufficiently simple and wild." In a passage quoted in Green's *Critical Biography*, he explains: "The civilized peoples have elaborated their child-like tales into the chief romantic myths, as of the Ship Argo, and the sagas of Heracles and Odysseus...European peasants keep them far more akin to the savage than to the Greek form" (83). So, after the first two fairy books, Lang does not adapt any more "high mythology" stories from Greece, or from Scandinavia—only folktales. (He did, nevertheless, retell Greek myths, for children, in later books.)

Lang included only two stories from the English tradition in *The Blue Fairy Book*—he believed them to be "so scanty" and of inferior quality. His friend Joseph Jacobs took exception to this view in the preface to his own *English Fairy Tales*, claiming he had gathered over 140 good English and Scottish stories. But Lang was referring to strictly *English* stories, stating in the preface to *The*

Blue Fairy Book that "they have been so flattened and stultified, and crammed with gross rural jests, in the chap books, that we can only give a decent if dull version of Jack the Giant Killer and Dick Whittington" (xxi). He held quite a different view of Scottish stories, and he included two at the end of his book, intended, he says, primarily for Scottish children. He admits that English children might be puzzled by the Scottish dialect in "The Black Bull of Norroway" and "The Red Etin," but he felt that "the Etin and the Bull are such very old friends of the editor's, that he could not omit them when the fairies were invited to the festival" (xxi). In some recent editions of *The Blue Fairy Book,* the Scottish dialect has vanished, replaced by standard English.

Readers of certain later editions of *The Blue Fairy Book* might be unaware that four of the original thirty-seven stories have been omitted, since the editors altered Lang's preface so as to make no mention of the missing stories. The deletions include a condensation and adaptation of *Gulliver's Travels,* and three stories from Galland's early eighteenth-century version of *The Arabian Nights:* "The Forty Thieves" (Ali Baba), "Aladdin and his Wonderful Lamp," and "The Story of Prince Ahmed and the Fairy Paribanou." Lang included the account of Gulliver and the Lilliputians (in a rigorously bowdlerized version, of course) primarily because it was a great favorite of young readers, at least when "the marvels are left and satire subdued." But some critics have strongly objected to the inclusion of Gulliver in a volume of fairy tales. J. R. R. Tolkien claims that "it has no business in this place" (he says it belongs to "the class of traveller's tales") (12), and even Green, one of Lang's strongest admirers, finds its presence "inexplicable"—"alien to anything in any of the fairy books" *(Critical Biography* 81). But why a tale involving "little people" and "giants"—so dear to hearts of fairy-tale readers—is "alien" is not made clear.

It is also unclear why the tales from *The Arabian Nights* should have been deleted (specifically, from the readily available series of color fairy books, with introductions by Mary Gould Davis, (first published in 1948.) In fact, *The Arabian Nights* seem to have been the object of a conspiracy of silence: not only is reference to these stories carefully excised from Lang's prefaces, but his two principal biographers, Roger Lancelyn Green and Eleanor De Selms Langstaff, omit Lang's *The Arabian Nights Entertainment* (1898) from their indexes and bibliographies. This work does receive mention in passing in Green's *Tellers of Tales,* but only to be dismissed as belonging to "other such complete and partial departures from the fairy kingdom" (144). But surely magic lamps, genies, "open sesames," and the Fairy Paribanou qualify for admission to that kingdom. The translations are all innocuous

144

enough, as Lang used the tidied-up adaptations from Galland rather than Richard F. Burton's unexpurgated versions; so one can only wonder at the reasons for the Arabian Nights exclusion. Perhaps the stories were not considered sufficiently edifying. Lang himself observed that there is nothing moral about these stories; both "The Forty Thieves" and "Aladdin" show the rewards of pure luck, "caprices of chance, or of love," but they are stories that he and countless others had enjoyed as young readers.

The deleted "Story of Prince Ahmed and the Fairy Paribanou" is also a typical Arabian Nights tale, involving a contest between three brothers as to who can bring home the most unique and valuable gift and so win the hand of the Princess. The gifts all turn out to be magical and of equal value, so the contest is a draw. The story then shifts to Prince Ahmed's involvement with the Fairy Paribanou, his outwitting of those who would destroy him, and his ultimate victory with the help of the Fairy's dwarfish but lethal brother. It is a good story, full of exotic Eastern details and enchantments, but much too long—a possible reason for its omission. One can, however, find all three stories in Lang's *Arabian Nights* (1898).

Lang's editing of *The Blue Fairy Book* was obviously a labor of love—even as an adult, he cherished fairy tales and retained a keen sense of childhood, and of the kind of stories children enjoy. He said that in reading and arranging the contents he experienced "perhaps, as much pleasure as the child who reads them or hears them for the first time.... 'Blue Beard,' that little tragic and dramatic masterpiece, moves me yet; I still tremble for Puss in Boots when the Ogre turns into a lion; and still one's heart goes with the girl who seeks her lost and enchanted lover, and wins him again in the third night of watching and tears" (xiii). In his own stories and in those he edited, he was offering to the young a "playful and fanciful excursion into another world," but the stories also had a more serious side: as Anita Moss suggests, they comment upon "the value of certain modes of human conduct," and "they provide encounters with evil and the means of eliminating that evil" (254). And he would have agreed with recent critics who maintain that fairy tales come closer to expressing symbolically the realities of human experience than most "adult" or "realistic" novels. Three years after publishing *The Blue Fairy Book*, in a review of some pallid "modern tales," he made some observations that deserve to be quoted in full:

In the old stories, despite the impossibility of the incidents, the interest is always real and human. The princes and princesses fall in love and marry—nothing could be more human than that. Their lives and loves are crossed by human sorrows. In many the lover and his lady are separated by a magic oblivion: someone has kissed the prince, and he instantly forgets his old love, and can only be recovered by her devotion. This is nearly the central situation of the *Volsunga Saga*, though there it ends tragically, whereas all ends well in a fairy tale. The hero and heroine are persecuted or separated by cruel stepmothers or enchanters; they have wanderings and sorrows to suffer; they have adventures to achieve and difficulties to overcome; they must display courage, loyalty, and address, courtesy, gentleness, and gratitude. Thus they are living in a real world, though it wears a mythical face, though there are giants and lions in the way. The old fairy tales which a silly sort of people disparage as too wicked and ferocious for the nursery, are really "full of matter," and unobtrusively teach the true lessons of our wayfaring world of perplexities and obstructions.

(Green, *Andrew Lang* 48)

Lang believed that teaching the "true lessons" of our world could include showing people at their best, as people all over the world like stories in which "loyalty and generosity are rewarded," both by humans and "grateful beasts," citing as examples the universally popular "Cinderella," "Toads and Pearls," and "The Bronze Ring." (For some unknown reason, Lang alternates between two titles: "Toads and Diamonds" and "Toads and Pearls"). He grants that some stories end badly, "a thing unknown in true popular fairy tradition": "The Yellow Dwarf" and "The Wonderful Sheep"; but he finds that their unhappy endings are balanced by their "wonderful touches of supernatural." In fact, "The Yellow Dwarf," in which evil triumphs, was one of Lang's favorites, partly for its marvelous enchantments and partly for its realism:

When the Princess awakens, after her betrothal to the Yellow Dwarf, and hopes it was a dream, and finds on her finger the fatal ring of one red hair, we have a brave touch of horror and of truth. All of us have wakened and struggled with a dim evil memory, and trusted it was a dream, and found, in one form or another, a proof, a shape of that ring of red hair. *(The Blue Fairy Book* xviii)

On the other hand, while he stresses the truths to be experienced in fairy tales, Lang was also aware that certain actions and consequences in early folktales are often unintelligible in modern versions, as they were based on ancient beliefs and taboos which have their equivalents all over the world, and usually involve some kind of disobedience. He cites as examples the disobedience and punishments of Blue Beard's wives, and the consequences, in "East of the Sun and West of the Moon," when the bride-to-be actually *sees* her husband. But perhaps the strangeness of some of these actions merely adds to the mystery and charm of the stories.

Critics have frequently noted that many "fairy tales" contain no fairies. This observation has been directed at Perrault and Grimm as well as Lang and is, of course, true. But while there may be no fairies literally present in some stories, they all take place in the "land of Faery"—the enchanted realm where the magical and the marvelous, free from the usual laws of nature, can work their imaginative wonders. *The Blue Fairy Book,* in the diversity of its original thirty-seven tales, is a testament to the riches that can be found in that land of Faery. Most of the themes, characters, and devices of fairyland are there. Moreover, the stories, for the most part, fulfil what seemed to be Lang's central criterion: each tale must be intrinsically interesting—it must stir the imagination and delight the senses through its lively detail and fanciful enchantments. While there is sometimes a similarity in basic plots, there is also a pleasing variety. A plot may please, for example, through a comfortable familiarity, a predictability, or through suspense and surprise. Predictability characterizes "The Princess on the Glass Hill," where there is little doubt as to the outcome, only as to how it is to be achieved. The structure is traditionally ritualistic: the narrative moves through a series of repeated refrains, mounting to the climax: the third brother, riding the third enchanted horse up the glass mountain, acquires the third apple (and the princess) on the third day of the contest. While seeing the resemblance to the Cinderella story (the hero is even called "Cinderlad"), a reader also enjoys the symmetry with which fatality works the transformation of the deserving young hero from a humble drudge to a victorious knight in gold armor. On the other hand, Lang offers stories of greater complexity and suspense, in which the outcome is uncertain until the end, as in "Blue Beard," and in "The Yellow Dwarf," where a sense of precariousness and menace hangs over the story up to the unusual (unhappy) resolution.

Lang seems less interested in advancing a specific moral (he omits the "moralities" Perrault appended to his tales) than in stimulating the imagination by means of the cherished devices of fairyland: talking animals and magical metamorphoses of man and beast; the fortunate appearance of "helpful animals," fairy godmothers, or wizards when the young hero or heroine most needs them; the discovery of a magic potion or artifact (a magic lamp, an enchanted ring, a cap that provides the wearer with invisibility). But in Lang's stories, fortuitous outside help is not usually sufficient: heroes and heroines must display exemplary behavior—courage, loyalty, steadfastness, unwavering love; otherwise success, even survival, will not be theirs. On the other hand, even the virtuous do not always triumph, as in "The Marvellous Sheep," whereas moral mediocrity, aided by chance or pure luck, may enjoy scarcely deserved rewards, as it does for Aladdin and Ali Baba.

Lang also prefers a kind of "symbolic realism," like that of the ring of red thread in "The Yellow Dwarf"—a realism that often appears as a logical working out of an earlier commitment or decision which imposes a future obligation in exchange for a present boon. A beleaguered character makes a promise—the relinquishing of a first-born child, or the hand of a daughter—to buy his or her way out of a crisis or to have an immediate reward, and then has to live with the consequences when the hour of payment arrives.

A wide range of personalities, ambitions, and desires is found in Lang's fairyland: it is a realm of hyperboles, of extremes. Characters are usually either impoverished woodcutters or millers, or they are ostentatiously wealthy kings and princes; they are either grotesquely ugly (like the long-nosed Prince Hyacinth and the various ogres, witches, and dwarfs) or they are the most beautiful and handsome in all the world (the standard prince and princess). The French writers especially love the extravagances of wealth—awesome quantities of gold and silver, exotic jewels and pearls, sumptuous coaches, elegant clothing, lavish foods, reflecting the values of the French royal court whose only equals in conspicuous consumption were the kings of the Arabian Nights. But even these extravagances, by their very excess, serve to enhance the sense of wonder and make-believe.

The charm of the tales is further enhanced by the illustrations by different artists in the various editions. But, one should seek out, if at all possible, copies or reproductions of the illustrations in the original edition of 1889—those by H. J. Ford and G. P. Jacomb Hood. They make a vivid and lasting impression, and possibly Green is right when he says that Ford has never been equalled as "the artist of Fairy Land." Hood is equally talented, but in one instance, rather inaccurate, prompting Lang, at the conclusion of his introduction, to chide his illustrator friend for depicting "Monsieur de la Barbe Bleue as a Turk," pointing out that one of the heroine's brothers was a "Dragoon" and the other a "Mousquetaire"—all French and Christians: "had he been a Turk, Blue Beard need not have been wedded to one wife at a time." In more recent editions, nevertheless, the villain continues to appear as a ferocious Turk.

Even though Lang's first two fairy books were extemely popular, he did not foresee that he would produce ten more such books in the next two decades. In fact, in the preface to *The Green Fairy Book* (1892) he described it as "the third, and probably the last, of the Fairy books of many colours," and he continued to publish other kinds of books for children, about a dozen of them, every year or so, such as *The Blue Poetry Book* (1891), *The True Story Book* (1893), *The Book of Romance* (1902), to name just a few titles; but popular demand for fairy tales persisted, and Lang was happy to comply. There seems to be general agreement that he will be remembered primarily for the fairy books, though there is understandable disagreement as to which volume is the best. Some readers have preferred the later fairy books, as they offer a wider choice of less familiar tales, and some might choose such editions as *The Rainbow Fairy Book* (1977), which represents a selection drawn from all the color books. But *The Blue Fairy Book* remains a perennial favorite. It offers young readers a fine introduction to the fairy tale, in excellent translations geared to the reading-level of the average child. A recent study has pointed out that the words rarely exceed two syllables (though the sentences tend to be longer and have more clauses than in modern writing), with the reading-difficulty level today ranging from the fifth to the ninth grades (ages ten to fourteen) (Langstaff 144). However, this "simplified" language retains all the essential vividness and color and seems quite appropriate to the tales being told.

The Blue Fairy Book, then, is not only important historically, for having influenced profoundly the course of children's literature, but it retains its value and popularity today. In the well-chosen variety of its tales, providing its readers with a pleasing mixture of the well known and the lesser known stories from several cultures, rendered in a lucid and lively style to be enjoyed by child and adult alike, the book has inspired a plenitude of imitations but has been replaced by none. It remains a model of its kind.

REFERENCES

Darton, Harvey. *Children's Books in England; Five Centuries of Social Life.* London: Cambridge U.P., 1932.

Dorson, Richard M. *The British Folklorists, A History.* Chicago: U. of Chicago Press; London: Routledge and Kegan Paul, 1968, 206-220.

Field, Mrs. E. M. *The Child and His Book.* London: Darton, 1892; rpr. Detroit: Singing Tree Press, 1968.

Green, Roger Lancelyn. *Andrew Lang, A Critical Biography.* Leicester, England: Edmund Ward, 1946.

. *Andrew Lang.* New York: Henry Z. Walck, 1962.

_____. "Epilogue." *The Rainbow Fairy Book*. Ed. Kathleen Lines. New York: Shocken Books, 1977.

_____. *Tellers of Tales: Children's Books and Their Authors from 1800 to 1968*. London: Kaye and Ward, 1946.

Lang, Andrew, ed. *The Blue Fairy Book*. London: Longmans, Green, and Co., 1889.

_____. ed. *The Blue Fairy Book*. New York: Dover Publications, 1969.

Langstaff, Eleanor de Selms. *Andrew Lang*. Boston: Twayne Publishers, 1978.

Moss, Anita. "Children and Fairy Tales: A Study of Nineteenth-Century British Fantasy." Diss. Indiana University, 1979.

Tolkien, J. R. R. *Tree and Leaf*. Boston: Houghton Mifflin Company, 1965.

Weintraub, Joseph. "Andrew Lang: Critic of Romance," *English Literature in Transition, 1880-1920* 18 (1975).

Edward Lear's *A Book of Nonsense:* A Scroobious Classic

by Mark I. West

In 1832, a twenty-year-old artist left London to take up residence in Knowsley Hall, a country manor not far from Liverpool. His name was Edward Lear, and he was hired by the owner of the manor, the twelfth Earl of Derby, to make drawings of Lord Derby's private collection of animals and birds. Assembling the large menagerie had long been one of Lord Derby's pet projects, and he wanted Lear to provide the illustrations for a book about the collection. Lear welcomed the opportunity. It not only bolstered his fledgling art career, but it also provided him with a degree of financial security, something that had been missing from his life since his father's bankruptcy in 1816. Because Lord Derby was in no rush and the menagerie was so large, Lear set to work at a leisurely pace, drawing out his work for more than four years. During that time, he dreamt that his creations would be recognized as significant. And some of them were; but they were not the creations that he hoped would win him fame. The detailed renderings of animals and birds that Lear labored over in the menagerie have all but been forgotten, while the creations that he hastily produced in the nursery to amuse the children of Knowsley Hall have won world-wide acclaim.

A number of children, including Lord Derby's grandchildren, lived in Knowsley Hall, and Lear often spent his free time with them. At first he had little choice in the matter. Lear was too young and unknown to be included among Lord Derby's own circle of companions, and the solitary nature of his work precluded much contact with the other employees. But the children took an interest in the young artist. Lear's unpretentious manner, absurd sense of humor, and ability to draw funny pictures soon made him popular with them. For his part, Lear tended to prefer their company over that of some of the stuffy adults who inhabited Knowsley Hall. Even after he became friends with Lord Derby, he often retreated to the nursery when he felt irked by what he called the "apathetic tone assumed by lofty society" (Davidson 17).

In addition to sharing jokes with his child friends, Lear would occasionally write a poem for them which he would illustrate with a humorous sketch. He invariably wrote limericks, a verse form that he adopted as his own after a friend introduced him to a limerick about an "Old Man of Tobago" who lived on "rice gruel and sago." Lear wrote his limericks one or two at a time over a period of several years. He wrote them only to delight the children, and he had no plans to publish them. The limericks eventually circulated throughout Lord Derby's household, and even the stuffy adults seemed to enjoy them. It pleased Lear that his limericks were popular, but he continued to think of himself as an artist, not as a poet. Still, he saved his limericks even after he left Knowsley Hall, and he wrote a few new ones when he returned for a visit or when he met other children.

Upon finishing his work for Lord Derby, Lear decided to make his living as a landscape artist. For the next several years, he traveled throughout Italy and a number of other European countries, producing many picturesque canvases but very few limericks. In 1845, he returned to England to oversee the publication of three of his books, all of which were brought out during the following year. As he saw it, the most important of these was a travel book entitled *Illustrated Excursions in Italy*. The other two stemmed from work that he had done a decade or so earlier. One, entitled *Gleanings from the Menagerie and Aviary at Knowsley Hall*, contained the drawings that Lord Derby had commissioned, and the other, which he called *A Book of Nonsense*, consisted of his limericks and their accompanying drawings.

It is not clear why Lear finally decided to publish these limericks. The children for whom Lear originally wrote them must have urged him to do so, and undoubtedly several of his friends concurred. Whatever the reason, Lear seemed to have some doubts about the wisdom of publishing his poems, for he refused to publish the book under his name, a practice that he did not follow with any of his other books. His use of the word "nonsense" was also indicative of Lear's ambivalence. As Emile Cammaerts pointed out in *The Poetry of Nonsense*, "Lear chose this word as an humble disparagement of his poems and as a plea for the public's indulgence" (3). But Lear soon discovered that he had no reason to worry. The book became an instant critical and commercial success, and has since come to be regarded as a pivotal work in children's literature.

Lear includes 112 limericks in *A Book of Nonsense,* and most share certain characteristics. An incredibly eccentric person, frequently an old man, appears in each limerick. These characters often look different from ordinary people, and they almost always engage in unusual activities. Several sit atop trees, others eat dishes or mice, and one old man dances with a raven. Many of the limericks also feature a nameless crowd that Lear simply refers to as "they." The main characters and "they" are usually at odds, but once in awhile "they" end up helping the main character. The limericks generally revolve around the peculiar things that happen to the eccentrics. For example, the man who consorts with a raven meets up with an unfortunate end:

> There was an Old Man of Whitehaven,
> Who danced a quadrille with a Raven;
> But they said—"It's absurd, to encourage this bird!"
> So they smashed that Old Man of Whitehaven.   (39)

Another character has an unpleasant experience while supervising his wife's cooking:

> There was an Old Man of Peru,
> Who watched his wife making a stew;
> But once by mistake, in a stove she did bake,
> That unfortunate Man of Peru.   (28)

Not all of Lear's characters expire. Some manage to survive even the most shattering of experiences:

> There was an Old Man of Nepaul,
> From his horse had a terrible fall;
> But, though split quite in two, by some very strong glue,
> They mended that Man of Nepaul.   (27)

Although Lear intended that the limericks be humorous, he never ends them with a clever punch line. The humor comes from the absurd nature of the characters and the situations that Lear describes.

Lear's illustrations greatly enhance the humorous impact of the limericks. His nonsense drawings are whimsical and remarkably modernistic in appearance. He uses very few lines and makes no attempt at realism. Playfully distorting the features of his characters, Lear drew men whose noses resemble elephant trunks and women whose limbs bend in unnatural directions. Often he ignores common rules of proportion. The old man who ends up in his wife's stove is a mere fraction of her size, and some of the birds and insects in the book are nearly as large as the people. Lear originally drew many of the pictures while surrounded by a roomful of excited children, and this undoubtedly contributed to the pictures' spontaneous and almost childlike quality. In short, Lear's absurd illustrations perfectly complement his nonsensical limericks.

When compared with most of the books that adults wrote for children during the first half of the nineteenth century, A Book of Nonsense is revolutionary. Lear completely dispenses with the didactic tradition that characterizes children's literature of this period. The book contains no thinly disguised sermons, lessons, or lectures, and none of the characters serve as a role model. Lear sought only to amuse his readers. Lear's ability to break away from the didactic tradition was tied, in part, to his unusual life. He had no children of his own, so he was not overly concerned about the problems of child-rearing. He shied away from organized religion, and consequently, he had no desire to teach religious lessons. Because he led an eccentric lifestyle himself, he did not think it necessary to instruct children about the importance of conforming to societal norms. As a child, he had never attended school, and he felt thankful that he hadn't. Thus, he felt no compulsion to praise traditional education. And finally, since his parents practically abandoned him when he was a young boy, he was not inclined to glorify adults. All of these factors served to distance Lear from most of his fellow authors of children's books.

Another difference between A Book of Nonsense and other children's books of the time is Lear's use of humor. Children's authors of this period did not generally emphasize humor, and those who did tended to mix a lot of cute sentimentality in with their jokes and funny stories. As a result, much of the humorous poetry written for children during the nineteenth century amused adults more than it did children. Lear's humor, however, did appeal to children. They liked the comical violence that ran through many of his limericks. They appreciated the nonsensical turn of events that Lear described, and they laughed at all of the preposterous adults who peopled his poems. In other words, children liked Lear's sense of humor because it was so similar to their own. In *Children's Humor: A Psychological Analysis,* Martha Wolfenstein argues that children often use nonsense to cope with common childhood anxieties. For example, in an attempt to quell their envious feelings toward grownups, children may rework adult commands into statements of pure nonsense (23-24). Similarly, Lear, through his use of nonsense, transforms several sources of children's anxieties (death, rejection, and powerlessness) into sources of amusement.

The drawings in *A Book of Nonsense* also set the volume apart from most nineteenth-century children's books. In a time when children's illustrators strove to create realistic pictures, Lear moved toward abstraction. His colleagues prided themselves on the detail that they included, whereas Lear sought to simplify. It was not until the twentieth century that many other children's illustrators began to follow his lead. Lear was also one of the few children's authors from this time period to illustrate his own writings, and perhaps the only one who could strike a perfect harmony between the literary and the visual images.

Lear's blend of limericks and simple line drawings met with tremendous success. Soon after its publication in 1846, *A Book of Nonsense* achieved the status of a bestseller. The resultant royalties provided Lear with an unexpected source of income, much of which he gave to charities or to his relatives. In addition to being popular with children, the book won high praise from prominent literary figures. John Ruskin, for example, wrote,

> The most beneficent and innocent of all books yet produced is the *Book of Nonsense,* with its corollary carols—inimitable and refreshing, and perfect in rhythm. I really don't know any author to whom I am half so grateful, for my idle self, as Edward Lear. I shall put him first of my hundred authors.
>
> (Davidson 265)

The response to his book gratified Lear, but it did not convince him to become a full-time writer of nonsense. He continued to devote most of his time to traveling, painting, and drawing. Still, he remained interested in nonsense, and often included nonsense writing in his letters to friends, which contained numerous puns, nonsense words, and words that he deliberately misspelled (Livingston). In 1861, he released an enlarged edition of *A Book of Nonsense,* and this time he published it under his own name. In fact, when he overheard a man on a train say that the book was written by another person who wrote under the pen name of Edward Lear, he insisted on correcting the mistaken gentleman.

In the 1870s, Lear finally brought out some new books of nonsense poetry. He published *Nonsense Songs, Stories, Botany and Alphabets* in 1871, *More Nonsense* in 1872, and *Laughable Lyrics* in 1877. *More Nonsense* consisted of limericks, but the other two books contained longer nonsense poems. Among the most famous of these were "The Owl and the Pussy-Cat," "The Duck and the Kangaroo," "The Jumblies," and "The Dong with a Luminous Nose." These longer poems are somewhat more sophisticated than his limericks, and as Ina Rae Hark suggests, they have a melancholic undertone that does not appear in *A Book of Nonsense* (52-53). Whereas his early limericks focus on individuals and their conflicts with society, his longer poems often deal with unusual couples who must flee from society in order to preserve their friendships. His limericks reflect the energy of a rebellious young man, while his longer poems express the frustrations and sadness of an aging homosexual in a sexually repressed society. Both his limericks and his longer poems are superb nonsense poetry, but because they differ in tone and content, they appeal to somewhat different audiences. Children can easily appreciate the limericks, but they might have more difficulty relating to the characters in Lear's longer poems. In many ways, these poems deal with specifically adult concerns and situations.

Following the publication of *A Book of Nonsense*, several other writers began to take an interest in nonsense poetry. Among these, Lewis Carroll, a mathematics professor, emerged as Lear's only serious rival. Carroll included a number of nonsense poems in *Alice's Adventures in Wonderland* (1865) and *Through the Looking Glass* (1872). Lear and Carroll not only shared a love for the absurd, but they also led similar lives. Both loved children but never had any of their own. Both viewed their writing as secondary to their other professions, and both, of course, were British. Curiously, they never met or even indicated that they knew of each other's work.

The twentieth century has seen a proliferation of nonsense poetry for children. During the first half of the century, A. A. Milne, Ogden Nash, and Laura Richards became known as nonsense poets. In more recent years, N. M. Bodecker, John Ciardi, Roald Dahl, Theodor Geisel (Dr. Seuss), Arnold Lobel, Karla Kuskin, David McCord, Theodore Roethke, Shel Silverstein, and many others have made significant contributions to the field of nonsense poetry. Like Lear, Geisel and Lobel have also illustrated their own poems. Nonsense poetry, in other words, has grown up around Lear and Carroll and is now a well established branch of children's literature.

But even though Lear's *A Book of Nonsense* now shares the shelf with other volumes of nonsense poetry, the stature of the book has in no way diminished. A few scholars sometimes quibble over the structure of his limericks. William Harmon, for example, argues that Lear's limericks "do not meet the standards of the perfect limerick" (70) because Lear usually combined the third and fourth lines and tended to end the last line with the same word that he used at the end of the first line. Although Harmon's charges are correct, only a rigid purist would feel that they weaken Lear's limericks. Most critics describe *A Book of Nonsense* as a work of genius. Authorities on illustration cite it as an example of a perfect picture book (Meyer 56). The book's humor remains as fresh today as it was in 1846, and its sales are just as brisk. It continues to delight children and to inspire poets and artists. It is one of the few children's books to start a tradition rather than follow one. Like a towering old oak tree in a grove of saplings, it remains a most impressive landmark.

REFERENCES

Cammaerts, Emile. *The Poetry of Nonsense.* New York: E. P. Dutton, 1926.

Davidson, Angus. *Edward Lear: Landscape Painter and Nonsense Poet.* New York: Barnes and Noble, 1968.

Hark, Ina Rae. *Edward Lear.* Boston: Twayne Publishers, 1982.

Harmon, William. "Lear, Limericks, and Some Other Verse Forms." *Children's Literature* 10 (1982): 70-76.

Lear, Edward.*A Book of Nonsense. The Complete Nonsense of Edward Lear.* Ed. Holbrook Jackson. New York: Dover Publications, 1951.

Livingston, Myra Cohn. *A Learical Lexicon.* New York: Atheneum, 1985.

Meyer, Susan E. *A Treasury of the Great Children's Book Illustrators.* New York: Harry N. Abrams, 1983.

Wolfenstein, Martha. *Children's Humor: A Psychological Analysis.* Bloomington, Indiana: Indiana University Press, 1978.

David McCord's Poems:
Something Behind the Door

by Myra Cohn Livingston

Inadequate form, George Steiner notes in *Tolstoy or Dostoevsky,* entails the "more significant dilemma of inadequate truth": "With the irruption of the unconscious into poetics" a real problem has arisen as "classical methods of narrative and discourse became inadèquate.... What we can hear of the language of the unconscious falls too readily into our own syntax. Perhaps we do not yet know how to listen" (222).

A reader, Theodore Roethke writes, must have curiosity and respect, must not be afraid to enter a world that is slightly different from his own. A reader, other voices whisper, must read well, must possess "suspension of disbelief." A reader must be liberal of spirit. An author, a poet waits for the "right reader" and cherishes him. Emerson tells us that it is the good reader who makes the good book.

We must be charitable therefore, we readers tell ourselves. We must try to listen, to keep our curiosity alive, to be alert to the voice of the new poetries and what they have to tell us about our fragmented world. We must try to recognize that we live in a time when the old centers do not hold. We hear for the thousandth time the echoes of Yeats, holding our breath for fear the falcon should not return. Yet we grow weary. After years of reading poets who would ask us to listen to their precious inner psyches, their confessions, dreams and lies, their poverty-stricken self-directed wishes, we realize we may have listened and tried to understand long enough. The country literally crawls with those who would engage us in worship of the incoherent, the urban scene with its tawdry images, its places of poverty and squalor. We are thrown back upon idiocy and babbling and the black arts, upon the romantic belief in the individual and a freedom untempered by self-discipline, upon the spillage of raw emotion, irrelevant imagery, ersatz primitivism and the ghosts of all the fears and nightmares and horrors of the inner mind, the inner life.

Until recent times, this poetry has managed to confine itself to those who are old enough to choose their reading from the San Francisco beats, the New York School of pseudo-surrealism, the midwest poets, the confessionalists, and the imagists, or to those who dabble in the Concrete and Found, and who attack the Academics with fury. But those who are interested know that eventually children's poetry must be affected. Within the past decade, the inadequacies of form and truth and glorification of the unconscious has been invading children's poetry, with a sort of "garbage delight" that assaults literature itself, if we think of this branch of art as one which offers children growth and enrichment. There are not many who would swallow whole the idea that children must be made to observe Dr. Watt's busy bee or listen to Blake's false nurse, crippled in a nursery where there is no play, no dreaming and a table without cherries and nuts. But it is equally true that some of us have ignored too long the werewolfs and ghouls, the insidious symbols of the irresponsible unconscious that are creeping into the garden where children play.

One of the latest to jump the garden fence is a book, recently published, which is intended to "make new" Dr. Heinrich Hoffman's *Struwwelpeter*. (Americans have a penchant for "making it new," as Horace Gregory observed.) Certainly we all remember the verse-tales of Slovenly Peter and their varying effects upon us and our peers. There is the long-haired, unkempt and dirty Peter himself, always staring from the cover. There is Frederick who tortures animals, birds and insects and is finally bitten by a dog, and there is Augustus, who refuses to eat his soup and dies of malnutrition. And there is Little Suck-a-Thumb, who must go through life with only eight fingers.

Dr. Hoffman's reasons for writing *Struwwelpeter* are of interest. Displeased by the "Long tales, stupid collections of pictures, moralizing stories, beginning and ending with admonitions, like 'the good child must be truthful' or 'children must keep clean,'" Hoffman wrote his book in order to calm young children whom he had occasion to treat as a physician. Too often had he heard parents threaten their children whose behavior was bad with warnings about how chimney-sweeps might carry them away, or how doctors come with their "nasty medicine." "The consequence is," he wrote, "that the little angel, when ill, begins to cry violently and to struggle as soon as the physician comes into the room. On such occasions, a slip of paper and a pencil generally came to my assistance and helped the little antagonist dry his tears and allow the medical man to do his duty." ("Introduction," *The English Struwwelpeter*).

Dr. Hoffman might well be shocked to know that his verses were a far worse threat to generations of children than any medical treatment. But he lived in a different country, a different time, and if Suck-a-Thumb ended up with missing thumbs or Johnny fell into the river, it was not due to lack of warning. The children only harmed themselves. In later years, Jim was also advised not to let go of nurse's hand, and the cautionary tale became, in Hilaire Belloc's verses, a *tour de force*, its energy still later sustained by Sendak's Pierre, who learned to say "I care." But we are back to the garden now, and to the new book, *The Terrible Tales of Happy Days School,* besides which *Struwwelpeter* pales.

For here are eleven contemporary children, six of whom are dead before the end of the book, who not only maim themselves but hurt their parents and friends with their slovenly ways. Jane, who will not eat the cafeteria food, leaves the principal of the school unconscious, if not actually dead, and lands on a fork. Melissa refuses to keep her hamster's cage clean and ends up, after her brother pinches her, inside the cage with the hamsters biting and chewing on her. Jerome, who refuses to wash, finally gets into a shower

> But since the grime adhered like glue
> The skin beneath it came off too.
> It's hard to keep your insides in
> When you are left without your skin,
> So with an anguished shriek of pain
> All of Jerome went down the drain. (21)

Nancy teases a dog so unmercifully that it finally

> Chewed her till she came apart
> And ate her liver and her heart. (29)

There are some who will say that all of this is simply in fun, and children themselves know it is nonsense. There are some who will say that children also know that ogres, werewolves, vampires and the like do not exist. But there are others, like myself, who believe that the irresponsible images of the unconscious may be understood by adults, but have no place in the child's world unless there is some helpmeet, some guide, something on which the child may fall back. The parents of the Happy Days School children are stupid and ineffectual; they smile at their children's idiosyncracies or view them with pride.

But other books that have been creeping into the garden are devoid of parents, and their symbols are grim; thus the inadequate form also gives an inadequate truth. Here is one of Jack Prelutsky's *Nightmares:*

> The gruesome ghoul, the grisly ghoul,
> without the slightest noise
> waits patiently beside the school
> to feast on girls and boys.
>
>   . . .
> He cracks their bones and snaps their backs
> and squeezes out their lungs,
> he chews their thumbs like candy snacks
> and pulls apart their tongues. (32)

The ghoul is but one of dozens of wraiths and creatures. There is the will o' the wisp in the forest who "summons you down to your doom," the vampire who comes in the open window, the werewolf who roams the streets beneath the child's bedroom; in Prelutsky's *The Headless Horseman Rides Tonight*, there is the zombie who "waits within your room" and "has come to take you in it arms

> And you shiver and you scream
> for you know it's not a dream
> as the zombie nears your bed.   (16)

Apart from the other-worldly there are those children of meagre spirit who play mean tricks on each other; there are creatures with silly sounding names who overeat, or squash each other; there are greedy overweight people who cannot subsist by food so eat whatever is in sight. They are not the true inhabitants of the nonsense world—the domain of Edward Lear and X. J. Kennedy, Lewis Carroll and N. M. Bodecker—they are, on the contrary, quite real, and their images speak of an incoherent fractured world because there is no center, no order, no true nonsense.

But just as irresponsible, perhaps, is a world that is bereft of dark symbolism of any kind. It is a child's garden where there is only good and light. Stripped of all nonsense, this garden offers no room for free will or choice. Here children have no need to be scared or shiver, because all evil is cast out, all questions answered, all truth made clear. Here all is peaceful, right and purposeful, as in this piece from Marjorie Ainsborough Decker's *Christian Mother Goose Book:*

Twinkle, twinkle, little star,
    God has placed you where you are;
Up above the world so high
    You're God's light placed in the sky.   (12)

Even in word play is the child assaulted:

Lavender's blue, dilly, dilly,
    Lavender's green,
Teach me to say, dilly, dilly,
    John 3:16.
God loved the world, dilly, dilly,
    He gave His son,
To give His life, dilly, dilly,
    For everyone.   (41)

160

Inadequate form is inadequate truth. To distort nonsense is to destroy the child's right to grow, to play with words, to sort out what is true and what is false. To present children with subjective images rather than meaningful symbols, to assault them with the spectres of the inner mind, to give them ghoul and zombie, bowed heads, holy men in trees, children poor in spirit, seems to some of us irresponsible and even immoral. For to grow, to understand, requires that the poet—and even the versifier—offer not those fleeting, evanescent images of the inner mind, the subjective self that can be understood only by one person, but symbols of universal communication. For only in this way is it possible to point to the evil inherent in man that prophesies his doom, dismemberment or death, or the joyous possibilities of life, the right of choice, the acknowledgement that while there is disorder, there is also wonder and hope. The poet who loses himself, who pays homage to the universals that all men can understand can make all the difference. He presents children with alternate possibilities.

Pablo Neruda writes,

> The poet who is not a realist is dead. And the poet who is only a realist is also dead. The poet who is only irrational will only be understood by himself and his beloved and this is very sad. The poet who is all reason will even be understood by jackasses, and this is also terribly sad. There are no hard and fast rules, there are no ingredients prescribed by God or the Devil, but these two very important gentlemen wage a steady battle in the realm of poetry, and in this battle first one wins and then the other, but poetry itself cannot be defeated.
>
> (265)

Neruda is right. The irrational poetry of those who listen only to their inner fears and inner images will always be with us. The poets who live only with reason will continue to sing their hymns, and there are many who will listen. But those who offer poetry to children must be those who retain some memory of childhood, the knowledge that the world is before the child, and that he can be led beyond his inner fears to a world in which there is a possibility of free will, free choice. This poet does not tell the child that the world is all good, nor that it is all evil. This poet, without moralizing, says to the child that each person has his failures and successes; and both are inevitable. This poet urges the child to use his curiosity, his imagination, to apprehend and gradually to comprehend the wonders of his existence. His symbols are those not of the bogeyman or the man in the tree, but symbols which are universal and eternal—those found in nature. For this is the symbol of a reality a child can see and touch, can explore and embrace. This poet does not emphasize the fears of his own existence, but he does not shun them either. This poet is not adverse to levity and nonsense, to the play of words, because he knows that this is the realm of the child, but he does not overlook that a child is also serious, and not to be continually left in the world of imagination. This poet realizes how glorious it is to be young, with the world of possibilities around the corner, under the ground, up in the sky, and he presents this world in images he has fashioned into symbols—which the child can understand.

This poet lives with himself as a man who knows that, in spite of all reality, no one can live only with reality:

> *Smokefall*
> Then, as if someone spoke
> And said, O smell the smoke!
> A little shift of breeze
> carried it through the trees
> And up to where I sat—
> It will always smell like that.
> I could gather it into my lungs:
> It talked with a hundred tongues
> Of what was hurt to hear
> When far is kin to near.
>
>   . . .
> We have pushed all over maps
> To the smokeless polar caps,
> And where the logic lay
> Is how many miles away?
> I want to climb my hill
> Where the fall flings yellow still,
> And half discover things
> That a leaf in smoulder brings.
> I want my world to square
> With what the mind can spare
> From hard industrial faith
> For blue and bitter wraith.
> I want no trail or guide
> To that other other-side. *(A Star by Day* 54)

This is not a poem for children, but you will hear in it the beliefs that lead us to remember Wordsworth's phrase, "The Child is Father to the Man." It is the poem of no less a man than David McCord, who retains those strong feelings, scents, memories of childhood. For the man who wrote the poem "Smokefall" in his book *A Star by Day,* and cries "O smell the smoke!" says to the child, years later, in *Take Sky,*

Oh kindle, day of days,
Unbroken blue in haze
The bitter burning sweet:
Sweet burning in our street.   (234)

Here are the echoes of the images, the feelings, the scents of childhood that "hurt to hear" when "far is kin to near," but that must be translated to the child in symbols he can understand. David McCord knows "How the leaf-firemaker felt," as he says in "Smokefall"; but he also knows that children are not ready to absorb concepts; they must have leaves that talk, leaves that may be gathered up and jumped in, leaves that die under the snow, leaves that on "October Street" lie like a jumping rope, "all curves and kinks" in a "ragged line," leaves that mirror the minds of children.

Even the leaves hang listless,
Lasting through days we lose,
Empty of what is wanted,
Haunted by what we choose.   (*One at a Time* 410)

This is the dark side, the realistic side which must be acknowledged, but it is not all—it is not everything, David McCord says. For when November comes, children can "part the leaves to see" the robin's nest. They must learn to live with the "full green leaves" that hide what is going on, but the possibility for exploration lives in dozens of poems that present the leaves and fire as symbols.

The poet who would be the realist and dreamer will tell adults that he is "half afraid" that he does not want to know everything; again in "Smokefall,"

I want my burning far
In the uplands as they are,
And not for me to trace
Such blent peculiar grace—
Leave that to time and chance
And the day's benevolence.

Instead, the poet who speaks to adults can say

I want to climb my hill
Where the fall flings yellow still,
And half discover things
That a leaf in smoulder brings.

McCord, the grown man, wants "no trail or guide/to that other other-side" because he knows that "hard industrial faith" is not the stuff of which the enriching, lifelong, important dreams are built. But he knows that children must have some help, some direction while they are still growing and discovering the difference between their inner lives and the externals, so he writes in symbols they understand: as he describes a swing in "The Walnut Tree," the very physiological rhythms of their bodies as they leave the reality that binds them to earth swing out, wonder at and discover what lies beyond:

> I swung from the past to the far dim days
> Forever ahead of me....
>
> ...Oh, I could guess
> From the backward No to the forward Yes
> That the world begins in the sweep of eye,
> With wonder of all of it more or less
> In the last hello and the first goodbye
> And a swing in the walnut tree is why.   (*One at a Time* 280)

Leaves, tree, sky, these are the externals of nature, and the swing will provide the first "flying journey from green to blue" which is greeted with both "scare and praise." The child is on his "verge of flight" and if there is a "Backward No," there is a "Forward Yes." McCord will not spare the child this knowledge either. He takes them to the place of the Backward No, to

> The worm talking tunnel
> And the mole saying mound.   (*One at a Time* 82)

He acknowledges that some must always live in darkness, but that for others light is possible—

> All's night for Moles
> Like us in holes.
>
> Me too! I surface,
> though, says Shrew.   (*One at a Time* 331)

Cellars underneath the earth can be filled with water to sail boats and boys, like the mole, can try to detect what is in the darkness of the earth. This is a different darkness than that given to children who tremble under the covers and who fear the cave of the ogre and the pit of the troll. David McCord's symbols do not dwell in the fears of wraiths where the child is alone and helpless, but neither does he give them a world without knowledge that darkness exists.

The Grasshopper

Down
a
deep
well
a
grasshopper
fell.

By kicking about
He thought to get out.
    He might have known better,
    For that got him wetter.
But
the
well
had
a
rope
that
dangled
some
hope.   (*One at a Time* 28-30)

The rope is there if only it can be found, and rope is made from the strong fibers of nature that even as it threatens to drown a creature of nature—the grasshopper or child—can be climbed.

The poet who is willing to say that a grasshopper can fall in a well is symbolizing for the child that reality is ever-present. The poet who leaves the grasshopper there to drown is the didactic moralist, the Watts who believed that grasshoppers *and* children have little time for play and none to dream, and should listen to reason and not nonsense. Watt's children would have to come face to face with the leaf-firemaker, choose the right trail, the perfect guide.

There are some writing today who want to see the grasshopper drown, to tell children that this is how it is and must be. There are others who will not allow the grasshopper to daydream and imagine, to fall into the well in the first place. There are also those who would like to torture the grasshopper once he is down there. Not only have these versifiers—I cannot call them poets—given an inadequate form to their work, a shabby form, but they have presented an inadequate truth. Do these people have any respect for children? Are the bogeyman, the child killed by a dog, the man in a tree symbols that are now being offered to children, the way to an enriching life experience? Or will they learn that the only thing to do is pull the covers tightly up over their heads, never exploring the possibilities of life for fear of falling?

David McCord tells children that there are wormy apples, but most are beauties; that fish will not always bite; that it is important to remember about the eggs that have been broken and make a mess, but that it is also important to remember that eggs neither broken or cooked hatch into chicks. David McCord, like the child, is a realist.

Cocoon

The little caterpillar creeps
Awhile before in silk it sleeps
It sleeps awhile before it flies,
And flies awhile before it dies,
And that's the end of three good tries. (*One at a Time* 59)

Look to nature, David McCord says. Take its symbols, the sky, the water, the seasons, the bugs and animals, the fruit and the fish. The echoes of "Smokefall" return:

Away and Ago

has the sound of over
the hills and far
away, but the rover
hasn't returned yet
for telling us what
it was that he met
with, or whether he got
there at all, or indeed
where it was that he chanced
to be choosing. So, losing,
no time, I've advanced
out ahead of him,
standing or sitting so still
my away and ago lay
just over one hill
and not very distant.
I hope that you'll mind
not to follow too close,
not to fall far behind. (*One at a Time* 278)

What lies beyond? David McCord stands there ready to turn his images into symbols that make sense to the child: to show them the difference between what is over the hill, whether he is in a swing or climbing

Up the pointed ladder, against the apple tree,
One rung, two rungs, what do I see?

A man by the roadside, his eye on me.
. . .
Seven rungs, eight rungs—I can't climb these.
The wobble's in the ladder, it isn't in my knees.
The man cries "Steady, boy!" And up comes a breeze.

Up comes a breezy "Now you come down slow!"
I offer him an apple, but he just won't go.
Well, it's all like that in the world below.   (*One at a Time* 132-3)

Children must climb, no matter how scary it may be, and they will
skin their knees and get scolded. Yet at the bottom there will
always be someone to call "Steady." The man, though temporarily
rejected, is still there. He won't go.

There is an adult in *Struwwelpeter,* but he does not seem to
understand the nature and curiosity of childhood; he speaks only
of the negative aspects of exploration. There is an adult in the new
Mother Goose who neatly removes, in totally inadequate form,
not only the nonsense by which a child learns, but free will. No
fear of ladders in her world, unless they lead directly to Heaven.
There are adults in the Happy Days School, but they are as
ineffectual as those who have never perceived any need for order
and structure in life itself. If there are adults who live in the world
of the other-worldly, they are ever invisible but their message is
clear; let the child work out his own fears—we have other things
to do.

There is an adult in *Take Sky,* in *Far and Few,* in *Every Time I
Climb a Tree,* in *All Day Long,* in *Away and Ago,* in *Speak Up,* in
One at a Time, who builds the swing, who attaches the rope, who
observes the caterpillar, who stands waiting on the hill and at the
bottom of the ladder, calling "Steady." David McCord knows of
the journeys to be made on earth, but they are journeys which are
part of earth. He knows that speed must be gathered to make a
leap, that "Farther is distance and further is time," and that some
things

> are always out of reach,
Like one last apple or one peach.
Quite visible up high, too far.
We think that way about a star.   (*Speak Up* 31)

David McCord's own "boyhood brook in a depth of wood" is
always close at hand. He knows the "selves of myself," "the life
ahead of life" and that, "Still climbing toward the light we slide
downhill." In his books of verse, *A Star By Day, Floodgate, The
Crows,* and many more—in his *Essays* and in his anthology, *What
Cheer,* he tells us of himself, of how he "smiled at the little boy in
him: the caged, imprisoned other self." In *A Star By- Day,* he
remembers a time "Under the Zodiac" when a seer spoke to him:

And long he looked, beyond and through
And out and up to where the mass
Of cloudy shapes against the blue
Controlled the shadows on the grass.

"My little man, as you grow up,
As you grow old, as you grow wise,
As you shall break the sterile cup,
As you may win to other skies,

"Asking, unanswered; telling, told;
Friendly, befriended; anxious, crossed;
Never forget that you behold
In the great sky the kingdom lost.

"Nothing you make but shall be made
More beautiful than love is fond
By wind and weather in the glade
That runs forever and beyond...."   (*Star by Day* 17)

How many times, we may all wonder, does the voice that bound
David McCord to the seer bind today's children—and tomorrow's
children—to his words as he asks them to "Take Sky"?

Now think of words. Take *sky*
And ask yourself just why—
Like sun, moon, star, and cloud—
It sounds so well out loud,
And pleases so the sight
When printed black on white.
        . . .
Remember, words are life:
Child, husband, mother, wife;
Remember, and I'm done:
Words taken one by one
Are poems as they stand—
Shore, beacon, harbor, land;
Brook, river, mountain, vale,
Crow, rabbit, otter, quail;
Faith, freedom, water, snow,
Wind, weather, flood, and floe.
Like light across the lawn
Are morning, sea, and dawn;
Words of the green earth growing—
Seed, soil, and farmer sowing.
Like wind upon the mouth
Sad, summer, rain, and south.
Amen. Put not asunder
Man's *first* word: wonder...wonder...   (*One at a Time* 125-7)

How many times have children been moved to wonder at the Firetender who rakes his coals, to look at the things of earth that are loved but not understood, the wind and sea, the clouds that

> are like a game
> that I don't seem to have to understand,
> played without rules, with no one in command.
>
> (One at a Time 259)

There are words to explore and worlds to explore beneath the water or just around the corner where fish and people, crows and locomotives all have their place. But there must be times that one must be alone, looking out on the unknown, and yet still bound to the earth by something solid in nature; something that offers security, some symbol that the child finds as his own:

> This is my rock
> And here I run
> To steal the secret of the sun.
>
> This is my rock,
> And here come I
> Before the night has swept the sky;
>
> This is my rock,
> This is the place
> I meet the evening face to face.   (One at a Time 41)

But most of all there must be times when there is someone to remind children that there is a pale green star that speaks but cannot be understood, that there is a broken star, that there are secrets never to be told, but that the journey must be made. The journeys of the swing and the ladder, the upward climb is a part of life that children cannot be denied, that must not be falsified, and there must always be faith. David McCord knows that these must be told truly. Why does he ask children—and us—to read "Dr. Klimwell's Fall" aloud? Why does he begin it with a quote from Emerson:

> We wake and find our-
> selves on a stair; there
> are stairs below us...
> there are stairs above us,
> many a one, which go
> upward and out of sight.

> *Dr. Klimwell's Fall*

> Down the star-stairs fell
> Old Dr. I. Klimwell.
> What he was doing there,

Climbing that kind of stair,
Staring down starry stone,
Standing (trust him) alone,
No one will ever know.
Stars, when you have to go
Where Dr. Klimwell did,
Hide away—hidden, hid
Under some stellar door;
But, if you've been before
(Doctors, of course, *have* been)
Knock, and they'll let you in.
   . . .

"There now, at last!" would cry
Old Dr. Klimwell. "My,
My, my, my, *my!* I smell
Leaves burning. Must be well
On towards...eh?...Halloween?
What is there in between?"
"Nothing. For someone's sick.
Climb, Dr. Klimwell, *quick!*"
Who could be sick above
Whom we'd be thinking of
Not knowing why or where
One could be sick up there?
Quick as the flight of thieves
Right by the rake of leaves,
Spiraling through the clear
Leaf-empty trees appear
Stones for the Doctor's climb
Time after sudden time
Just when your laggard glance
Spies, as it will by chance,
Something you want to see:
Dragonflies floating knee-
High over sandy shore;
Something behind the door,
Something inside of tents,
Something that won't make sense,
Something before your face,
Something from outer space,
Something you've heard of, just—
Something the rain might rust,
Something you don't quite trust
Something... (*One at a Time* 125, 7)

No one will ever know, the poet David McCord tells us, why Dr. Klimwell is alone, what he was doing on those stairs, why he had to go in the first place. No one will know why the stars hide away under some stellar door and only let in doctors and a few who have been there before. If Dr. Klimwell is very much like all of us, loving the things of nature, remembering the images of life, looking back, all "things worlds and winds away" and enjoying the "little happy things," why does he climb alone, and why does he cry "at last!" and smell leaves burning? Why does he rush by a rake of leaves, and leaf-empty trees, and who, indeed, could be sick up there?

In his introduction to *One at a Time*, David McCord speaks about the labors and duties of men who know "perfectly well, even before breakfast" about their duties. Most people, he writes, have "a fairly positive plan for the work ahead from day to day."

> But the poet—what is he? Why, he is more like a fireman waiting for a fire; the ambulance driver waiting for an accident, an illness, or a tragedy; a policeman in his cruise car waiting for a call over the intercom for immediate and possibly dangerous action. (vii)

The poet, David McCord tells us, is a man who does not write on a fixed schedule, but, "Once he has the idea for a poem he will also have, if he is any good at all, an immediate urge to write it. This may happen anytime, any place, day or night, on land or sea or in the air." It may, of course, take shaping, tinkering, adjusting as to rhyme and accent, and a "desperate search for the right word in a difficult line, and may stretch into days, even, alas! into weeks. Only on rare occasions does an idea for a poem have to be stored away in the mind for months or possibly for years before the writer...can put pen to paper."

Who is Dr. Klimwell and why, when he has just fallen, when he is most enjoying the smell of leaves burning, should he race up the stairs again? And what is the something behind the door, something inside of tents, something that won't make sense, something before your face, something from outer space, something you've just heard of, just—something the rain might rust, something you don't quite trust, something—

We all know and probably remember the first time we came upon him, on the starry stones with, "The Star in the Pail:"

> I took the pail for water when the sun was high
> And left it in the shadow of the barn nearby
>
> When evening slippered over like the moth's brown wing,
> I went to fetch the water from the cool wellspring
>
>   . . .

But every star was far away as far can be,
With all the starry silence sliding over me.

And every time I stopped I set the pail down slow,
For when I stooped to pick the handle up to go

Of all the stars in heaven there was one to spare,
And he silvered in the water and I left him there.

(*One at a Time* 13)

How do we show our love, David, for someone who brings us back a star?

REFERENCES

An earlier version of this essay was the David McCord Lecture given at the Boston Public Library, November 7, 1983.

Decker, Marjorie Ainsborough. *The Christian Mother Goose Book.* Grand Junction, CO: Decker Press, n.d.

Duncan, Lois. *the Terrible Tales of Happy Days School.* Boston: Little, Brown, 1983.

Hoffman, Dr. Heinrich. *The English Struwwelpeter.* London: Griffith, Farran, Okeden & Welsh.

McCord, David. *One At a Time.* Boston: Little, Brown, 1974.

_____. *Speak Up.* Boston: Little, Brown, 1980.

_____. *A Star By Day.* New York: Doubleday, 1950.

Neruda, Pablo. *Memoirs.* New York: Farrar, Straus & Giroux, 1977.

Prelutsky, Jack. *Nightmares.* New York: Greenwillow, 1976.

_____. *The Headless Horseman Rides Tonight.* New York: Greenwillow, 1980.

Steiner, George. *Tolstoy or Dostoevsky.* New York: Knopf, 1959.

A. A. Milne's *When We Were Very Young* and *Now We Are Six:* A Small World of Everyday Pleasures

by Anita Wilson

Like Robert Louis Stevenson, A. A. Milne began his first book for children as a diversion during a dismally wet summer holiday. He had already written "Vespers," and Rose Fyleman had encouraged him to write a book of verses after he sent her "The Dormouse and the Doctor." Working in a summerhouse in Wales, Milne began what was to become a perennial best-seller of children's literature as he reflected upon childhood—his own, and his son's: "...there on the other side of the lawn was a child with whom I had lived for three years...and here within me were unforgettable memories of my own childhood" (*Autobiography* 280). Although Milne dedicated *When We Were Very Young* to Christopher Robin, the child in the poems is sometimes Christopher Robin, sometimes A. A. Milne as a child, and sometimes "the child," or any child. In fact, Christopher Robin appears by name in only four of the forty-four poems in *When We Were Very Young*, which owes as much to Milne's imagination and memories as it does to his son's childhood:

> As a child I kept a mouse; probably it escaped—they generally do. Christopher Robin has kept almost everything except a mouse. As a child I played lines-and-squares in a casual sort of way. Christopher Robin never did until he read what I had written about it, and not very enthusiastically then. But he did go to Buckingham Palace a good deal (which I didn't) though not with Alice.... (*By Way of Introduction* 196)

As for who is speaking the verses, Milne says in the Preface to *When We Were Very Young* that if you are not sure, it is probably "Hoo,"—"one of those curious children who look four on Monday, and eight on Tuesday, and are really twenty-eight on Saturday...." The blending of Milne's voice and memories with Christopher Robin's experiences continues in *Now We Are Six*, which features a slightly more mature Christopher Robin and gives Pooh a more prominent role in the poems.

Nor were Milne's poems based upon a close relationship between father and child. While nannies figure in a number of the poems and parents in general are mentioned occasionally, only one poem out of both books portrays Christopher Robin and his father. In "Sand-Between-the-Toes," they take a walk on the beach together, more like two children, each with sixpence from Nurse, than parent and child: "We clambered over the humping sand—And Christopher held my hand" *When We Were Very Young* (75). Ordinarily there would be nothing unusual in this closeness between parent and child, but the emphasis given the final line of this verse creates a rather wistful tone and suggests that Christopher and his father had few such moments. In his autobiography, Christopher Milne indicates that during his nursery years, his father remained in the background; a close and rewarding father-son relationship developed later, when Christopher was a schoolboy and well beyond the Winnie-the-Pooh stage. Ironically, it was this distance between Milne and his son which stimulated him to write poetry for children; the poems were a substitute for, rather than a reflection of, an intimate bond between father and child: "My father was a creative writer and so it was precisely because he was *not* able to play with his small son that his longings sought and found satisfaction in another direction. He wrote about him instead" (36).

Not all of Milne's poems are about children, but most are, in some respect, about childhood. Milne transforms kings and knights into humorous figures in whom the child can see himself; King John is "not a good man," but Father Christmas provides his heart's desire, "a big, red, india-rubber ball," anyway. Kings can exercise power as children would like to; another royal figure in one of Milne's most popular poems, "The King's Breakfast," won't settle for marmalade instead of butter just to make things easier for everyone else. King Hilary looks forward to sugar-plums in his Christmas stocking and dismisses his snobbish Chancellor. These characters do as they please, acting out the fantasies of the child who says, in "If I Were King," "I often wish I were a King/And then I could do anything" (*When We Were Very Young* 100). "Bad Sir Brian Botany," on the other hand, is a grownup bully who meets with poetic justice. "The Knight Whose Armour Didn't Squeak" is wise by a child's standards; he can write letters and multiply up to four. The grownups in these poems combine a child's perceptions with an adult's prerogatives. Other verses not featuring children include a few nature poems, mostly in *When We Were Very Young*. On the whole, these are not among Milne's best, for they lack his characteristic verve and humor. He seems most natural and at ease in depicting rather homely and ordinary scenes, as in "Summer Afternoon," where "Six brown cows walk down to drink" (*When We Were Very Young* 67), or "The Invaders," where the cows make another appearance as they tramp through the woods in early morning.

Milne's antecedents in the area of children's poetry include Christina Rossetti's *Sing-Song* (1872) and Stevenson's *A Child's Garden of Verses* (1885). He surpasses both in wit and verbal ingenuity, although he never achieves the depth of feeling found in a lyric such as Rossetti's "Sea Sand and Sorrow." A few of Milne's poems reflect well-known works by his predecessors; "Wind on the Hill" resembles Rossetti's classic "Who Has Seen the Wind?" and "Daffodowndilly" borrows her name for the daffodil, while Milne's "Swing Song" is reminiscent of Stevenson's "The Swing." Like Rossetti and, particularly, Stevenson, Milne focuses his poetry around cheerful images of a young child's everyday experiences. His poems are not derivative, however; in their deft humor and irresistible rhythms, they are inimitably his own. Milne's work is distinguished above all by his disciplined and inventive light verse, which at its best gives an impression of effortless humor and grace. He did not toss off trifles for the nursery; as he observed in his *Autobiography,*

Whatever else they lack, the verses are technically good.... *When We Were Very Young* is not the work of a poet becoming playful, nor of a lover of children expressing his love, nor of a prose-writer knocking together a few jingles for the little ones, it is the work of a light-verse writer taking his job seriously even though he is taking it into the nursery. (282)

The same philosophy that children deserve the best is evident in *Now We Are Six* also.

Indeed, Milne's craftsmanship is impeccable, and his ingenious use of rhyme, meter, and typography is a trademark of his verses. Sound and sense are perfectly matched in the rollicking rhythm of "James James Morrison Morrison Weatherby George Dupree" or the refrain from "Busy," the "threeish" poem in *Now We Are Six:*

Round about
And *round* about
And *round* about I go—
All around the table,
The table in the nursery—   (9)

or in the quieter, more contemplative mood of "Halfway Down," where, as Zena Sutherland notes, the pattern of the verses mimics Christopher Robin's stopping firmly on the middle step:

Halfway down the stairs
Is a stair
Where I sit.
There isn't any

Other stair
Quite Like
It. (*When We Were Very Young* 83)

Finding ingenious ways to keep the strict rhyme and meter essential to light verse was a challenge which Milne clearly relished; in "The Christening," for example, a rhyme creates a pun in the first verse:

What shall I call
    My dear little dormouse?
His eyes are small,
    But his tail is e-nor-mouse.

(*When We Were Very Young* 7)

A common speech pattern of small children, doubling plurals, is carried to comic extremes in "The Three Foxes:" "They went to a Fair, and they all won prizes—/Three plum-puddingses and three mince-pieses" (*When We Were Very Young* 42). The appearance of the poem on the page is also often important; Christopher Robin, in "Politeness," says that he always answers grownups' questions,

If they ask me
Politely....
BUT SOMETIMES

I wish

That they wouldn't. (*When We Were Very Young* 43)

The small print of the last line suggests Christopher whispering his rebellious thoughts, too softly to be heard. The repeated refrain and varied typeface in the closing lines of "The Little Black Hen" highlight the child's egocentric delight at being more important than the adults:

Berryman and Baxter,
    Prettiboy and Penn,
And Old Farmer Middleton
    Are five big men.
All of them are wanting
    An egg for their tea,

But the Little Black Hen is much too busy,
The Little Black Hen is *much* too busy,
The Little Black Hen is MUCH too busy...
    She's laying my egg for me! (*Now We Are Six* 66)

The child in Milne's verses is in many respects a typical child with universal qualities that have not changed in half a century. He (or she) is curious, egocentric, imaginative, sometimes

176

perplexed by the seemingly pointless demands and questions of adults. Less typically, perhaps, he is a rather solitary figure. Only two poems out of both volumes are about children playing together; in *Now We Are Six,* "Buttercup Days" and "The Morning Walk" portray Christopher and his closest childhood friend, Anne Darlington, to whom *Now We Are Six* was dedicated. Other than his nurse, the child's usual companions are animals, real or stuffed. The child in *When We Were Very Young* christens his dormouse, revels in the rabbits which he finds on the common, and romps in the hills with a puppy, who "got talking" when they met—like most small children, Christopher is quite able to believe that animals can speak. The bear Pooh of Milne's classic novels plays only a minor role in this volume, but comes into his own in *Now We Are Six,* where he is Christopher's best friend. The poems about friendship, "The Friend," and "Us Two," feature Christopher and Pooh, not Christopher and another child:

> So wherever I am, there's always Pooh,
> There's always Pooh and Me.
> "What would I do?" I said to Pooh,
> "If it wasn't for you," and Pooh said: "True,
> It isn't much fun for One, but Two
> Can stick together," says Pooh, says he.
> "That's how it is," says Pooh.   ("Us Two," *Now We Are Six* 37)

Although Christopher's solitude eliminates a slice of life from these verses—there are no poems about school, or other activities involving groups of children—it allows Milne to concentrate upon the child's inner world, particularly as expressed in imaginative play. Role-playing is portrayed as a way of experimenting with one's identity, which is fluid and offers infinite possibilities. In "Nursery Chairs," after impersonating a hunter, lion, and sailor, Christopher Robin plays at being a three-year-old in his own chair; in play, this identity is no more "real" than the various roles which he slips in and out of. "Busy" presents a similar game of role-playing: "Perhaps I am a Postman. No, I think I am a Tram./I'm feeling rather funny and I don't know *what* I am—" (*Now We Are Six* 9). By age six, Christopher has a firmer sense of self as he ponders the differences between himself and a younger child: "If I were John and John were Me,/Then he'd be six and I'd be three" ("A Thought," *Now We Are Six* 71). He still has an active imagination, however, as he slays dragons in his suit of armor and creates Binker as an alter-ego and imaginary companion in a sometimes frustrating world:

> Well, I'm very fond of Daddy, but he hasn't time
>   to play.

And I'm very fond of Mummy, but she sometimes
   goes away,
And I'm often cross with Nanny when she wants to
   brush my hair...
But Binker's always Binker, and is certain to be
   there.   (*Now We Are Six* 20)

Like all young children, Christopher Robin lives in a world largely controlled by adults, whose values and requirements often make little sense to him. He pities the tradespeople in "Market Square" who do not have a rabbit, which is far more important to him than the saucepans and mackerel for sale. In a number of poems, Milne blends humor with a sensitive awareness of the child's point of view. Adults sometimes emerge as a collective, anonymous "they" who, as Christopher says in "Independence," "don't understand." They ask foolish questions, burden him with precautions ("Not up there, dear!") and dismiss his attempts to share his discoveries. "Come Out with Me" contrasts the child's excitement about what he has seen with the grownups' disappointing lack of interest:

There's wind on the river and wind on the hill...
You can hear the sea if you stand quite still!
There's eight new puppies at Roundabout Farm—
And I saw an old sailor with only one arm!
   But every one says, "Run along!"
   (Run along, run along!)
All of them say, "Run along! I'm busy as can be."
   Every one says, "Run along,
   There's a little darling!"
If I'm a little darling, why don't they run with me?
                    (*Now We Are Six* 59)

Here sentimental clichés enable adults to diminish the child's importance under a veneer of affection. Elizabeth Ann, one of the occasional female children in *Now We Are Six*, receives similar responses when she asks how God began—admittedly a tough question: "Now then darling, it's time for bed," and "Well, what put *that* in your quaint little head?" ("Explained" 80, 82) Even Alice, who watches the changing of the guard with Christopher, listens without genuine interest and stifles his question cheerfully but decisively: "Do you think the King knows all about *me?*" "Sure to, dear, but it's time for tea" (*When We Were Very Young* 5). Adults focus on their own priorities rather than the child's. They find no purpose in climbing a hill when "There's nothing to see," and they want to know the child's plans for a beguiling spring morning when, like Pooh, he plans only to enjoy whatever the day may bring:

178

Where am I going? I don't quite know.
What does it matter where people go?
Down to the wood where the blue-bells grow—
Anywhere, anywhere, *I* don't know.
("Spring Morning," *When We Were Very Young* 37)

The children in *When We Were Very Young* and *Now We Are Six* can be more than a match for the adults, however. One of Milne's attractive qualities is his lack of didacticism; his poetical children are not taught lessons about good behavior, and the grownups are far from infallible. Jane, "The Good Little Girl," in *Now We Are Six*, is a far cry from Robert Louis Stevenson's "A Good Boy," who goes to bed with a clear conscience because he's been obedient all day—since she has no intention of incriminating herself, she wonders why her parents bother to ask if she's been good:

Well, what did they think that I went there to do?
And why should I want to be bad at the Zoo?
And should I be likely to say if I had?
So that's why it's funny of Mummy and Dad,
This asking and asking, in case I was bad,
    "Well?
Have you been a *good* girl, Jane?" (70)

Ernest Shepherd's illustrations, which show Jane standing on a lawn with a "Keep Off the Grass" sign and feeding an animal next to another sign forbidding the same, make clear that her parents don't know as much as they think they do. Similarly, Mary Jane's well-intentioned nurse tries to placate her with presents and can't see what is obvious even to the youngest reader: "*And it's lovely rice pudding for dinner again!—/*What *is* the matter with Mary Jane?" ("Rice Pudding," *When We Were Very Young* 53) The notion of parental authority and contol is turned completely upside-down in "Disobedience," where James James leads his errant mother home on a leash and reprimands her in a delightfully dictatorial fashion: "You must *never* go down to the end of the town without consulting me" (*When We Were Very Young* 34)

Although the children in Milne's poems may be occasionally vexed or baffled by the inscrutable ways of grownups, these are a source of annoyance, not anguish. Milne chose to emphasize the joyous aspects of childhood; disappointments and frustrations are handled with a light touch which makes them humorous rather than devastating. As in the novels about Pooh, nothing bad ever happens to anybody; losing Alexander Beetle is the closest Christopher Robin comes to a crisis. The poems do not deal with the darker side of childhood—such emotions as fear, anger, or jealousy are entirely absent. Christopher never has nightmares, but enjoys being alone in the dark, where he can imagine anything he likes. The bears waiting to eat him at the street corner hold no terrors; he complacently defeats them by stepping over the pavement squares. He never loses his temper, breaks a toy, or has a fight and, despite his occasional impatience with adults, Christopher never causes trouble for them. He emerges as a remarkably happy and well-behaved child, inhabiting a sedate and benevolent world.

While Milne undoubtedly gives a one-sided picture of childhood, he excels at cheerful and spirited evocations of everyday joys:

> I've got a nice new pair of braces,
> I've got shoes with new brown laces,
> I know wonderful paddly places.
>   Who's coming out with me?
> ("Growing Up," *When We Were Very Young* 99)

An adult, or an older child than three-year-old Christopher, may smile at his ecstasy over these small symbols of growing up, but Christopher is not made fun of; throughout Milne's poems, the laughter is affectionate, not sardonic, and the child's perspective is respected. Christopher's struggles with "Dates and Pounds-and-ounces and the names of funny Kings" are amusing, but his worries reflect every child's anxiety over schoolwork: "And I know they'll think me silly if I get the answer wrong" ("The Friend," *Now We Are Six* 67). And readers of any age can identify with the egocentric dream-world of "The Island": "There's nobody else in the world, and the world was made for me" (*When We Were Very Young* 39). Milne's attitude is not one of amused condescension; he respects the child. As he said in his *Autobiography* regarding *When We Were Very Young*, "It seems that the nursery, more than any other room in the house, likes to be approached seriously" (282).

Milne can lapse into sentimentality, however, when he tries to render children charming to adults, rather than portraying them naturally and with a touch of humor. The baby-talk which appears in some of the poems is one of their less attractive characteristics; even at three, Christopher Robin seems too old for "nuffin" and "nosserus" and "portant"—happily, there is less of this in *Now We Are Six*. In "Buttercup Days," however, Christopher and his friend Anne appear as miniature lovers, innocently acting out adult roles. Anne is twice described as "little," a description Milne rarely applies to children in his poems, and her attachment to "her man," as Christopher is called, is depicted in a coy fashion which reduces both children to adorable figures for the sentimental pleasure of adults. "The Brownie," in *When We Were Very Young,* also seems excessively sweet; brownies "wriggle off at once because they're all so tickly/(Nanny says they're tickly too)" (16). The accompanying illustration reinforces this contrived tone, showing Christopher Robin peeking behind the curtain in his dainty smock and girlish coiffure. The facing page provides a refreshing contrast with "Independence," where Christopher gleefully swings on a tree branch, his curls in disarray, while complaining that grownups always spoil the fun with "Now take care, dear!" or "Hold-my-hand" (17).

Probably the most notorious of Milne's poems is "Vespers": "Hush! Hush! Whisper who dares!/Christopher Robin is saying his prayers." Although this is the last poem in *When We Were Very Young,* it was one of the first that Milne wrote. He gave it to his wife, "telling her that if she liked to get it published anywhere she could stick to the money" (279). As Milne wryly observed some years later, it turned out to be an expensive present. In his autobiography, Christopher Milne acknowledged that "Vespers" brought him "more toe-curling, fist-clenching, lip-biting embarrassment" than any of his father's poems (28). Yet Milne did not intend the poem to be sentimental; in fact, he saw it as a humorously realistic description of a child whose dutiful prayers mean little to him:

> Not "God bless mummy, because I love her so," but "God bless Mummy, I know that's right"...not even the egotism of "God bless Me, because I'm the most important person in the house," but the super-egotism of feeling so impregnable that the blessing of this mysterious god for Oneself is the very last thing for which it would seem necessary to ask. (285)

Egotism and heartlessness were qualities which Milne perceived as natural to children, if not necessarily attractive. He considered "Buckingham Palace" another example of the former, and "Disobedience" a portrait of the latter; when James James Morrison's mother disappears, his only reaction is to tell his other relatives "Not to go blaming *him.*" This seems a rather solemn reading of a poem which comically inverts the roles of parent and child, but it shows that Milne was not oblivious to the less endearing characteristics of young children.

The enduring appeal of Milne's poems rests neither upon sentimentality nor uncompromising realism, but upon his light-hearted yet sympathetic portrayal of a child's everyday world. Milne made no exaggerated claims for his verses, even after the overwhelming success of *When We Were Very Young* and *Now*

We Are Six. His intention was to entertain, with wit and grace, and his poems are one-dimensional, straightforward, and cheerful. They are clever and amusing, not intense or profound, and they unapologetically reflect the snug and sometimes smug atmosphere of a middle-class English household in the 1920s; the uniformed nannies, the orderly nursery life, the decorous trips to the park and the zoo now have an old-fashioned flavor, and the attitude of "all's right with the world" which permeates the poems may now seem complacent, particularly to adults. Milne's limitations become strengths, however, as he creates unpretentious but memorable images of childhood, simultaneously humorous and affectionate. As in the Pooh stories, he does not attempt to offer a comprehensive vision of life or of childhood, preferring to depict a small world of everyday pleasures where good humor and happy endings are the rule. He rejoices in ordinary happenings and, wisely, does not strive for the extraordinary. Thomas Burnett Swann quotes a review of Milne's last book, four years before his death, that epitomizes Milne's achievement as a writer of children's literature: "He has perfect vision out of a small window..." (148).

REFERENCES

Milne, A. A. *When We Were Very Young.* London: Methuen; New York: Dutton, 1924.

_____. *Now We Are Six.* London: Methuen; New York: Dutton, 1927.

_____. **"Introducing Shepard."** *By Way of Introduction.* London: Methuen; New York: Dutton, 1929. 33-37.

_____. **"The End of a Chapter."** *By Way of Introduction.* 195-202.

_____. *Autobiography.* New York: Dutton, 1939. American edition of *It's Too Late Now,* London: Methuen, 1939.

Milne, Christopher. *The Enchanted Places.* London: Eyre Methuen, 1974; New York: Dutton, 1975.

Sterck, Kenneth. "The Real Christopher Robin: An Appreciation of A. A. Milne's Children's Verse." *Children's Literature in Education* 11, 2 (Summer, 1980):52-61.

Sutherland, Zena, Dianne L. Monson, and **May Hill Arbuthnot.** *Children and Books.* 6th Ed. Glenview, IL: Scott, Foresman, 1981. 286-287.

Swann, Thomas Burnett. *A. A. Milne.* New York: Twayne, 1971.

Rev. of *Year In, Year Out,* by A. A. Milne. *The New York Herald-Tribune Book Review,* 29 (November 16, 1952):5.

The Nursery Rhymes of Mother Goose: A World without Glasses

by Perry Nodelman

Of all the great works of children's literature, the oddest is the body of poetry surrounding the name of Mother Goose. It is amorphous. It is various. Above all, it is absurd.

The canon of Mother Goose is so amorphous that trying to pin it down might be something like doing a bibliography of the complete works of Anonymous. In Iona and Peter Opie's *Oxford Dictionary of Nursery Rhymes,* there are 550 different rhymes (not including variants); in William and Ceil Baring-Gould's *The Annotated Mother Goose* there are 884. The reason for this uncertainty about how much Mother Goose wrote is obvious—there is not now and there never was a Mother Goose, at least not one who wrote poetry.

That has not prevented scholars from trying to invent one. Their candidates have ranged from Charlemagne's Mother Bertha (who went by the nickname "La Reine Pedauque," or Queen Goosefoot, and who has become confused with another Queen Bertha, blood relative and wife of Robert II of France, who is said to have given birth to a goose-headed child) to one Elizabeth Foster Goose (or maybe Vergoose or Vertigoose) of Boston, Massachusetts, who may or may not have recited rhymes to her grandchildren in a manner that suggested the cackling of geese. Somehow, somewhere in history, the idea of literature for the young became connected with the name Goose; it seems to have already been an old idea when Perrault subtitled his collection of fairy tales "CONTES DE MA MERE LOYE"—stories of Mother Goose—in 1697. But where or how the connection was first made nobody knows.

What we do know is what goes under the name of Mother Goose—a body of verse that has become separated from its original contexts, and therefore, its original authors. In some instances, we either know or can guess some of those authors: we know that "Twinkle, Twinkle, Little Star" first appeared in Jane and

Ann Taylor's *Rhymes for the Nursery* in 1806, and that Sarah Catharine Martin had something to do with *The Comic Adventures of Old Mother Hubbard and Her Dog* published in 1805; if she didn't make it up, at least her version of it was what first made it popular. And we know that no less a literary figure than the great Samuel Johnson was responsible, not just for compiling the dictionary and providing James Boswell with an object of worship, but for

> If a man who turnips cries,
> Cries not when his father dies,
> It is proof that he would rather
> Have a turnip than his father.   (Opie 284)

That the sententious Dr. Johnson improvised this as an example of bad writing may say less about the quality of the verse ascribed to Mother Goose than it does about Johnson's taste; a similar lack of appreciation backfired on Samuel Griswold Goodrich, better known as "Peter Parley," when the rhyme he made up in the eighteen-forties as a parody of the irrationality of Mother Goose rhymes also entered the canon:

> Higglety, pigglety, pop!
> The dog has eaten the mop;
> The pig's in a hurry,
> The cat's in a flurry,
> Higglety, pigglety, pop!   (207)

The Opies suggest that many of the rhymes ascribed to Mother Goose may have been written by professionals: "we believe that if all the authors were known, many more of these 'unconsiderd trifles' would be found to be of distinguished birth, a birth commensurate with their long and influential lives" (3).

But scholars have not often been able to identify authors, for a simple but important reason. Whoever wrote these verses in the first place, and whatever the occasions of their having been written, they are the kinds of words that get stuck in human minds, so that people can pull them out on those occasions when they need to say or sing something that sounds pleasant or just plain interesting. Whatever their sources, then, people who found these verses easy to remember remembered them, and passed them on to others by word of mouth; and so, the poems became part of an oral tradition that cares much less for authorship than it does for memorability.

As a result, we can't figure out exactly what Mother Goose wrote; and because memory tends to be eclectic in its tastes, we can't any more easily determine the characteristics of her work. This body of verse includes everything from gentle prayers like

"Now I lay me down to sleep" to counting out rhymes like "Eena meena mina mo," from parts of old ballads like "Lavender's blue, diddle diddle" to tongue twisters like "Peter Piper picked a peck of pickled peppers. "Obviously, this variety of rhymes had a variety of difference sources, mostly in forms of jollity of the sort that people used to enjoy in their free time, in the days before soap operas and singles bars. Some rhymes were intended as riddles or jokes, some were parts of mummer's plays, some were drinking songs or just pleasant songs to sing at parties; and some were words that allowed reluctant performers to get out of singing at parties:

> There was an old crow
> Sat upon a clod;
> That's the end of my song.
> That's odd. (138)

"Oh where oh where has my little dog gone?" was originally a comic ballad, "Der Deitcher's Dog," published by Septimus Winner in 1864; luckly, its transition to the oral transition divested it of its tasteless mock-German accent and its cheap jokes about "very goot beer" and sausage made "mit dog" and "mit horse."

Some of the rhymes had less playful origins. Some, like "Hot cross buns" and

> Young lambs to sell! Young lambs to sell!
> I never would cry young lambs to sell
> If I'd as much money as I could tell,
> I never would cry young lambs to sell (264)

were once street cries; and the stern advice to

> Come when you're called,
> Do as you're bid,
> Shut the door after you,
> Never be chid (136)

seems to have been directed at servants before it was inherited by children.

Not surprisingly, this grab-bag of various types of verse ranges widely in tone and effect. There is somewhat imbecilic absurdity of

> Goosey, goosey gander
> Whither shall I wander?
> Upstairs and downstairs
> And in my lady's chamber. (191)

But there is also the mysterious beauty of

Gray goose and gander,
    Waft your wings together,
And carry the good king's daughter
    Over the one-strand river.   (190)

There is the smarmily gentle

I love little pussy,
    Her coat is warm,
and if I don't hurt her
    She'll do me no harm.   (356)

But there is also the bloodyminded nastiness of the boy who drowns another pussy in a well, the farmer's wife who amputates the tails of defenseless handicapped mice, and numerous other tales of sometimes breathtakingly brutal violence:

When I went up sandy-hill,
I met a sandy-boy;
I cut his throat, I sucked his blood,
And left his skin a-hanging-o.   (377)

(Somehow, it doesn't help to know that this is a riddle, and that the sandy-boy is merely an orange.) There is the wistful sadness of

The north wind doth blow
And we shall have snow
And what will poor robin do then?
    Poor thing.   (426)

But then there is the raucous vulgarity of another verse about a robin, as it appeared in the first known collection of nursery rhymes, *Tom Thumb's Pretty Song Book,* in 1744:

Little Robin Redbreast
Sat upon a rail
Niddle noddle went his head
and Poop went his hole.

In modern versions designed more for the adult sense of decorum than the juvenile sense of humor, the last line is "Wiggle waggle went his tail." But even when the vulgar bits have been expurgated, a free spirited breeziness survives everywhere in Mother Goose, in references to "dirty sluts" (297) and "Greedy-guts" (390) and to a disrespectfully described "gaping wide-mouthed waddling frog" (181).

But more often than not, the most widely known verses of Mother Goose are merely absurd—absolutely and unreservedly absurd. What are we to make of poems that express no surprise or alarm about weird events like cows that jump over the moon or people that jump over candles, or weird characters like groups of tradesmen who climb into small containers intended for bathing and husbands who incarcerate their wives in large vegetables? What are we to make of a logic which assumes that a refusal to submit oneself to the divine will is grounds for having one's lower extremities grabbed by a large domesticated fowl and being tossed down the stairs, or that the thought of having one's cradle blown out of a tree by the wind should comfort an infant and assist somnolence? (Nor does "Rockabye Baby" express an attitude unusual in Mother Goose; there is also

> Baby, baby, naughty baby,
> Hush, you squalling thing, I say.
> Peace this moment, peace, or maybe
> Bonaparte will pass this way
>
> And he'll beat you, beat you, beat you,
> And he'll beat you all to pap,
> and he'll eat you, eat you, eat you,
> Every morsel, snap, snap, snap.   (59)

Pleasant dreams?)

Furthermore, what are we to make of poems that do the opposite, and instead of taking oddities for granted, imply that there is great significance in quite obviously insignificant events, such as a child falling asleep half-shod, or another child pulling a plum out of a plum pie, or a couple who

> walked on their feet
> And 'twas thought what they eat
> Helped, with drinking, to keep them alive!   (171)

Given their history, of course, these verses may once have made sense. Before the vagaries of memory distorted them, they may have been associated with events that explained them, or had further verses that eventually offered rational explanations for some of the bizarre behavior they describe. But once these verses have been divorced from those contexts, there is no question about it: they are unquestionably loony.

That lunacy interests, and bothers, a lot of adults. Here are words that we have in our heads, words as familiar to us as our own names and telephone numbers, words we seem to have always known, for we probably can't remember when we first heard them; but if we stop to think about it, these ever-so-familiar words make no sense at all. A lamb going to school? A garden with pretty maids growing in it? A blackbird that bites off noses? How could something so familiar—something we all know and take for granted—be so strange? So irrational? So just plain loony?

187

That strangeness bothers some people so much that they invent all sorts of theoretically rational explanations for it—ways of accounting for the lunacy by denying it. Sure, they say, Mother Goose rhymes *sound* strange—but they actually have hidden meanings, and once you know what those meanings are, then they aren't strange at all anymore. About once a year or so, I get a phone call, usually late in the evening, from someone who asks, in a slightly slurred voice over a background of tinkling glasses and loud music, for the guy who knows all about children's literature. When I admit to being that guy, the slurred voice says, "You don't know who I am, but we're having an argument here and somebody said you could settle it. Isn't that there rhyme 'Georgie Porgie, pudding and pie' all about one of them kings of England back in the olden days, and, like, he had all these mistresses and he killed them all, like Henry the Eighth?" When I say that, no, it isn't, that in fact old versions don't even have the name George in them (the Opies report that the first printed version, in Halliwell's *The Nursery Rhymes of England* of 1844, is about "Rowley Powley") and that in any case these rhymes rarely have that kind of secret allegorical meaning, the slurred voice gets a little angry, and says, "But I heard it from a guy who says he read it in a magazine somewhere—so it must be true. I thought you professors were supposed to know everything."

In asking about the hidden meaning of nursery rhymes, my callers are partaking in another significant aspect of oral culture, the transmission of pseudo-scholarship by rumor and word of mouth. Some of the demystifying explanations of nursery rhymes they ask me about have a long history of their own, going back at least as far as 1708, when William King included speculations about who the original King Cole might have been in his *Useful Transactions in Philosophy* (Opie 134). In 1834, John Bellenden Ker published *An Essay on the Archeology of Popular English Phrases and Nursery Rhymes;* almost a hundred years later in 1930, Katherine Elwes Thomas' published *The Real Personages of Mother Goose,* which, the Opies say, expressed "a cheerful determination to prove that the nursery characters were real persons regardless of what the sources quoted say" (29). This book formed the basis of an MGM documentary which probably put these silly theories into popular circulation, where, as my phone calls reveal, they still survive.

One of the main delights of the *Oxford Dictionary of Nursery Rhymes* is the Opies' levelheaded discussions of these theories, which are often more absurd than the rhymes themselves—and just as entertaining. The Opies say, "Much ingenuity has been exercised to show that certain nursery rhymes have had greater significance than is now apparent.... It should be said straightway that the bulk of these speculations are worthless" (27). Thus, Ker himself invented the early form of Dutch which he claimed that the rhymes were actually Anglicized versions of, so that "Ding Dong Bell" was originally

Ding d'honig-beld,
Die kaetst in de weld
Hwa put heer in?
Lyt'el Je haen, Je Grjn   (Opie 28)

which supposedly meant, "It is the honey-bearing image that brings this revenue, it is this that affords all this wealth. Who is it takes it out? That curse to us all, the sneering bully (the monk)"— an attack on the Catholic Church by early Dutch Protestants, it seems. In 1866, the Rev. Sabine Baring-Gould proposed that Jack and Jill were originally Hjuki and Bil of the Norse Edda; he could only explain how Bil became Jill by suggesting that one of the children ought to have a female name, and he conveniently forgot the much simpler explanation that Jack and Jill have often been used as generic names for boys and girls, as in Shakespeare's "Jack shall have Jill; nought shall go ill" (*Midsummer Night's Dream* 3.2.461-2). A particularly rich example of the wild extremes to which pseudo-explanation has gone is the Opies' list of sources proposed for "Hey diddle diddle," which begin with James Halliwell taking seriously the practical joke of someone who presented him with a parallel to the verse in supposedly ancient Greek:

some other of the 'origin' theories that may safely be discounted are (i) that it is connected with Hathor worship [whatever that is]); (ii) that it refers to various constellations (Taurus, Canis Minor, &c.); (iii) that it describes the flight from the rising of the waters in Egypt (little dog, the Dog Star, or 'Sohet'; fiddler, beetle, hence scarab; cow jumping over moon, symbol of sky, &c.); (iv) that it portrays Elizabeth, Lady Katherine Grey, and the Earls of Hertford and Liecester; (v) that it tells of Papist priests urging the laboring class to work harder; (vi) that the expression 'Cat and the fiddle' comes (a) from Katherine of Aragon (Katherine la fidele), (b), from Catherine, wife of Peter the Great, and (c) from Caton, a supposed governor of Calais (Caton le fidele). (203-5)

Alternately, the Opies suggest that "The sanest observation on this rhyme seems to have been made by Sir Henry Reed, 'I prefer to think,' he says, 'that it commemorates the athletic lunacy to which the strange conspiracy of the cat and the fiddle incited the cow.'"

This perfectly logical explanation for one particular rhyme points to an important generalization about all the works of

Mother Goose. Since most of us remember these rhymes without knowing or caring about their original reasons for existence, any satisfactory explanation of their significance will not depend on their origins. Because we know them and treasure them in apparently meaningless forms, we must account for their lack of meaning instead of attempting to find meaning in them.

A good way of doing so may be found in the circumstances in which they have been remembered. The British call these verses nursery rhymes because they have a history of having been often said or sung to young children by people with no books handy. Somewhere in the history of each of the rhymes of Mother Goose there is probably a nanny or a mother trying to calm down a child, and plucking some words out of her brain in order to do so. In these circumstances, the original purpose of the words is quite beside the point; as the Opies say, "the mother or nurse does not employ a jingle because it is a nursery rhyme *per se*, but because in the pleasantness (or desperation) of the moment it is the first thing which comes to her mind" (6). I can recall my own mother singing to my younger brother about how he'd wonder where the yellow went when he brushed his teeth with Pepsodent; if other mothers also sang it, and if their children remember it and later pass it on to *their* children, then someday that verse may turn out to be a nursery rhyme, for people who haven't the vaguest idea about who or what Pepsodent might once have been.

In fact, the *real* explanation for the often absurd nature of nursery rhymes is less often a forgotten historical significance than it is merely the vagueness of memory. Again and again, the Opies report that familiar rhymes are actually parts of simpler versions of older songs—most often their openings or their choruses; and the rest of the song often grounds the apparent nonsense in quite logical circumstances. For instance, Mother Goose tells us merely that

> Elsie Marley is grown so fine,
> She won't get up to feed the swine,
> But lies in bed till eight or nine
>   Lazy Elsie Marley.   (159)

But a later verse of the original verse of the original song Mother Goose borrowed these lines from provides the reason for this indolence: Elsie can afford to be so lazy because she's become rich on the proceeds of booze, and maybe even prostitution:

> Elsie keeps wine, gin and ale,
> In her house below the dale,
> Where every tradesman up and down,
> Does call to spend his half-a-crown.

The memories of those who brought rhymes to the nursery were not just selective; they were often inaccurate. "Goosey Goosey Gander" is as illogical as it is because the last four lines about throwing an old man down the stairs actually have a separate source:

> They are much the same as the lines which school-children address to the cranefly ("Daddy-long-legs"), sometimes pulling off its legs as they repeat,
> > Old father Long-Legs
> > > Can't say his prayers;
> > Take him by the left leg,
> > > And throw him downstairs. (191)

An even vaguer memory than the one that joined these two separate bits of memorable verse into one strange poem is the one responsible for "Rub a dub dub" as we now know it. This story of three men in a tub is based on

> Hey! rub-a-dub, ho! rub-a-dub, three maids in a tub,
> And who do you think were there?
> The butcher, the baker, the candlestick-maker
> And all of them gone to the fair. (376)

Replacing "were there" with "they were" makes for a whole different story: the sordid and less memorable truth behind the memorable nonsense is that the three tradesmen weren't taking the bath themselves; it was their minds that were dirty, for they were just spectators of the tub scene, apparently at a side-show involving three, count 'em, three beautiful wenches.

The fact that easy (if sometimes confused) memorability is what made a rhyme part of the nursery canon is an important clue to the significance of Mother Goose rhymes as touchstones for children's literature—especially children's poetry. These rhymes have that insidious insistence that writers of popular songs aspire to—we find them running through our thoughts even when we'd rather forget them altogether. The important question is, why are they so insistent? What makes them so memorable? Knowing that should tell us much about how poetry in general affects and delights us.

The first thing to be said is that the memorability of these rhymes has little or nothing to do with their content; the mere fact that so many of them make so little sense should tell us that. In some cases, in fact, the content is quite literally something we would otherwise find hard to remember, so that the rhymes have the express purpose of assisting memory, of helping us to recall the days of the month in "Thirty days hath September" or the letters of the alphabet in

A was an archer, who shot at a frog,
B was a butcher, and had a great dog.   (48)

Rhymes like these allow us to remember otherwise unmemorable information because they use patterns of language, rhymes and rhythms, that place the useful information into predictable slots; all we have to do is remember the frog in the first line, and we're well on the way to remembering the rhyming "dog" in line two, and thus, the butcher who owned him and the letter B that begins the word "butcher." The information survives because it is carried within an easily recognizable and highly repetitive structure. It is accompanied by a great deal of what theorists of information call "redundancy": that part of our communications with each other that we already know, for paradoxically, we cannot communicate anything new without reminding ourselves of a great deal that we know already:

> A written message is never completely unpredictable. If it were it would be nonsense. Indeed, it would be noise. To be understandable, to convey meaning, it must conform to rules of spelling, structure and sense, and these rules, known in advance as information shared between the writer and the reader, reduce uncertainty. They make the message partly predictable, compelling it to carry extra luggage in the form of superfluous symbols. Rules are a form of redundancy....
> (Campbell 68-9)

Because nursery rhymes often don't conform to rules of sense, they might seem to lack this sort of redundancy; but in fact, their obvious patterns of rhyme and rhythm and repetition quickly become redundant, and thus, help us to remember the nonsense they contain. According to Jeremy Campbell, psychologists have discovered that people "are poor at remembering sequences which contain little or no redundancy...most people can sense a distinct change that occurs when unorganized strings of words acquire structure. Some sort of barrier is crossed, with powerful effects on the effectiveness of memory" (218).

Nursery rhymes often have very short lines, so that the rhymes comes frequently and thus, are hard not to notice:

> Jack be nimble,
> Jack be quick,
> Jack jump over
> The candlestick.   (226-7)

They also tend to have strong, assertive rhythms, as in

> American jump, American jump,
> One—two—three   (55)

and strongly repetitive patterns of language, so that nouns and verbs appear at the same place in series of lines:

> He *put* in his thumb,
> And *pulled* out a plum,
> And *said*, What a good boy am I!   (234)

Here the second word in each line is a verb, "put in" is balanced by "pulled out," and "out a" is echoed by "what a." Sometimes, the patterns are all reversals:

> As I went over the water,
> The water went over me.   (220)

There are also often repeated words or phrases, repeated refrains or choruses as in "There was a man lived in the moon, lived in the moon, lived in the moon" (52) or "Curly locks, curly locks" (140) or "Pussy cat, pussy cat, where have you been?" (357) When all of these rhymes and patterns and reversals and repetitions combine in one short verse, the result is hard to forget:

> Hickory, dickory, dock,
> The mouse ran up the clock.
>> The clock struck one,
>> The mouse ran down,
> Hickory, dickory, dock.   (206)

But redundancy makes, not just for memorability, but also, and more significantly, for enjoyment: as their long history of service in the nursery shows, we recall these rhymes in circumstances in which we wish to give pleasure, to both ourselves and to children. They are a pleasure to hear, and they are a pleasure to say.

That they are a pleasure to hear accounts for the rhymes that the Opies call "infant amusements": words meant to accompany games that adults play with babies, such as "This little piggie went to market," designed as an accompaniment to tickling, or this rhyme meant to be said while hiding an object in one of two closed fists:

> Handy dandy, riddledy ro,
> Which hand will you have, high or low?   (197)

The pleasure is not just the physical activity, but the silly sounds that go with it: the mere fact that the words make no sense focuses attention on their patterns, and it is these satisfying structured patterns that gives listeners pleasure. When my own children were younger, they were particularly fond of our own variation of one such game:

> This is the way the lady rides—
> > Easy, easy;
> And this is the way the gentleman rides—
> > A gallop a trot, a gallop a trot;
> And this is the way the farmer rides—
> > Hobbledy hoy, hobbledy hoy;
> And this is the way the maniac rides—
> > Eeeeee—AW!

The traditional game consists of holding the child's hands and of jumping it up and down ever more quickly on one's knees; at the end of the last verse, which I made up myself, I'd toss the child up into the air—and that toss, accompanied by a high pitched scream, always got more laughs than a toss without a scream, and without a redundant pattern of every quickening nonsense syllables preceding it.

That the rhymes are a pleasure to say is also apparent in games like these; "A gallop a trot" is a wonderful workout for the tongue, and it's hard not to want to say it, and then say it again. And it's easy to understand why children like to choose sides with counting out rhymes that are as much fun and as challenging to say as

> Inter, mitzy, titzy, tool,
> Ira, dira, dominu,
> Oker, poker, dominoker,
> Out goes you.   (223)

Some of the rhymes are even more obviously intended to be fun to say—among them tongue twisters like "Peter Piper picked a peck of pickled peppers" or

> I need not your needles, they're needless to me,
> For kneading of needles is needless, you see.
> But did my neat trousers but need to be kneed, I then should
> have need of your needles indeed.   (326)

In all these rhymes, basic characteristics of language—for instance, the fact that words or sounds that are similar to each other create rhythmic patterns—have been exaggerated, so that they become much more obvious than they usually are in speech or in written prose. Having been exaggerated, they become the center of attention: these tongue twisters are less about their apparent subjects than about the pleasure of the patterns formed by the words used to describe those subjects. And to some extent, that is true of just about every rhyme in the Mother Goose canon.

But the qualities of words in themselves can be foregrounded in this way exactly because the meanings of the words in these rhymes is so relatively unimportant. Like conversations in languages we don't understand, we can hear the music better when we aren't conscious of the significance of the words. Not knowing Italian, I used to think that Puccini's aria "Mi chiamano Mimi" sounded extravagantly romantic—until I read a translation of the libretto for *La Boheme,* and discovered that all it meant was, "People call me Mimi, and I live by myself in a chilly room making artificial flowers."

That part of the effect of Mother Goose rhymes depends on their lack of meaning becomes particularly obvious when we consider the works of poets who try to imitate Mother Goose, like the Canadian poet Dennis Lee. When he writes absurd nonsense, the rhymes and patterns become as significant as they are in the originals, and Lee creates some magnificently persuasive rhymes:

> Mississauga rattlesnakes
> Eat brown bread.
> Mississauga rattlesnakes
> Fall down dead.
> If you catch a caterpillar
> Feed him apple juice;
> But if you catch a rattlesnake
> Turn him loose!   (16)

But when he uses almost the same rhythms for poems that try to convey realistic emotions, they only seem shoddily sentimental, more Eugene Field than Mother Goose:

> I've got a Special Person
>   At my day-care, where I'm in.
> Her name is Mrs. something
>   But we mostly call her Lynn.
>
> Cause Lynn's the one that shows you
>   How to Squish a paper cup.
> And Lynn's the one that smells good
>   When you make her pick you up.
>   She smells good when she picks you up.   (24)

What is interesting however, is not just that the nonsense of the first example allows sound patterns to become apparent—it is that it is, unlike the second example, satisfyingly mysterious—a strange set of events delightful both because they are strange and because the patterns of their saying make them seem so inevitable, so to be taken for granted.

The same is true of all the important works of Mother Goose. They are memorable not just because they are highly patterned, but also because they are so successfully strange. Their main strangeness is that they use quite sensible language in the service of quite nonsensical situations, as in the story of a man who lived in the moon.

> And his hat was made of good cream cheese, good cream cheese, good cream cheese,
> And his hat was made of good cream cheese,
> And his name was Aiken Drum.

> His breeches were made of haggis bags, haggis bags, haggis bags,
> His breeches were made of haggis bags,
> And his name was Aiken Drum.

This is redundancy without any comprehensible information to convey—the use of the very means which make communication possible to communicate nothing sensible. It becomes interesting and pleasurable exactly because the meaning it conveys is so unrecognizable. Short-sighted people will understand when I say that the work of Mother Goose is something like taking your glasses off and enjoying what you see, or rather, don't see—wrongheadedly using your eyes, your tools of vision, to see unclearly, and enjoying the mysterious and meaningless world you see.

There is, of course, some pleasure in putting your glasses back on again, and realizing that that wonderful reddish cloud with green and yellow bits was just an ordinary phone booth after all. It's something like solving a riddle: that which seemed so peculiar, so absurd, so entirely inexplicable, had a quite commonplace explanation after all. That may explain why so many people try so hard to find explanations for these rhymes: they are so strange that we assume they must be riddles—that they must have quite rational explanations after all, if only we could apply our ingenuity and figure out what they are.

And of course, many of the rhymes are actually riddles—very weird descriptions with very ordinary explanations:

> Four stiff standers
> Four dilly-danders.
> Two lookers, two crookers,
> And a wig-wag.   (397)

To a nasty mind like mine that sounds exceeding sexual; but in fact it's just a cow. Or how about

> Little Nancy Etticoat
> With a white petticoat,
> And a red nose;
> She has no feet or hands,

The longer she stands
The shorter she grows.   (326)

This apparently deformed Elephant Girl is actually just a candle.

But so what? What is most revealing about the riddles of Mother Goose is that their answers are not very memorable. It's the riddling descriptions themselves that capture our attention, so much so that in a few cases we have even forgotten that the verses we take such pleasure in reciting started life as riddles. One example is

Little Dicky Dilver
Had a wife of silver; He took a stick and broke her back
And sold her to the miller;
The miller wouldn't have her
So he threw her in the river.   (148)

This apparently gruesome tale of horror is part of a longer ballad which makes it clear that Little Dicky Dilver's wife is actually a grain of wheat, whose travels after the miller breaks her back are chronicled in a series of verses. An even more telling example of a riddle now divorced from its answer is one of the most famous of the rhymes: few people who recite the story of "Humpty Dumpty" realize they are giving a riddling description of an egg.

Like most of Mother Goose's riddles, "Humpty Dumpty" really needs no answer. It's the peculiar description, the strange world evoked by language used in an unusual way, that gives it its power. When we do find out the answer of a Mother Goose riddle we've not heard before, we tend to immediately go back and consider the riddle again, and only partially to see how the answer explains what seemed so weird; the other reason we return is to enjoy the pleasure or familiar things turned so strange, so magical—the world of the commonplace made wonderful by magic. Knowing that it's a phone booth, we take our glasses off again to enjoy how it becomes a strange red cloud. Knowing that it is a description of an egg only heightens the mysterious intensity of this extravagantly beautiful description:

In marble halls as white as milk,
Lined with a skin as soft as silk,
Within a fountain crystal-clear,
A golden apple doth appear.
No doors there are to this stronghold,
Yet thieves break in and steal the gold.   (196)

And the fact that it represents something so mundane as teeth and gums does nothing to dispel the magically mysterious behavior of

Thirty white horses
Upon a red hill,
Now they tramp,
Now they champ,
Now they stand still.   (212)

The irony in the history of attempts to explain away, conventionalize, normalize nursery rhymes is that the absurdity that so disturbs a certain kind of adult mind may be exactly what most delights those children and adults who most enjoy these rhymes. It is an anarchic absurdity, a defiance of convention and normalcy; it's no accident that Mother Goose's version of the old proverb

A man of words and not of deeds
Is like a garden full of weeds (286)

should continue with a series of absurd statements that send up the seriousness of the proverb:

When the weeds begin to grow,
It's like a garden full of snow;
when the snow begins to melt,
It's like a ship without a belt;
When the ship begins to sail,
It's like a bird without a tail.

(I've changed the tense here to fit the first verse, which, not surprisingly, has been discarded in many modern versions.) To explain away this sort of deliberate absurdity is merely to restore the pomposity of the proverb, merely to replace the wonderful image of stamping horses with a picture that could delight only a dental hygienist.

Like the story about the garden or the riddle about the horses, Mother Goose's best work contains nothing much that we aren't familiar with—although its daily acquaintance with cows and candles makes it even more magically foreign for us than it once was for our ancestors. But it combines common words for common objects in such a way that they become strange; due to accidents of history, furthermore, or sometimes due only to our lack of knowledge about their origins, even those rhymes that once did make sense have come to be mysterious. Making the ordinary seem weird is a way of shooting holes in our usual vision of the world—focusing our attention on things we are otherwise so familiar with that we no longer even notice them. Above all, in making the ordinary noticeable and strange, the language of Mother Goose draws attention to its own power, its own mystery. In these ways, in revealing the power of language to make the ordinary wonderful and to be wonderful in and for itself, the rhymes of Mother Goose offer their young hearers an introduction to the main pleasure of poetry—indeed, of all literature.

The rhymes of Mother Goose have given rise to a vast body of pictures, including many by great children's illustrators from Caldecott and Greenaway and Crane in the last century to Maurice Sendak and Nicola Bayley in more recent years. While many of these illustrators have produced fine books based on Mother Goose, new creations that result from combinations of these old words with new pictures, their work never adequately represents the rhymes themselves. This is not just a question of our being better able to imagine our own pictures without the interference of Caldecott or Sendak; the fact is that *any* specific picture at all, even one we invent for ourselves, is bound to destroy some of the special impossibility, perhaps even unimaginability, of the images evoked by the rhymes themselves.

Consider the thirty white horses: while a picture of a set of dentures would obviously deflate the grand mystery of the image, a picture of thirty horses doesn't serve much better, for looking at a bunch of horses is not the same as having words evoke them for us; and in any case, the illustrator would have to resort to a hill covered with red posies or something equally literalizing. The fact is, the best picture is an impossible one that could be both teeth and horses at the same time—and not as silly as that sounds, but grandly strange. The pictures evoked by most Mother Goose rhymes are equally impossible. Breeches made of haggis bags? Somebody sitting on a tuffet (especially when there is no such word or thing as a "tuffet")? Boys made of frogs and snails and puppy-dog's tails? All are equally unimaginable to the eye but easily understandable to the mind.

But most illustrations for nursery rhymes are anything but impossible; illustrators tend to explain the rhymes away in the same doggedly singleminded way that scholars have tried to allegorize them. Sometimes this makes for good jokes, as when Randolph Caldecott or Maurice Sendak turn simple rhymes like "This is the house that Jack built" or "Hector Protector" into long, complicated narratives in an extended sequence of pictures; the effect of these is something like the relationship between complex riddles and their commonplace answers, except in reverse: the riddling words are relatively simple, the pictures that provide the answers complex. But more often than not, literalizing illustrations merely make the rhymes seem pointlessly commonplace rather than magically absurd. The actual silver bells growing on the plants in both Blanche Fisher Wright's and Nicola Bayley's gardens look manufactured, like chintzy Christmas ornaments; and the athletic lunacy of the cow in "Hey diddle diddle" seems hardly even worth noting when illustrators again and again depict it as an optical illusion—a matter of a cow in the foreground seeming to jump over a moon low in the sky in the background. Either taking these rhymes literally or attempting to literalize them, as Wallace Tripp does when he makes the fox who "gives warning/It's a cold frosty morning" into a TV weatherman, results in a flattening of their mystery.

Consequently, while children should certainly have access to the many ingeniously humorous stories that good illustrators have made out of Mother Goose, we shouldn't allow the existence of those stories to deprive children of the quite different pleasure of the rhymes on their own—the pleasure of hearing or of saying these enjoyable and evocative words without the interference of accompanying illustrations. For this purpose, any large collection of the rhymes will do; but since the main audience for Mother Goose is likely to be those too young to be able to read the rhymes for themselves, the best collection will be one that offers the most to the adult readers who will actually speak the rhymes.

Like many other editions, the Opies' *Oxford Dictionary of Nursery Rhymes* gives adults access to a lot of fine rhymes to read aloud to their children; unlike most other editions, it has the added virtue of explaining the rhymes in a sensible and useful way—offering answers to the riddles, and easily followed directions for the infant amusements. As an added bonus, the *Dictionary* offers careful scholarship that doggedly traces rhymes back to often fascinating origins, happily debunks silly ideas—and meanwhile, offers a rich ragbag of delightfully useless information about subjects as diverse as American slang and Old Norse deities. Reading the *Dictionary* is like exploring the attic of an old house— there is lots of stuff to rummage through, and most of it is just useless and dusty, and some of it is useless and fascinating, and some of it is not just fascinating but useful indeed. The *Dictionary* is much like the rhymes it contains—it has a lot to offer because it's more than a little crazy.

REFERENCES

Baring-Gould, William S. and **Ceil.** New York: Bramhall House, 1962.

Bayley, Nicola. *Book of Nursery Rhymes.* Harmondsworth, Middlesex: Penguin Puffin, 1981.

Caldecott, Randolph. *The Randolph Caldecott Picture Book.* London and New York: Frederick Warne, 1976.

Campbell, Jeremy. *Grammatical Man: Information, Entropy, Language, and Life.* New York: Simon and Schuster, 1982.

Lee, Dennis. *Alligator Pie.* Toronto: Macmillan, 1974.

Opie, Iona and **Peter.** *The Oxford Dictionary of Nursery Rhymes.* Oxford: Oxford Univ. Press. 1951; rpr. 1984.

Sendak, Maurice. *Hector Protector and As I Went Over the Water.* New York: Harper and Row, 1965.

Tripp, Wallace. *Granfa' Grigg Had a Pig and Other Rhymes Without Reason from Mother Goose.* Boston: Little, Brown, 1976.

Wright, Blanche Fisher. *The Real Mother Goose.* Chicago: Rand McNally, 1916; rpr. 1974.

The Fairy Tales of Charles Perrault: Acute Logic and Gallic Wit

by James Gellert

Writing nearly two and a half centuries after the first publication of the fairy tales of Charles Perrault, the respected author, critic, and fellow countryman of Perrault, Paul Hazard, rhetorically asked:

> At what moment did the thought first occur to someone that children might wish for other reading than school work, for other books than catechisms or grammars? What revolutionary first became aware of the child's existence and dared to sanction it? What perspicacious observer noticed children? What benefactor procured for them the joy, multiplied to infinity, of owning a book at last that was truly theirs?" (6-7)

These questions are obviously critical to the development of children's literature; Hazard answers them by identifying the "moment" as the century of Louis XIV, and the "revolutionary" and "benefactor" as the French Academician, Charles Perrault. With the publication of Perrault's *Histoires ou Contes du temps passé, avec des moralitez* in 1697, adds Hazard, "Mother Goose came out of the sheds and barns and strutted about Paris; then and for the first time, French children, and later all the children in the world, had a book after their own heart, a book so lovely and so fresh that they were never willing to give it up" (8).

While Hazard's panegyric does reflect the unique importance of Perrault's contribution to children's literature, it also raises fundamental questions about Perrault and about his famed publication. What were the sources of the tales? To what extent was Perrault pandering to current literary tastes? For whom was he writing the tales? Was Perrault the sole author of the tales? And, most pertinent of all, why is it that this particular collection has endured with children, whereas many others written about the same time have not?

Some of the answers to these questions are provided in Roger Sale's investigations of the evolution of the written fairy tale when he writes,

> Perrault's *Histoires* stands out, for two reasons. First, his was a pivotal period in the history of the invention of childhood, and thus of children's literature, when traditions of both oral and written tales were taking a turning. Second, of all the many collections of fairy tales that were written and collected in France around the turn of the seventeenth century, Perrault's were the ones most clearly designed to be read to children." (50)

Sale's comment points to the particular significance of Perrault's publication, and suggests why the tales have endured with young readers for nearly three centuries.

Considering that the literary reputation of Charles Perrault rests almost exclusively upon his prose tales, it is somewhat surprising that at the time of their publication in 1697, Perrault was sixty-nine years of age. Moreover, although Perrault did publish three verse tales prior to 1697, these too were published, and probably written, in his declining years. But as Barchilon and Flinders show, before turning his hand to fairy tales, Perrault had led, by all contemporary standards, a very successful public career. A graduate in law (he practised little), he held posts as a tax collector and as an advisor on artistic and literary affairs to the influential minister of finances in the court of Louis, Jean-Baptiste Colbert. In 1671 Perrault was elected to the prestigious French Academy, and became its *Directeur* in 1681.

Throughout his life, Perrault experimented with numerous literary genres, first writing burlesque poems, then the trendy "precieux" poetry so popular in France in the 1660's and 70's, before dabbling in occasional verse—a medium he employed to eulogize the happy occurences and highlights of the rein of Louis XIV. By the late 1680's, Perrault had become embroiled in the artistic *cause célèbre* of the century, the contentious "Quarrel of the Ancients and Moderns," in which he vigorously championed fellow artists such as Molière and Corneille, while disparaging

Homer, Plato, and other past masters. Perrault's published contributions to this protracted debate, in which Boileau played an active antagonistic role to Perrault, was four books, the last of which appeared in the same year as the eight prose tales.

Always a follower of literary fashion, Perrault also found time in the final decade of the century to capitalize on a lively interest in written fairy tales. He had come under the influence of the literary salon of his niece, Mademoiselle L'Héritier. This eminent coterie, which included Mesdames D'Aulnoy and Murat, regaled themselves and their aristocratic audience with the retelling of fairy stories, many of which were current in the nursery. The rage in fairy tales carried impressive sanction, and there is evidence that courtiers such as Colbert and even Louis himself retained an interest in the genre long after their childhood (Barchilon 78-79). The charm of these tales for the lords and ladies of Louis' court existed not only in their inherent simplicity and engaging didacticism, but, as Andrew Lang observed some hundred years ago, in their welcome contrast to the "weariness" inspired by the "long novels and pompous plays of the age..." (xix). So Perrault was very much following the fashionable literati of his time when he published his fairy tales, although his particular response to the craze was unique—so much so that while most of the versions of his contemporaries are obscure today, his are still universally known and enjoyed.

Perrault's first full-fledged attempts at writing fairy tales (some of his earlier writings contain allusions to the genre) were the three verse tales of "Griselidis" ("Patient Griselda"), published in 1691, "Les Souhaits ridicules" ("The Ridiculous Wishes"), published in 1693, and "Peau d'Ane" ("Donkey-Skin"), published in 1694. These verse tales, all of which had antecedents in popular tradition, are sometimes published today along with the better known prose tales. The prose stories, the *Histoires ou Contes du temps passé*, often referred to as the "Tales of Mother Goose" from the inscription on the volume's frontispiece reading "Contes de ma mère l'oye," were printed together for the first time in 1697, although five had appeared in a dedication manuscript in 1695, and "Sleeping Beauty" had been printed separately in the periodical *Mercure Galant* in 1696. The eight tales, at least five of which are known to children all over the world, were "La Belle au bois dormant" ("Sleeping Beauty"), "Le petit chaperon rouge" ("Little Red Ridinghood"), "La Barbe bleüe" ("Bluebeard"), "Le Maître Chat, ou le Chat Botté" ("Puss in Boots"), "Le Fées" ("The Fairies"), "Cendrillon, ou la petite pantoufle de verre" ("Cinderella"), "Riquet à la Houppe" ("Ricky of the Tuft"), and "Le Petit Poucet" ("Tom Thumb"). In addition to the frontispiece, which depicts three enthralled children listening to an aged female story-teller, crude woodcuts introduced each tale in the collection.

Judging from contemporary notices and the number of subsequent early editions published both in France and in other European countries (numerous pirated editions appeared in Amsterdam, for example), the *Contes* seem to have been a virtual instant success; moreover, they have enjoyed a continuous popularity since the initial publication in 1697. That popularity began for young British readers in 1729, when Robert Samber translated a 1721 French edition of the tales "corrected" by the widow of Perrault's printer. Included in this first English version of the eight tales was an additional story, "The Discreet Princess," by Mademoiselle L'Héritier. After Samber's translation, the prose tales found their way into German, Dutch, Italian, and Russian editions before the end of the eighteenth century. The first complete American edition was published by Peter Edes in Haverhill, Massachusetts in 1794. Notable subsequent editions include an 1862 version with illustrations by Gustave Doré; Andrew Lang's 1888 edition, which includes the verse and prose tales in French and a comprehensive introduction in English; a popular American translation by A. E. Johnson in 1921 (reissued in 1969 with the Doré illustrations); a 1961 edition translated by Johnson "and others" with illustrations by W. Heath Robinson (this edition includes the verse tales as well as three stories not linked to Perrault); and a 1967 translation by Angela Carter, again of both the verse and prose tales. Partial editions of Perrault's tales have also proven popular, such as that by Marianne Moore featuring "Sleeping Beauty" and "Cinderella," which was published in 1963.

Today, with the association between fairy tales and younger readers, it is easy to forget Perrault's original primary audience. Many jokes and innuendoes in the tales, which include jibes on social snobbery, courtly marriages, the duplicity of lawyers, and even aristocratic culinary tastes, imply an informed, sophisticated readership. It is telling that when "Sleeping Beauty" was first published in the *Mercure Galant,* itself an avant-garde magazine aimed squarely at an adult audience, a note was appended to the tale stressing that the story was not intended primarily for children (Thelander 468). This directive contrasts sharply with the opinion of Robert Samber, who in the dedication to his 1729 translation writes that, while "those of Maturity" might find the tales pleasing, "they are designed for Children." Samber's edition, with its clear emphasis on the child audience, began the final stage in a circular journey for the tales from the traditional story-tellers (many of whom told their tales in the nursery), to the salons of fashionable Paris, and ultimately back to the nursery through post-seventeenth century editions and translations.

While Robert Samber seems comfortable in his attribution of the eight prose tales to Charles Perrault, the matter of authorship is by no means a clear-cut issue. The uncertainty arises from the fact that the dedication for the 1697 edition is signed "P. Darmancour," Darmancour being the name adopted by Perrault's third son, Pierre. The attribution was perpetuated in unauthorized editions printed in Amsterdam, until the 1721 edition noted above named "M. Perrault" as the author. Early opinions on the authorship question vary from the definitive claim for the father in Samber's edition, to the same for the son in an 1876 collection edited by Paul Lacroix (Lang xxviii). Andrew Lang favored a collaboration theory, arguing that the precocious son (only seventeen years old when the dedication manuscript appeared in 1695) sketched out the tales he heard from solicitous nurses, but that "the elderly Academician and *beau esprit* touched [them] up, here toning down an incident too amazing for French sobriety and logic, there adding a detail of contemporary court manners, or a hit at some foible or vanity of men" (xxx). More recent commentators have also debated the authorship conundrum. Percy Muir "unhesitatingly cling[s]" to the sponsorship of the son (40), while Gilbert Rouger opines that after suffering the insults of Boileau for writing fairy tales, Perrault diffidently designated his son as the author to obviate further disapprobation (xxxi). Marc Soriano advances the more complex theory that Perrault senior welcomed and participated in a collaboration because his son unconsciously represented his own twin brother, who had died at six months of age (340-64). Iona and Peter Opie cautiously support the father, basing their verdict both on the evidence of the corrected 1721 edition and on the reflection that, "whereas children rarely let it be assumed that work which is theirs was produced by a parent (however much the parent assisted), fathers are commonly happy to attribute work of theirs to their children, no matter how little the offspring assisted in it" (29). Perhaps the closest one can come to an answer to this contentious question is provided by Jacques Barchilon and Peter Flinders, who write, "For nearly three hundred years scholars have debated the question: 'father or son?' In our opinion, it is a vain question that can be answered: 'both,' but we will never accurately know what proportion each of the collaborators contributed.... We tend to believe, on the strength of the numerous references in other works...that it must have been mostly Perrault" (89).

As Iona and Peter Opie lament in *The Classic Fairy Tales*, Perrault would today probably be considered the father of folklore, if only it had occured to him to state where, when, and under what circumstances he had obtained the material for his tales (26-27). But Perrault was not a folklorist, an anthropologist, or a professional linguist. Instead, as a writer, he adapted and embroidered traditional stories and motifs for his courtly readers. There are antecedents (either oral, written, or both) for all of the verse and prose tales of Perrault, and it would certainly be a mistake to regard him as the creator of characters such as Sleeping Beauty and Cinderella. Like Shakespeare, he culled his sources and reshaped the tales to meet the perceived tastes of his audience. The three verse tales ("Griselidis" is more strictly a *nouvelle*) existed in popular tradition prior to Perrault's treatment of them. As for written sources, "Griselidis" has analogues in Boccaccio, Petrarch, and Chaucer; "Peau d'Ane" in the anonymous fourteenth century novel, *Perceforest,* and in the Italian collections of Straparola and Basile; and "The Ridiculous Wishes" in Oriental renditions (see Barchilon 90-95). In reference to the prose tales, with the exception of "Little Red Riding Hood," for which only a probable oral source has been identified (Zipes 28), and "Bluebeard," for which only the motifs of the forbidden chamber and the magical key come from earlier popular tradition, Perrault may have been indebted, in varying degrees, to Italian, Greek, Indian, German, Egyptian, English, and earlier French written sources. Two tales, "The Fairies" and "Ricky of the Tuft," were actually printed before 1697 by female members of Perrault's literary circle. In addition to the versions of his contemporaries, many of these earlier written sources must surely have filtered down to Perrault; but the precise details of his reliance on earlier printed material will likely never be known.

Perrault's motives for introducing the kind of changes he does in his reworkings of oral and written sources have intrigued researchers and critics who have imputed, on behalf of Perrault, many different rationales for the versions as we now know them. Writing from the perspective of a social historian, for example, Dorothy Thelander claims that Perrault's tales "reflect the serious concerns of particular social and intellectual circles in late seventeenth-century France, and that they reveal a mood of hostility or ambivalence toward important elements in the official culture of the age of Louis XIV" (492). For Robert Darnton, the vestiges of folk traditions in the tales imply "a world of raw and naked brutality," and a story such as "Tom Thumb" suggests a Malthusian vision of "the problem of survival during a period of demographic disaster" (15,30). In contrast to Thelander and Darnton, who see Perrault's tales as reactive to political and social realities, Jack Zipes views them as proactive, and argues that the tales were tools of socialization, "providing behavioral patterns and models for children...based on gender" and designed "to reinforce the standards of the civilizing process set by upper-class French society" (23,26). For females, then, Perrault proseletyzes an ideal who is "beautiful, polite, graceful, industrious, properly groomed, and knows how to control herself at all times"; males, on the other hand, are celebrated as having "remarkable minds, courage, and deft manners" (25-26).

All three of the critics cited here may be correct to some extent, for each of their theories can be adequately defended with reference to the tales. What is certain, however, is that whether Perrault was subtly engaging in political sedition, underscoring social inequities, or prescribing behavioral models for aristocratic young men and women, once the tales had been translated into English and other languages, and had circulated sufficiently in France, they began to reach another audience and to fulfill a much more meaningful and lasting role as literature for children.

If, as Lillian Smith avers, fairy tales have slight, if any, appeal to children merely because they are old (63), it is likely that the attraction for children to Perrault's tales specifically rests not in their status as socio-historical tracts, but rather because they possess the inherent qualities of good literature. Moreover, in spite of his writing primarily for an aristocratic, adult audience, Perrault was probably well aware of how the genre and his versions particularly might appeal to children. In the third volume of the "Quarrel of the Ancients and Moderns" published in 1692, Perrault had written on the charm of fairy tales, and had referred to their intrinsic attractions and eclectic appeal:

> the old wives tales, like those of Cupid and Psyche, provide the most beautiful subjects and give more pleasure than the most complicated theatre plots.... These kinds of fables...have a way of delighting all sorts of people, the greatest minds as well as those of the lower classes, the older men and women as well as children.... (quoted in Barchilon 81-82)

In keeping with the penchant for simplicity characteristic of the traditional tales, Perrault avoids the extravagant descriptions and lengthy story-lines found in versions by contemporaries like Madame d'Aulnoy, whose tales, in the opinion of the Opies, are "wild, undisciplined, almost feverishly imaginative" (30), or like Mademoiselle L'Héritier, whose "The Discreet Princess" runs for some sixty pages in Samber's 1729 edition. Instead, Perrault favors a more restrained, simpler, and far shorter medium for the popular stories.

This emphasis on simplicity does not mean that Perrault was perfunctory or careless in his writing. As Jacques Barchilon and Peter Flinders have demonstrated, a comparison between the 1695 dedication manuscript and the 1697 printed text of the tales reveals a fastidious craftsman at work, one who pruned and amended, always working towards a more precise, economical presentation (103). Perrault's debt to French classicism is exemplified in the terse, pithy exchanges between primary characters, such as those involving Sleeping Beauty and her prince, Red Riding Hood and the wolf, and Puss and his master, and also in his refusal to indulge in long-winded explanations or character analysis which might interfere with fundamental plot development. In addition, Perrault excises the bawdiness common in some earlier collections. For example, instead of the indelicate ravaging of the sleeping princess by a married king in "Sleeping Beauty"—an incident found in an Italian version by Basile—we find the romanticized meeting of the princess and prince now familiar to most readers.

In keeping with Perrault's general tendency to simplify, his characters are, for the most part, free of psychological complexity or depth. Cinderella is good, Puss is clever; Bluebeard is a murderous villain, the wolf in "Red Riding Hood," is temptation and evil incarnate. What character description exists in the tales is abbreviated and vivid. The effect of Perrault's descriptive technique, especially on young readers, is to immediately and indelibly stamp the essence of a character. Cinderella, for example, is introduced as possessing "an exceptionally sweet and gentle nature." Perrault's terse elaboration on her character is limited to "She got this from her mother, who had been the nicest person in the world" (*Tales* 67). This same direct characterization is present in the opening of "The Fairies," where one daughter is irrevocably labelled disagreeable and arrogant, while the other is declared to be gentle and sweet.

Some of Perrault's characters, and particularly the males, are extremely adroit and clever, and exhibit what Paul Hazard terms the French "national traits" of acute logic and wit (123). Ricky of the Tuft is born clever, and displays the combined rhetorical skills of Cicero and Cyrano in winning the hand of his princess. Puss and Tom Thumb likewise illustrate logical, agile minds, the former in securing wealth and a good marriage for his penniless master, the latter in saving his brothers from a heartless ogre. Even the fairies in the tales, whom more than one critic has described as "Cartesian" (see Hazard 123), dispense their magic with a kind of rigid logic, whether that magic results in a hundred year sleep in return for an oversight, or a disagreeable daughter spewing out snakes and toads because of her incivility.

This emphasis on logic is apparent in another way in the denouements of many of the tales, where Perrault strives to round off or tidy up the plots. In "Sleeping Beauty," the ogress queen is devoured by the very hideous creatures she gathered to consume the heroine—thus assuring that the princess and prince really will live "happily ever after." In "Bluebeard," the surviving wife marries "a very worthy man" who is perfunctorily drawn into the story to guarantee her a blissful future. Cinderella graciously provides for her erstwhile tormentors by marrying the jealous step-sisters to courtiers—a striking contrast to their fate in the version by the Brothers Grimm, where they mutilate their feet in vain attempts to fit the prince's slipper and are never reconciled to Cinderella. Even Puss, who is but a mechanism in "Puss in Boots" not unlike Aladdin's genie in the Arabian Nights cycle, is not forgotten by Perrault. After the miller's youngest son finds wealth and happiness through the machinations of Puss, the tale ends with the clever feline's welfare certain: "Puss became a personage of great importance, and gave up hunting mice, except for amusement" (*Tales* 56).

Perrault's stories contain conventions and motifs common to many folk tales; we encounter fairies and ogres, magic boots and keys, idealized princesses and hateful siblings, formulaic descriptions and miraculous escapes. But Perrault flavors these traditional elements with a certain Gallic cynicism, and a sardonic humour which further adds to the uniqueness of his versions. In its simplest forms, this touch can be seen in the macabre pun in "Tom Thumb" when the hungry ogre instructs his wife to "go upstairs and dress those little rascals"—he is thinking in terms of his next meal, she of helping Tom and his brothers put on their clothes (*Tales* 111)—or in the numerous aphoristic chestnuts found throughout the tales: "The more [sense] one has, the more one fears it to be wanting;" or it is "like a woman to have the knack of saying the right thing, but not the trick of being always in the right" (*Tales* 84, 99).

In its subtler forms, Perrault's wit thrusts in various directions, although contempory manners and courtly foibles seem to especially interest him. At times he lampoons the vanity of courtly ladies, as in "Bluebeard" and "Cinderella," where the secondary female characters are chiefly preoccupied with admiring themselves, usually in full-length mirrors. In "Tom Thumb," Perrault satirizes courtly marriages and spousal fidelity, when in the epilogue of the tale, he reports that Tom used his seven league boots to carry letters from ladies of the court to their lovers, and this proved to be "his greatest source of income." As for letters from wives to husbands, the result is far different: "[the wives] paid him so badly, and this branch of the business brought him in so little, that he did not even bother to reckon what he made from it" (*Tales* 115). Other courtly allusions surface in the tales, including a reference in "Sleeping Beauty" to a culinary delight,

"Sauce Robert," that was much enjoyed by King Louis. The fact that in the story the sauce was intended to flavor the children of the princess in order to satisfy the palate of an ogress-queen would no doubt prompt knowing titters amongst the king's favorites (the reference to Sauce Robert is removed from most modern editions, although it was retained in Samber's). In the opening lines of "Puss in Boots," Perrault hits at that most ubiquitously satirized of all institutions, when the narrator, after noting that the family legacy was quickly absorbed by two elder brothers on the death of the father, adds, "you may be quite sure that neither notary nor attorney were called in to help, for they would speedily have grabbed it all for themselves" (*Tales* 47). Finally, Perrault sends up the very traditions of the fairy tale genre itself, when the just awakened princess in "Sleeping Beauty" greets her savior as follows: "Is it you, dear prince...? you have been long in coming!" (*Tales* 13). In its most subtle forms, Perrault's cynical humour might well be beyond the grasp of children; but in a more general way it imbues the tales with a freshness and a mischievous wit to which readers of all ages can respond.

The diversity of Perrault's tales also plays an important part in their appeal to children. In addition to the well-known plots and themes of "Sleeping Beauty," "Red Riding Hood," "Bluebeard," "Puss in Boots," and "Cinderella," "The Fairies" is a straight-forward exemplum on the rewards of kindness, "Ricky of the Tuft" celebrates intelligence and the power of true love to look beyond physical appearances, and "Tom Thumb" follows a "Hansel and Gretel" plotline and once more emphasizes the worth of an agile mind. The three verse tales also rework tried and true traditional themes: "Griselidis" teaches the virtue of patience in wives, "Peau d'Ane" is a variation on the Cinderella theme, and "The Ridiculous Wishes" moralistically urges the reader to accept his lot in life.

When all of the elements of Perrault's tales are considered— the diversified but traditional plots, the unambiguous charac-terizations, the presentation of basic themes, the simple and economical language, and the infectious humor—the overall emotional appeal they may have for children can well be appreciated. Paul Hazard cites the range of this emotional appeal as encompassing pity, fear, anguish, hope, terror, and joy (8). This catalogue of emotions, which Hazard believes "stirs the souls" of children as they read Perrault's tales, closely anticipates the feelings associated with "faërie," Tolkien's secondary, sub-created world with its attendant fantasy, recovery, escape, and consolation (46-70).

Although a lucid exploration of human emotions is basic to the appeal of Perrault's tales, their unvarnished didacticism is no less significant. "Avec des moralitez" reads the 1697 title, and the dictum of John Locke—to entertain and to instruct—is apparent throughout the collection. "Bluebeard" and "Red Riding Hood" are both cautionary tales. The former ends benignly enough; the latter is decidedly more emphatic in its instruction, since in Perrault's version, the trusting heroine is gobbled up and is not rescued as in the softened variation by the Brothers Grimm. The patent didacticism of "The Fairies" is reinforced by the rigid bipartite structure of the tale (one daughter fails her test with a fairy, the other passes hers)—a structure similar to that in many fables. Although the morals in the other prose tales are not so forcefully represented in the stories themselves, all carry moral tags to guide and instruct the reader. "Sleeping Beauty" demonstrates both that "true love comes by fairy-lot" and "young blood must when young blood will"—a dual message consistent with Perrault's tendency of informing his appended verse morals with several insights. The morals added to "Puss in Boots," "Ricky of the Tuft," and "Tom Thumb" reiterate Perrault's emphasis on the value of a keen mind, while in "Cinderella" the morals extol grace and sweetness in women. What is most evident about Perrault's didacticism is that however much he propagates sexual stereotyping in the tales (and the tales do support this reading), he was writing from what was, for him, a vision of a morally coherent universe.

Finally then, Roger Sale's suggestion that Perrault's tales were clearly designed to be read to children reveals their abiding significance. Perrault's achievement can be evaluated in at least three ways. First, whether the tales were initially directed at adults or children, Perrault's collection was the first to present the tales in a form which children truly enjoyed. This in itself represents a fundamental breakthrough in the history of children's literature. Second, Perrault's spontaneous treatment of the traditional stories make his versions interesting and appealing as literature in their own right. Third, Perrault's successes in the genre have inspired others to turn to fairy tales as entertainment for children. Hans Christian Andersen, Andrew Lang, Walter de la Mare, and in another medium, Walt Disney, all demonstrate an indebtedness to Perrault. Finally, however nagging some of the uncertainties surrounding the tales might be (who wrote the tales? what were the sources? who was the intended audience?), it remains true that the tales as published in Paris in 1697 and attributed to Charles Perrault in the first English translation in 1729, have become immortal favorites in the reading of children, favorites to which they continually return.

REFERENCES

Barchilon, Jacques, and **Peter Flinders.** *Charles Perrault.* Boston: Twayne Publishers, 1981.

Cott, Jonathan, ed. *Beyond the Looking Glass Extraordinary Works of Fairy Tale and Fantasy.* New York: Pocket Books, 1978.

Darnton, Robert. *The Great Cat Massacre and Other Episodes in French Cultural History.* New York: Basic Books, Inc., 1984.

Hazard, Paul. *Books Children and Men.* Trans. Marguerite Mitchell. Boston: The Horn Book, Inc., 1944.

Lang, Andrew. *Perrault's Popular Tales.* Oxford: Clarendon Press, 1888.

Muir, Percy. *English Children's Books.* London: B. T. Batsford Ltd., 1954.

Opie, Iona and **Peter.** *The Classic Fairy Tales.* New York: Oxford University Press, 1980.

Perrault, Charles. *Perrault's Fairy Tales.* Trans. A. E. Johnson. New York: Dover Publications, Inc., 1969.

_____. *Histories or Tales of Times Past.* Trans. Robert Samber. New York: Garland Publishing, Inc., 1977.

Rouger, Gilbert. *Perrault: Contes.* Paris: Éditions Garnier Frères, 1967.

Sale, Roger. *Fairy Tales and After.* Cambridge, Mass.: Harvard University Press, 1978.

Smith, Lillian. *The Unreluctant Years.* Chicago: American Library Association, 1953.

Soriano, Marc. *Les Contes de Perrault.* Paris: Éditions Gallimard, 1968.

Thelander, Dorothy. "Mother Goose and Her Goslings: The France of Louis XIV as Seen Through the Fairy Tales." *The Journal of Modern History* (Sept. 1982):467-96.

Tolkien, J. R. R. "On Fairy-Stories." *The Tolkien Reader.* New York: Ballantine Books, 1966.

Zipes, Jack. *Fairy Tales and the Art of Subversion.* New York: Wildman Press, 1983.

Howard Pyle's *The Merry Adventures of Robin Hood:* The Quintessential Children's Story

by Taimi M. Ranta

If Bennett A. Brockman correctly defines children's literature as "imaginative literature marketed to children and designed for their amusement as well as their edification," then *The Merry Adventures of Robin Hood* stands at the apex of children's literature; indeed, the author-illustrator Robert Lawson once called it "the most perfect of children's books." It embodies all of the significant ingredients of a successful story, regardless of a reader's age. The language befitting the characters of twelfth century England, the pastoral setting, and the lyrical tone all elicit the involvement of a reader or listener. The theme of good triumphing over evil helps the story fuse into a memorable work of fiction. Moreover, Pyle's picturesque, detailed illustrations add special texture and fabric to the story; Selma Lane writes, "There are lovers of fine books who feel Pyle's *Robin Hood* represents the highwater mark of American bookmaking."

The folk hero Robin Hood has been celebrated in popular tales and ballads as far back as the Middle Ages. From this reservoir of unrelated, often conflicting ballads, Pyle, in his own words, "snipped, clipped and tied together again in a score of knots" stories in a loose episodic sequence which nevertheless forms an artistic whole. The book has ten parts, each with two or three chapters containing numerous single episodes of Robin Hood's indefatigable courage, unmatched skill at archery, and daring deeds in his quest for justice for the poor. They depict Robin Hood, the unifying element, progressing merrily through life from the time he becomes an outlaw in the Prologue until his death in the Epilogue. While the order of most of the episodes in the cycle could be shifted without disturbing the sense of wholeness, there is some progression because additional characters are added as the story unfolds who then are involved in later episodes. Also, some sense of chronology is achieved by the succession of kings: Henry II, Richard I, and John. The underlying theme of the cycle is the glaring gap between legal and social justice which Robin Hood personally accepts as his life's challenge.

Born in 1853, Howard Pyle had his first success at the age of twenty-three, when *Scribner's Monthly* bought an illustrated story about the annual wild pony roundup on the island of Chincoteague. That same year, 1876, Pyle moved to New York City and took a job with *Harper's,* one of the great magazines of the day. He worked as their visual idea man, his rough sketches being developed by more experienced staff members. But Pyle was dissatisfied with this work, so he spent several weeks working on a melodramatic sketch, "Wreck in the Offing," which publisher Henry Harper reproduced as a double page showpiece in the magazine. As a result, Pyle soon became the most popular and sought-after magazine illustrater in America.

Following this artistic and commercial success, Pyle left New York and returned to his home in Wilmington, Delaware, where he founded the Brandywine School of Illustrators. His school assisted the development of some of America's most renowned illustrators and painters, including N. C. Wyeth, Violet Oakley, Jessie Wilcox Smith, Maxfield Parrish, and Frank Schoonover. Pyle, meanwhile, devoted his free time to working on his epic masterpiece, the retelling and illustrating of *The Merry Adventures of Robin Hood.*

Although Pyle also completed the text and illustrations for such widely known books as *The Wonder Clock, The Story of King Arthur and His Knights,* and *Otto Of The Silver Hand,* his work on *The Merry Adventures of Robin Hood* is his main gift to American Literature. Indeed, his Robin Hood is one of the all-time quixotic heroes, at once Sir Lancelot, Cyrano de Bergerac, Don Quixote, Huck Finn, Tom Sawyer—a Medieval English hero with surprising resemblances to the romantic outlaws of legendary America.

The opening sentences of the prologue to *The Merry Adventures of Robin Hood* lyrically sets the stage for this hero:

> In merry England in the times of old, when good King Henry the Second ruled the land, there lived within the green glades Sherwood Forest, near Nottingham Town, a famous outlaw whose name was Robin Hood. No archer ever lived that could speed a gray goose shaft with such skill and cunning as his nor were there ever such yeomen as the seven-score merry men that roamed with him through the greenwood shades. Right merrily they dwelt within the depths of Sherwood Forest, suffering neither care nor want. (1)

It is Robin Hood's skill as an archer that first gets him into trouble with King Henry, and begins the action. At the age of eighteen, Robin unwittingly kills one of the King's deer, reason enough to cause him trouble. But when he kills one of the King's lackies in the dispute that follows, not only does it make him an outlaw, it fills his heart with despair:

Robin Hood ran through the greenwood. Gone was all the joy and brightness from everything, for his heart was sick within him, and it was borne in upon his soul that he had slain a man...(but) even in his trouble, he remembered the old saw that, "What is done is done; and the egg cracked cannot be cured. (4)

The Sheriff of Nottingham pledges to bring Robin to justice for this dastardly deed done against the King and against the existing order of things—and also, against himself, for the man Robin slew was a relative of the Sheriff. Robin is mortified by his own deed.

And so he came to dwell in the greenwood that was to be his home for many a year to come, never again to see the happy days with the lads and lasses of sweet Locksley Town; for he was outlawed, not only because he had killed a man, but also because he had poached upon the King's deer, and two hundred pounds were set upon his head, as a reward for whoever would bring him to the court of the King. (4)

Many outcasts from the King's favor gather around Robin and choose him as their leader. They live by a code that deems they help poor people treated unjustly because of the exorbitant taxes, rents and fines levied by the King. In reprisal, Robin levies a toll upon any abbot, knight, or esquire who travels through Sherwood Forest.

In most children's books, there are one or two characters who stand out as memorable; in *The Merry Adventures of Robin Hood,* there are several imposing characters: "...Robin Hood lay hidden in Sherwood Forest for a year, and in that time there gathered around him many others like himself, cast out from other folk for this cause and for that...all, for one cause or another, had come to Sherwood to escape wrong and oppression" (4). Among this "legion of damned" synonymous with Robin Hood in the annals of classic literature: Little John, Will Stutely, Will Scarlet, Arthur a Bland, Allan a Dale, and Friar Tuck. Each is distinctly drawn—what E. M. Forster called "round characters" as opposed to "flat characters." Their exploits make up the body of the story, in connecting episodes that tell of their merry outrages against the King, the Sheriff of Nottingham, and the existing social order.

Pyle's vigorous illustrations etch the main participants and events in the story into a reader's mind. These illustrations are detailed black and white pen and ink drawings, including many animated full-page plates with decorative borders that reflect Pyle's keen interest in nature, many delightful vignettes and head- and tail-pieces, and many illuminated initial letters. Each illustration enhances character and action, much like a word-picture. The ones of the merry Friar carrying Robin across the water on his back and of Robin on the log bridge looking down at the tall stranger struggling in the water up to his neck among the lily pads reflect the good humor that permeates the stories. Another illustration renders Robin as a Sir Lancelot-like warrior, standing next to a tree with his archery accoutrements strapped to his svelte body. It is a strong yet poetic figure, one which admirably expresses the romance of a warrior steadfast in his resolve to do battle against the forces of evil.

The language that makes up the story is in perfect harmony with the pictures, and often makes pictures itself:

> The day was bright and jocund, and the morning dew still lay upon the grass. Under the greenwood tree sat Robin Hood; on one side was Will Scarlet, lying at full length upon his back, gazing into the clear sky, with hands clasped behind his head; upon the other side sat Little John, fashioning a cudgel out of stout crab-tree limb. (115)

This passage offers a vivid word-picture of this merry band of men relaxing in the idyllic setting of Sherwood Forest on a sultry day, a sort of "laid back" period of peace and restoration before striding forth once again to do battle against the foes who are opposed to better life for all of the people in the King's domain.

If imitation is the sincerest form of flattery, then parody may be the sincerest revelation of the importance of a work of fiction. Even before Pyle adapted them, stories of Robin Hood had been popular enough to parody. Mark Twain, for instance, showed how the fabled adventures of Robin Hood were grist for the individual drives of Tom Sawyer and Huck Finn against the constrictures and hypocrisy of small town midwestern life. Although Tom and Huck are equipped with rapscallion qualities, they also manifest some of the positive values Robin Hood represents when they confront oppression. In Chapter Eight of *The Adventures of Tom Sawyer*, Mark Twain writes of Tom roaming through a glen and having illusions of Robin Hood, a scene of childhood fantasy that expresses the need of young people to escape from the literal world of adults:

> He (Tom) said cautiously—to an imaginary company: "Hold, my merry men! Keep hid till I blow."
>
> Now appeared Joe Harper, as airily clad and elaborately armed as Tom. Tom called: "Hold! Who comes here into Sherwood Forest without my pass?"
>
> "Guy of Guisborne wants no man's pass. Who art thou that— that—"

"Dares to hold such language," said Tom, prompting—for they talked "by the book," from memory...

As Twain wrote, Tom and his merry band of young friends "would rather be outlaws a year in Sherwood Forest than the President of the United States forever." High praise indeed by one of America's greatest writers for the ever-appealing Robin Hood material that Pyle would recreate a few years later.

If, as Tom Sawyer seems to do, one considers Robin Hood's exploits as a drive against social and political evil, then it is easy to see connections between the Robin Hood legend and the infamous outlaws who played an intricate part in the settling of the American West. Although most outlaws were involved in their lawless deeds for personal gain, there was a quixotic aura about the actions of some of these legendary personas. History and folklore tell us that some outlaws sensed a calling to aid people who were being coerced by powerful political elements. History tells us that Jesse James and "Billy the Kid" were in opposition to those who would pervert justice for their own personal gain, just as Robin Hood, in the twelfth century, was opposed to King Henry the Second and his repressive reign. In the case of Jesse James, and his brother Frank James, there is historical evidence that they returned to Missouri from the Civil War and discovered their home state overrun by predators of all sorts: carpetbaggers, greedy landowners, and Unionists. Much of this is conjecture, but it is worth considering when discussing the significance of the Robin Hood legend in the American consciousness—a signifiance implied in Twain's work and stated forcefully by Pyle.

Like all quixotic heroes in literature, Pyle's Robin Hood seems confronted by almost insurmountable forces in his drive for truth and justice. Although the King is the power behind those human forces, the personification of evil for Robin Hood is manifested in the person of Guy of Gisbourne. Robin had heard of Guy of Guisbourne and all his infamous deeds; when he actually meets him in Sherwood Forest, all of the tribulations that have beset Robin seem present in this man:

> ...he pushed the cowl back from his head and showed a knit brow, a hooked nose, and a pair of fierce, restless, black eyes, which altogether made Robin think of a hawk as he looked on his face. But beside this there was something about the lines on the stranger's face, and his thin cruel mouth, and the hard glare of his eyes, that made one's flesh creep to look upon.

(257)

Following this stark characterization is a fight in which Robin Hood slays Guy of Gisbourne. Afterwards Robin becomes an

217

to King Richard of the Lion's Heart. A favorite of the King, Robin Hood rises in rank to become chief of the yeomen, eventually regaining his rightful heritage as the Earl of Huntingdon. As in many movies and TV shows that express key elements of the American consciousness, one good man and his friends can eventually win out over corrupt, powerful forces.

The Merry Adventures of Robin Hood is still significant reading for children. The prose is such that it would interest even young readers who may not be accustomed to such a florid style; and the simplicity, gaiety, and morality of the story make this an incomparable book for teachers who wish to introduce their students to a classic milestone of children's literature. *The Merry Adventures of Robin Hood* is tasty enough to be palatable in and of itself but also complex enough to be a steppingstone to many other great books in world literature.

Nevertheless, teachers may be bewildered by the number of collections of Robin Hood stories that are available, even editions of the Pyle version. A recent *Children's Catalog* (1981) lists both Pyle's *The Merry Adventures of Robin Hood of Great Renown in Nottinghamshire* and his *Some Merry Adventures of Robin Hood of Great Renown in Nottinghamshire,* which was adapted by Pyle himself from his longer work; it contains only twelve of the original twenty-two stories, and some of these Pyle shortened or condensed for easier reading, without losing the spirit of his masterpiece of epic retelling. Nevertheless, the Dover edition of *The Merry Adventures of Robin Hood* is the best choice, for it is an unabridged and unaltered republication of the work originally published by Charles Scribner's in 1883. It includes Pyle's delightful borders for large full-page plates, his pleasing vignettes, and his decorative initial letters, all of which are such an integral part of the total illustration, and all of which were removed in the multilated and still available 1946 edition. In the Brandywine Edition that Scribner's Sons issued in 1983 to celebrate the hundredth anniversary of the publication of *The Merry Adventures of Robin Hood,* Pyle's work is intruded upon by additional illustrations by former Pyle pupils. Many school versions are cheap substitutions that cheat the students out of a true experience of Pyle's work.

Children should become aware of the living, changing nature of language instead of thinking of it as a static entity; and teachers should use carefully selected pieces of choice literature to develop awareness of these changes. In my own teaching, Pyle's version of the Robin Hood stories has been a key example of such changes, specifically for the Middle English flavoring that Pyle sought to capture.

Yet students today are attuned to the greater dependence of our English upon word order for meaning than was the language of Robin Hood's day. So, Pyle's text may sound somewhat foreign to modern ears and be slower to read than recently published adventure fiction. But since the sometimes archaic language is part of the book's charm and authenticity, it lends itself to reading aloud, at least in part, by the teacher and by better readers in a fifth or sixth grade class. Many of the children will know Robin Hood as a hero, but usually only through screen renditions, lesser versions, or hearsay. Expressive oral reading will convey the spirit of the Pyle version and recreate some of the flavor of the original oral tradition from which the stories stem. I often follow my own presentation of Pyle's version to upper elementary or middle school children, and also to college students in children's literature classes, with a short presentation of ballads, first some that Pyle used as source material and then other folk and literary ballads, including some modern ones.

I often hear the lament, "Where have all our heroes gone?" Robin Hood is the very definition of the hero for children. He embodies the basic characteristics of the epic hero, those of courage, justice, and control. A book recommended for teaching should always say something important to students at that phase of their lives, and not be assigned merely to prepare them for some future goal in literary experience. Pyle's *The Merry Adventures of Robin Hood* does both. It involves the students in the exploits of an ageless hero of the people and leads them into the study of the ageless heroes like King Arthur, Beowolf, and Odysseus.

In summary, the study of *The Merry Adventures of Robin Hood* provides children with (1) the pleasure of reading a rollicking good adventure story, (2) an introduction to one of the great traditional folk cycles in English literature, (3) an opportunity to weigh values of courage, justice, honor, and loyalty without didactic overtones, (4) some awareness of how their mother tongue has evolved over the centuries, and (5) a natural steppingstone to other great literary experiences.

Writing some years ago in *A Critical History of Children's Literature,* Ruth Hill Viguers said, "Many fine books that deserve to be read generation after generation may be lost in the confusion of pendantry, technology, and good intentions that confounds the mid-century." They plague us even more in the late twentieth century. This must not happen to Pyle's Robin Hood. Children should be encouraged to follow the Piper when Pyle himself in his preface says, "And now I lift the curtain that hangs between here and No-man's-land. Will you come with me, sweet Reader? I thank you. Give me your hand."

In his introduction to the first edition of that same text on the history of children's literature, Henry Steele Commager quotes the great author-artist Howard Pyle himself: "My ambition in days gone by was to write a really notable adult book, but now I am glad that I have made literary friends of the children rather than the older folk. In one's mature years one forgets the books one reads but the stories of childhood leave an indelible impression, and their author always has a niche in the temple of memory from which the image is never cast out to be thrown into the rubbish-heap of things that are outgrown and outlived." *The Merry Adventures of Robin Hood* does leave an indelible impression, Mr. Pyle.

REFERENCES

Abbot, Charles D. *Howard Pyle: A Chronicle* (New York: Harper and Brothers, 1925).

Brockman, Bennett A. "Robin Hood and The Invention of Children's Literature," *Children's Literature* 10(1982):1-17.

Cech, John. "Pyle's Robin Hood: Still Merry After All These Years," *Children's Literature Association Quarterly* 8 (Summer 1983):11-14, 34.

Lanes, Selma. "The Brandywine Legacy," *Portfolio* (May/June 1981):70-77.

Lawson, Robert. "Howard Pyle and His Times," *Illustrations of Children's Books*. Compiled by Bertha E. Mahoney and others. Boston: Horn Book, 1947.

Meigs, Cornelia, Anne Eaton, Elizabeth Nesbitt, and **Ruth Hill Viguers.** *A Critical History of Children's Literature*. Rev. Ed. New York: Macmillan, 1969.

Pyle, Howard. *The Merry Adventures of Robin Hood of Great Renown in Nottinghamshire*. New York: Dover Publications, 1968.

_____. *Some Merry Adventures of Robin Hood of Great Renown in Nottinghamshire*. New York: Charles Scribner's Sons, 1954.

Steckmesser, Kent L. "Robin Hood and the American Outlaw: A Note on History and Folklore." *Journal of American Folklore* (April/June 1966):348-355.

Howard Pyle's *The Story of King Arthur and His Knights:* A Backwards Look at Chivalry

by Jill P. May

My fascination with Howard Pyle's version of the King Arthur legends began only after I had become an adult, so I cannot claim that I can remember their childhood appeal, and that I am now returning for a look in terms of my adult response. And since Lloyd Alexander once confessed to me that he had *never* read the versions by Pyle, I cannot even say that Pyle has been a direct influence on all later authors of fantasy. Yet I think that Pyle's King Arthur series indirectly established a tradition, for it was the first of many multiple-volumed sequential fantasy tales based upon new interpretations of Arthurian materials. And I believe that modern children's versions of these materials do contain adventures and characters similar to those found in Pyle's story. In fact, Pyle's historically significant role in the continual process of reinterpretation makes the first volume of his series on King Arthur (as well as the following ones) archetypal in children's literature.

Pyle took a backwards look at the old tales and created a new version for his modern audience. He sought to write a tale of Arthur which would be acceptable to his contemporaries. Today I look backwards at Pyle, knowing something about his sources, his plans, and his Arthur, and realize that I am looking at his work as an adult just as the adult Pyle looked at his own source materials when he determined to re-create Arthur for children. Like Pyle, I remember other versions of Arthur, only mine are both older and newer than his.

Northrop Frye once wrote, "We cannot in practice study a literary work without remembering that we have encountered many similar ones previously. Hence after following a narrative through to the end, our critical response includes the establishment of its categories, which are chiefly its conventions and its genre. In this way the particular story is seen as a *projection* of the theme, as one of the infinite number of ways of getting to the theme ("The Road of Excess" 15). Thinking about that comment I am struck by its similarity to Pyle's own belief in what he was doing with the King Arthur legends, and to his recognition that he was *reshaping* earlier mythic and historic legendary tales, transforming tales of chivalry not yet available to young readers of English either in North America or the British Isles into an American romance.

Pyle had already read much of what was available on Arthur in English; since he took German in grade school and since he owned some reference books in German, it is possible that he had read or heard other versions. Pyle wrote to Edith Dean Weir that there was much in the legends which disturbed him, much he planned to leave out, and went on to say that he hoped to develop a new version which would be enjoyed by his readers. He wrote: I must follow the thread of the better known legends, for it is not advisable for me to draw upon the less well-known narratives. So I try to represent those which are known in the best light (Abbott 128).

Earlier, Pyle had woven the remnants of Robin Hood legend into a continual hero story. That book was extremely popular from the day of its release, for heroic legend was in vogue with American audiences. Pyle lived among fanatic readers of Sir Walter Scott; the Waverly novels were popular with the young boys of the Wilmington area. Pyle had probably read Scott's comment that the Arthurian tales were full of "dull repetition and uninteresting dialect" within a "confused story" as well as his judgement that, nevertheless, the stories contained "passages of interest" and "specimens of spirited and masculine writing" ("Essay on Romance" 186). Aware of Scott's popularity and encouraged by publishers, Pyle began to rewrite the loosely joined Arthurian legends into an easily followed chronological narrative. The episodes he chose are still those most often found in more recent children's versions of the Arthurian tales, and usually, the characters' personalities in these newer fantasies resemble the people in Pyle's version; for these reasons, the books must be considered archetypal in characterization.

The Story of King Arthur and His Knights was the first in a set of four books by Pyle about King Arthur's court and his knights. It sets up all of the patterns now familiar in questing hero stories. As such, it is the groundwork for establishing the courtly intrigue and the final collapse of Arthur's rule which are the subjects of the later books.

Each time Arthur or his knights go to battle during this first book, Pyle describes the countryside and the scene in detail. He sets most of the major battles between knights in glens within a woods, which the knights reach on horseback. The physical battles are not held inside the court; while help is sought from the court, the actual fighting occurs outside of the "civilization" of Arthur's rule. A knight on quest must leave Arthur's rule, travel into the unknown, seek adventure in the name of honor, and return home after an honorable fight. The highest battles are those which are fought to preserve the courtly system, save a damsel from disgrace, or revenge unknightly conduct. The low battles unworthy of glory are those involving power struggles between two knights. A knight will not fight a foe of lesser strength, and he cannot turn down a virtuous maiden's plea for help. In order to keep the peace established after a battle, Arthur takes the favorite son of his conquered enemy with him "to serve in court" (or to serve as ransom).

The covenant of the Round Table, Pyle writes, demands of the knights

> That they would be gentle unto the weak; that they would be courageous unto the strong; that they would do terrible unto the wicked and the evil-doer; that they would defend the helpless who should call upon them for aid; that all women should be held unto them sacred; that they would stand unto the defense of one another whensoever such defense should be required; that they would be merciful unto all men; that they would be gentle of deed, true in friendship, and faithful in love. (145-146)

Today's fantasy stories based on Arthurian traditions and written for children still contain questing male heroes who are gentle, faithful, true; Pyle did not say that a masculine hero needed to be intelligent, and no demands of intelligence are placed on later male heroes either. Taran, Lloyd Alexander's hero in the Prydain series, begins his quest with no knowledge concerning his adventure, gains friends he would defend at all costs, and in the end says, "I ask no reward. . . I want no friend to repay me for what I did willingly, out of friendship and my own honor" (218). Alexander's hero fits into the code as easily as Pyle's heroes.

But knights are not all alike in Pyle's *The Story of King Arthur and His Knights.* Heroes are clearly differentiated from one another in the Pyle books. Many of these heroic personalities were already defined in the earlier versions, but Pyle reformed them to fit his needs. Within the first volume, for instance, Pyle establishes his character portrayals of Merlin, Sir Pellias, and Sir Gawaine. Each has an unique personality which is based in the earlier legends and is itself the basis for characters found in renditions created after Pyle's series.

Gawaine represents the earthy, hot headed young knight who is at times vain and brutal. The early French romances depicted Gawain as both knightly in battle skills and lascivious and cruel (Barber 95). Pyle realized that in his story of Gawaine, he must explain why so noble a hero would act in less than virtuous ways when dealing with others. He decided to "try to represent Gawaine as proud and passionate, quick to anger, but with a broad basis of generosity and nobility" and admitted that he would "modernize Sir Gawaine" (Abbott 128). Pyle lets his readers know that Gawaine is a proud young man full of high spirits by describing him as such, and by having the courtly action center on him during a balmy afternoon when he is the "most gayly clad" of the court and is busy entertaining the others with song. Suddenly the queen's favorite greyhound runs in, jumps up and soils Gawaine's clothes. Pyle writes: "At this Sir Gawaine was very wroth, wherefore he clinched his hand and smote the hound upon the head . . ." (242). Thus, Gawaine's high spirits drive him away from the court when he displeases Guinevere. But even the queen does not break his will. Once Guinevere orders him away he complies, saying, "Nor will I return thitherward until thou art willing for to tell me that thou art sorry for the discourteous ways in which thou has entreated me now and other times before my peers" (243). In the end it is a fay who tames Gawaine, with her devoted love. After Gawaine is wedded to duty, Pyle tells the reader, he is one of the most virtuous of knights. Nevertheless, the reader is likely to remember that Guinevere sent him away, and to hold some suspicions that the two are not true friends.

Sir Pellias, on the other hand, foreshadows two knights still to come: Launcelot and Galahad. Pyle calls Pellias "the gentle knight," and has him go questing for Queen Guinevere's sake. He is a noble young man who would hold that the queen's honor is sacred, yet, unlike Launcelot, he would not honor the queen above all womankind, and, unlike Galahad, he would not sacrifice his belief in the powers of the fay in honor of the Christian God. In Pellias, Pyle has established a prototype of the two noblest of knights, and he has given the reader a sense of what it means to be the greatest warrior of chivalry. In this first book, Pellias has fallen in love with a dishonorable maiden who has used magical powers to bewitch him; he is saved by a fay who gives him another magical element, the water of life. Once he receives it, Pellias declares, "Thou hast given life unto me again, now do I give that life unto thee forever" (274). Sir Pellias travels with his companion to the land of Avalon, the self-same land where Arthur will go upon his death. Pellias is a representation of Pyle's own ambivalence concerning the Christian belief in eternity and the Celtic land of death—Avalon. Pyle's story continually brings the best of knights who express the old ideals of chivalry to Avalon. Pellias will be joined by Arthur; Gawaine is married to a fay who chooses to become human for his sake.

The other character who reflects Pyle's modern beliefs is Merlin. In Pyle's version, the magician decides to share his knowledge with Vivien, a decision which Pyle calls a misuse of his God-given powers (*The Story of King Arthur and His Knights* 152). Part of this may be Pyle's own philosophy; he had earlier expressed a disinterest in training women artists and sought to separate his creative world into two parts, one in which masculine peers worked side by side as artists, and the other the intellectual ambiance of the afternoon soirée attended by both sexes. Considering that, it is difficult when reading about Merlin's failing to decide whether Pyle objects to Merlin's sharing knowledge with Vivien because she is evil, or because she is female.

Pyle's attitude towards his heroines is always interesting; it is both a backwards look at earlier legends and a modernized Pyle interpretation of woman's role in society. His version of the quest valorizes the female as heroine at home or villain when traipsing about the countryside, the male as the quester in journey or the wise leader while at home, and magic as somehow amoral yet most appealing.

Pyle successfully weaves together the Celtic and the Christian tales, but he does it at the expense of his female characters. He chooses to ignore the fact that Arthur is the bastard younger brother of Morgana, and to separate the Lady of the Lake's powers from Morgana's by making the Lady and her fays' motives ambigious, Morgana's evil. Yet, he has Morgana rule Avalon, and says, "This island of Avalon was a very strange, wonderful land, such as was not to be seen anywhere else in all the world. For it was like a Paradise for beauty.... Avalon would float from place to place according to the will of Queen Morgana le Fay, so that sometimes it would be here, and sometimes it would be there, as that royal lady willed it to be" (159-60). In the end, he has Morgana return for Arthur upon his death and take him away with her to Avalon, implying some kind of sibling tie of loyalty or love. In this first book, however, Pyle calls Morgana cunning, and gives her no real motive for her outbursts of jealousy other than that she wishes to have power over Arthur's kingdom and respect from Arthur. Since the reader has no real knowledge of Morgana's claim to Arthur's throne, she seems petty and mean.

Pyle is not ignoring earlier legend in his retelling. Geoffrey of Monmouth in *Vita Merlin* had described Avalon as an "otherworld" and had named Morgan chief of the land (Barber 54), and Malory had laid most of the blame for the courts failure upon Guinevere, choosing to ignore the earlier legends that made Mordred Arthur's bastard son conceived with his half-sister. While Celtic legend had placed women enchantresses in esteemed positions, there is no evidence that Pyle had read these versions. What Pyle did was to represent "all that is noble and high and great" and omit "all that is cruel and mean and treacherous" (Abbott 128) in terms of male supremacy and the Christian masculine code of honor. And so, he depicted Morgana as the dark side of religious beliefs representing black magic, and placed the saving Christian graces in the male hero Galahad.

This interpretation is not new with Pyle, but it was solidified in children's literature by him. Pyle's tradition of a series which depicts an evil queen and a gentle but forceful male ruler is seen again in C. S. Lewis's Narnia series, and is also followed in Alexander's Prydain series. The pattern was not to be broken until women fantasy authors such as Cherry Wilder returned to the Celtic legends as source materials for their fantasy series.

Pyle's interpretations of women are never flattering. Even Guinevere is less than perfect. She knows that Arthur is more than a gardener's boy when he appears in her father's garden, and she purposely exposes him to her ladies in waiting. Pyle writes:

> And after that time, whenever the Lady Guinevere would come upon the gardener's lad in the garden, she would say unto her damsel in such a voice that he might hear her speech: "Lo! yonder is the gardener's lad who hath an ugly place upon his head so that he must always wear his cap for to hide it."
> Thus she spake openly, mocking at him; but privily she bade her damsels to say naught concerning these things...
>
> (88)

Later, when she discovers that he is King Arthur and that she is to be wed to him, she says, "Lord, I am afeard of thy greatness." Pyle has Arthur play the perfect courtly gentleman when he replies, "...thy kind regard is dearer to me than anything else in the world, else had I not served for these twelve days as gardener's boy..." (134).

The women, then, are more ornamental or meddlesome than they are comforting. The only noble spirits in this first volume are the fay, and they are aloof for the most part.

Pyle's Arthurian cycle is firmly established in the first book. He has created a court for his king, has established the women as troublemakers within the court, and has repeatedly shown the conduct of a worthy knight in battle. His choice of ignoring the Celtic and Welsh ideals of women as leaders and spiritual guides, and of showing Arthur as a hero "as pure as snow," probably stemmed from his background reading. He had read Malory and Scott; it is not certain that he read the Mabinogian. Even if he had, he knew that youngsters were reading Sir Walter Scott and his version of Robin Hood. His intended American audience, with its full blown optimism and its thirst for heroism, would have been more receptive to a manly version of the quest.

What Pyle established for future writers was a chronological adventure story which wove the various legends into a consistent story. Years later, English reading audiences would not only have newer versions in children's fantasy but also could see theatrical representations of the continuous story in *Camelot* and *Excalibur*. Pyle's books have inspired many young boys to play act knightly quests based, whether they knew it or not, upon his ritualistic pattern. Today's youth use these character types when they participate in Dungeons and Dragons.

Pyle's *The Story of King Arthur and His Knights* was greeted with high praise in his own time. It brought together old legends, and created a romantic adventure that captured the hearts of its readers. Full of jousts and courtly activity, it glorifies an aristocracy based on male honor and feminine beauty. Northrop Frye has called the medieval chivalric romance "a ritualized action expressing the ascendancy of a horse-riding aristocracy", one which "expresses that aristocracy's dreams of its own social function, and the idealized acts of protection and responsibility that it invokes to justify that function" *(The Secular Scripture* 56). Pyle's turn of the century volumes gave his youthful reading audience that tradition. The entire cycle was strongly conservative in its attitudes. It firmly supported the established code of ethics found within American society. Within his Arthurian cycle, Pyle was able to bring alive the old ideas of a code of honor, of the virtues in serving a worthy cause, and the glories of battle. He also sought to show male readers the pitfalls of putting trust in a woman's advice or becoming too infatuated with the woman you serve (unless she happens to be fay). And so, the questing hero was born in children's literature.

That hero is found several times on the ChLA list of Touchstones. Though he may look slightly different, he can be seen in Lloyd Alexander's books, in C. S. Lewis' Narnia series, and in T. H. White's *The Sword in the Stone*. As part of a literary tradition continuously being reinterpreted, Pyle's first children's version of Arthur is an essential beginning in our understanding of the Arthurian cycle and its significance in children's literature.

REFERENCES

I would like to thank Perry Nodelman for his patience, encouragement, and editing.

Abbott, Charles D. *Howard Pyle: A Chronicle.* Harper & Brothers, 1925.

Alexander, Lloyd. *The Book of Three.* Yearling. 1964.

Barber, Richard. *The Figure of Arthur.* Great Britain: Longman, 1972.

Frye, Northrop. "The Road of Excess." *Myth and Symbol: Critical Approaches and Applications.* Ed. Bernice Slote. Univ. of Nebraska Press, 1963.

_____. *The Secular Scripture: Critical Approaches and Applications.* Harvard Univ. Press, 1976.

Pyle, Howard. *The Story of King Arthur and His Knights.* Dover, 1965.

Scott, Sir Walter. Essays on Chivalry, Romance and Drama. Books for Libraries Press, 1972.

Contributors

Norma Bagnall is a member of the English department at Missouri Western College, St. Joseph, Missouri; she has done extensive research on teaching literary criticism to children.

Yancy Barton's thesis for Stephen F. Austin University, Nacogdoches, Texas, was on the work of Padraic Colum.

Glenn S. Burne teaches in the English department at the University of North Carolina at Charlotte; his work in the area of children's literature has appeared in the *ChLA Quarterly.*

John Cech, a past president of the Children's Literature Association, is a member of the English department at the University of Florida and Review Editor for *Children's Literature.*

James Gellert teaches in the English department at Lakehead University, Thunder Bay, Ontario. He is Assistant Editor of the *ChLA Quarterly.*

Caroline R. Goforth is a member of the English department at Clemson University, Clemson, South Carolina; her criticism has appeared in the *ChLA Quarterly.*

Alethea Helbig, a past president of the Children's literature Association and co-author of *A Dictionary of American Children's Fiction* (Greenwood), teaches in the English department at Eastern Michigan University.

Nancy Huse, a member of the English department at Augustana College, Rock Island, Illinois, has published a number of articles on children's fiction.

Hugh T. Keenan is a member of the English department at Georgia State University; he edited the children's literature and narrative theory issue of *Studies in the Literary Imagination.*

Myra Cohn Livingston has written widely about poetry for children and has also produced many fine volumes of children's poetry.

Joanne Lynn is Professor of English at California State University, Fullerton; her criticism has appeared in the *ChLA Quarterly.*

Jill P. May, chair of ChLA Publications, teaches in the Department of Education at Purdue University; she has published widely on the work of Howard Pyle.

Nina Mikkelsen, a consultant in children's literature, is a frequent contributor to the *ChLA Quarterly.*

Perry Nodelman, Professor of English at the University of Winnipeg, has published widely on numerous aspects of children's literature.

Taimi M. Ranta, a past president of the Children's Literature Association and Professor of English at Illinois State University, specializes in the children's literature of Finland.

Kay Unruh DesRoches, a member of the English department at the University of Winnipeg, specializes in drama, particularly the work of the Norwegian playwright Henrik Ibsen.

John Warren Stewig, author of *Children and Literature* (Rand McNally), teaches in the Education department at the University of Wisconsin-Milwaukee.

Joyce Thomas teaches in the English department at Castleton State College, Vermont; she has published in *Children's Literature* and in the *ChLA Quarterly.*

Mark I. West, a member of the English department at the University of North Carolina at Charlotte, has done extensive research on the censorship of children's literature.

Anita Wilson, a member of the English department at Miami University of Ohio, wrote on A. A. Milne's novels in volume one of this series.